The Couriers
A Memoir of Bible Smuggling

L. D. CARROLL

Copyright © 2018 L.D. Carroll.

All rights reserved. No part of this book may be used or reproduced by any means, graphic, electronic, or mechanical, including photocopying, recording, taping or by any information storage retrieval system without the written permission of the author except in the case of brief quotations embodied in critical articles and reviews.

Scripture taken from the NEW AMERICAN STANDARD BIBLE®, Copyright © 1960,1962,1963,1968,1971,1972,1973,1975,1977,1995 by The Lockman Foundation. Used by permission.

Scripture taken from the New King James Version®. Copyright © 1982 by Thomas Nelson. Used by permission. All rights reserved.

This book is a work of non-fiction. Unless otherwise noted, the author and the publisher make no explicit guarantees as to the accuracy of the information contained in this book and in some cases, names of people and places have been altered to protect their privacy.

WestBow Press books may be ordered through booksellers or by contacting:

WestBow Press
A Division of Thomas Nelson & Zondervan
1663 Liberty Drive
Bloomington, IN 47403
www.westbowpress.com
1 (866) 928-1240

Because of the dynamic nature of the Internet, any web addresses or links contained in this book may have changed since publication and may no longer be valid. The views expressed in this work are solely those of the author and do not necessarily reflect the views of the publisher, and the publisher hereby disclaims any responsibility for them.

Any people depicted in stock imagery provided by Thinkstock are models, and such images are being used for illustrative purposes only. Certain stock imagery © Thinkstock.

ISBN: 978-1-9736-0842-4 (sc)
ISBN: 978-1-9736-0843-1 (hc)
ISBN: 978-1-9736-0841-7 (e)

Library of Congress Control Number: 2017917764

Print information available on the last page.

WestBow Press rev. date: 02/16/2018

"All I have seen teaches me to trust the Creator for all I have not seen."
Ralph Waldo Emerson

Dedication

This is dedicated to the Christian dissidents who maintained their faith and endured the hardships placed upon them by the Communists in Eastern Europe during the Communist Era and those who suffer for the Good News around the world even today. It is also dedicated to the mission teams who served persecuted Believers during the 1980s and to those who serve the persecuted now.

This is a Special Remembrance for my mom and her close friend, Margie, who had a love for people in other countries and for missions. They planted seeds for service in many lives.

Author's Note

This account contains memoirs of a guy who wanted to help the Eastern European Believers who lived under the yoke of communists during the 1980s. The people, their stories, the events, and places in this story were real. It is based upon accounts taken from my journal, notes, the best of my recollection, and a few published brochures and books. These events occurred at a time before the advent and convenience of cell phones, internet, smart phones, and social media—a time during the 1980s, when primary communication was conducted via "snail mail" letters, telegrams, land line telephones, and radio. Compact cell phones were a fantasy found only in episodes of the historical *Star Trek* TV series. Communications capabilities have greatly increased since that time. Emails and video conference via PCs were a few years away from being in common use. Mailgrams from the U.S. usually took about seven to ten days, or sometimes more, to cross the Atlantic and arrive at our mission base.

Other than known historical figures, incomplete names or pseudonyms are used for individuals in this story. Names have been altered to shield the privacy of those mentioned. The men and women referenced that I worked with were truly individuals who had a love for justice, the Lord, and others. It is a story about deliverances. The number of times the phrase, "Thank you Lord!" was quietly uttered in thanks for His protection and provision is innumerable. There are many people who have their own stories who worked helping those persecuted by communists behind the Iron Curtain. This is just one man's story. It is shared for the next generation, lest some events should be forgotten.

Contents

Introduction 1
Toward the Curtain 13
Reflections 23
Making It to Europe 31
Bibles for Romanians and Russians 43
Books for Czechoslovakian, Hungarian, and Russian Believers 91
Down on the Farm 105
The Typewriter 109
VBs, the STB and ZOMOs 125
More Important Than Gold, Silver and Precious Jewels 171
The Texas Medic and the Romanians 177
The Wall Comes Down 199
Ethics of Taking Bibles into Closed and Restricted Countries .. 207
Reliability of the Bible 213
Epilogue 225
A Special Thanks 229
Appendix I   Organizational Contacts 231
Appendix II   Excerpts from the Former Soviet Criminal Code
                Related to Religious Regulations 233
Appendix III   Recommended Reading List 237
Endnotes 239
Bibliography 241

Introduction

This story transpired during the 1980s, during the time of the Cold War between the communist Eastern European Warsaw Pact and the Western European NATO allies. It happened in a time prior to the fall of the Berlin Wall, which separated Eastern and Western Europe after World War II. It was during the 1980s, before the time when communist governments began to topple across Eastern Europe in 1989.

These events occurred during the last year of Jimmy Carter's Presidency and during the term of Ronald Reagan, who was elected and followed as the fortieth President of the United States. President Reagan's tenure continued from January 1981 to January 1989, when Leonid Brezhnev, Yuri Andropov, and Mikhail Gorbachev presided as some of the last rulers of what was the now defunct Soviet Union. Andropov and Gorbachev had relative short times as the leaders in the top spot as Secretary Generals over the USSR.

This all happened not long after the Union of Soviet Socialist Republics (USSR), under Brezhnev, had invaded Afghanistan in 1979. In December of that year, fifty thousand Soviet troops under Brezhnev's direction poured across the Afghan border to prop up the failing communist regime there. Brezhnev was a hardline communist in charge of the USSR when it invaded Afghanistan, but historically he was also a driving force involved with crushing the Czechoslovakian *Prague Spring* in 1968. That Czech pro-freedom movement had been an attempt by the Czechoslovakian people to break off the yoke of communism. It was crushed by the USSR under Brezhnev. The Soviet Union, along with four other neighboring Warsaw Pact nations, invaded Czechoslovakia with tanks, armored personnel carriers and troops, smashing the efforts of the

Czech and Slovak peoples' movement to realize autonomy. That effort was squashed by the USSR among others, led by Brezhnev. Brezhnev ruled over the USSR for eighteen years.

In November 1982, Breshnev, who was the Secretary General of the Soviet Union, died. Another hardline communist, and former member of the KGB, Yuri Andropov, took Brezhnev's spot at the helm of the USSR. Andropov had been appointed as Chairman of the KGB in 1967. In the late 1960s he enacted measures to increase pressure on the religious dissidents within the USSR and its satellites. As a former Soviet Ambassador to Hungary, he had been one of the influential individuals involved with crushing the 1956 Hungarian revolt against communism in that country. He was also a leading proponent of the invasion of Czechoslovakia in 1968. After Brezhnev's passing in the early 1980s Andropov, as the Secretary General of the USSR, continued the hardline Soviet presence in Afghanistan, enforcing communist rule there as well as in the Eastern European satellites. He also continued to maintain policies of persecution against people of faith.

From the end of World War II to the 1990s communist leaders in Eastern Europe and the former Soviet Union utilized propaganda, terror campaigns, secret police, and the military for conquest and enforcement of socialistic communist ideology. What was known as the Cold War between the USSR, its allies, and the U.S. with its allies was in full swing.

It is fairly well known that communists as global socialists embraced the concept of atheistic socialism. No matter what they called themselves, that ideology remained basically entrenched. During the 1980s, Russia and its neighboring communist satellite countries claimed to provide religious freedom for citizens. But there was a deeper truth behind that propaganda story line. While on the surface freedom to worship was flaunted, even written into the Constitution of the USSR, the civil rights abuses against Christians and Jewish people of faith was not disclosed by communist media propagandists. A visitor to Eastern European countries might be led to believe that religious freedom was truly allowed in that land when taken on a tour by the communist government employee. But what was revealed to the visitor was only a portion of the truth. The casual observer saw only a bit of the truth. Complete reality was more than what was seen by the undiscerning eye. The Believers who lived in those countries and actively practiced belief in God, studied the Bible, participated in home group Bible studies, met in unregistered house churches, printed Bibles or religious books and distributed literature, taught their children about God or were active in their faith were usually discriminated against, often viewed as criminals, persecuted, and prosecuted.

Churches and religious practices were strictly regulated by the Soviet State, which considered itself to be the supreme arbiter over faith and religious affairs. One of the tools the communists utilized to control Christianity and religion were Departments of Religious Affairs. These State Departments not only existed to control the religious expression of the people in the Soviet Union, but existed within the Warsaw Pac communist satellite countries as well. However, there were differing degrees of intolerance toward Christianity in each communist Eastern European country.

Government agencies dedicated to the regulation and repression of the Christian and Jewish religions were the overseers of faith. Only those groups or organizations which complied with the State Edicts regarding religion were tolerated. The State dictated what was allowed within the context of the church, what was taught, and who could attend. For example, in some places it was illegal to teach out of certain books of the Bible, including portions of Romans or the Revelation. Home Bible studies and prayer meetings were illegal and not permitted. I previously had read about and then met people who had to meet covertly in order to attend home Bible studies or prayer meetings. People who wanted to worship God, as part of a small Bible study group, home prayer meeting, or house church had to be discreet in attendance as they faced fines or imprisonment for doing so. Participants found it necessary to arrive at meeting places at different time intervals. Only one or two people at a time would go to the designated house. They approached the location on foot from a distance, entering discreetly from different directions. Several vehicles at one home was an invitation for an investigation. Having those unauthorized home meetings was not permitted by the communist authorities. Those under eighteen years of age were not allowed to receive instruction about God or be baptized. If parents were caught teaching their children about God, they were subject to punishment from the State.

Bibles and study aids were rarely printed and only in limited quantities, and Christian book stores were non-existent. Bibles may have occasionally been found as a rare exception in the state-controlled bookstores. Those were generally a showcase item in limited supply. The freedom of the press and religion as an American concept as put forth in the First Amendment to the U.S. Constitution was a foreign concept. It did not exist there as practiced in the United States. Censorship of printed material was the norm. The press was State controlled and monitored. Censorship was the rule. Theological works published by state-approved clergymen were printed on state-controlled printing presses and adhered to communist dictates and philosophy. Only those censored and approved by the Communist State were placed into print. Christian literature was an anathema to the communists.

While the Church, was allowed to operate within the Soviet Union, it was heavily regulated and monitored. At times, church buildings were destroyed, leaving the congregations no place to meet for worship. Home Bible studies and prayer meetings including non-denominational congregations were not sanctioned. But the communists insisted they had religious freedom and no state religion. However, the evidence led to the conclusion that religious freedom was heavily regulated, extremely limited and only tolerated because of outside pressures. The practice of state-controlled religious belief was not only the situation in the USSR, but also in the communist countries within the sphere of Soviet influence. The nations of Albania, Bulgaria, Czechoslovakia, East Germany, Hungary, Poland, Romania, and Yugoslavia were places where people of religious faith were heavily regulated, oppressed, and persecuted, and at times suffered from human rights abuses from 1948 through 1989.

In the appendices of this book the reader will find copies of Soviet regulations used to regulate Christianity. Appendix II contains an *Index of Criminal Charges,* from statutes of the Soviet Criminal Code which was copyrighted by the *Society for the Study of Religion Under Communism* in 1981, published by Keston College, in Kent, England, in the booklet titled *Soviet Christian Prisoner list, 1981.* This booklet also contained the names, dates of birth, denominational affiliation, the severity level of concentration camps and places of incarceration of hundreds of Christian prisoners.

The extreme Marxists were mostly atheists and agnostics, many being strong proponents against the existence of God. Evidences of the historical persecution of Christians in Eastern Europe may be found in the books, *Tortured for Christ* and *Was Karl Marx a Satanist,* by Richard Wurmbrandt, as well as a multitude of other books and magazines. Dozens and dozens of documented events, circumstances, testimonial accounts, and books attest to the facts that Marxist socialists were intolerant of Christianity and belief in God. Most communists believed that those who practiced belief and faith were lesser, weak-minded individuals. Many of the Christians who actively practiced their faith were placed in prisons and psychiatric hospitals, most especially during the period from 1948 to 1955 in what was known as the Time of Terror. During that time, communists attempted to eliminate the influences of religion in society. Persecutions were harsh[8]. Many persecutions continued from 1955 until 1989, although at times to somewhat of a lesser extent.

In the 1992 book *Praying with the KGB* by Philip Yancey, on page 67, Yancey quotes Mikhail Gorbachev, who when meeting with a delegation of North American Christian leaders, stated the following: "We have treated this book like a bomb," he said, holding up a Bible. "Like contraband material, we have not allowed Bibles into our country. Now we realize how wrong that was." [1]

Earlier in his book, Mr. Yancey relates the terror of Soviet style communism as follows:

> They stripped churches, mosques and synagogues of religious ornaments, banned religious instruction to children and imprisoned and killed priests. The government (Soviet) opened Forty-Four anti-religious museums, and published a national newspaper called *The Godless*. Using government funds, first the League of Militant Atheists and then The Knowledge Society organized, "unevangelism" campaigns of lectures with the specific aim of stamping out all religious belief. Vigilantes known as "The Godless Shock Brigades" went after the most stubborn believers [2].

If the reader can obtain a copy of the out of print book, *The Persecutor*, by Sergei Kourdakov, they will discover that the biography tells of shock brigades which raided Bible studies and prayer meetings in private homes. These house church raids resulted in beatings of the men and sometimes women and children. Home owners and church leaders were arrested and many were placed in prisons or concentration camps; personal property including homes were confiscated by the State.

Another example of Christian persecution by the Soviet Communists can be found in the book, *Vanya*, by Myrna Grant. This book is about a Russian soldier who was persecuted by the Soviet Army and allegedly killed by the KGB.

In the literary work, *The First Guidebook to the USSR, Prisons and Concentration Camps of the Soviet Union* by Avraham Shifrin, the author details lists of concentration camps in the Soviet gulag system, and categorizes them as to type. The book was copyrighted in 1980 by Stephanus Edition Verlags AG, CH-Seewis/GR, Switzerland, and was translated from the Russian.

In that little known work, it is documented by Shifrin, that from the 1950s to 70s, there were over two thousand concentration camps in the USSR. In that group, forty-one camps were considered death camps. No, the communists did not gas and burn the prisoners as the Nazis had done. The death was a slow agonizing death, due to harsh, hazardous working conditions, poor nutrition and sanitation, inadequate medical care, and radiation poisoning. Many of those sentenced to these camps did not come out, except in a casket. Many political prisoners, including Christians, were sentenced to those camps. These prisoners were put to work in Uranium mines or forced to work cleaning the nozzles and parts of nuclear powered submarines without protective gear or necessary precautions. Life expectancy for those held in such camps might be as much as five years, often times much less. Death from radiation sickness occurred frequently.

Shifrin's researched book also contains many personal testimonials of individuals held captive in the Soviet concentration camps during the 1970s. On page 94 of that book, Shifrin includes the photo of a young Jewish man named Feldman who was placed in a KGB camp simply because he applied for an exit visa to Israel.

On page 95, Shifrin's book includes photo documentation of the ruins of a Baptist family's home which was bulldozed and destroyed because a prayer meeting was regularly held at the house. What follows is a partial testimonial found on page 103, from a man known as LB. He was a former prisoner of the Moldavian camp system. Here, LB reports on his experiences in camp Krikovo:

> We were brought to this strict regime camp in 1975. There were a number of Jewish prisoners like myself

here. We were arrested on various false charges after having received our visas to Israel. Our first day at the camp began with the confiscation of our books and personal belongings. Those who showed any resistance were immediately beaten up and thrown into an isolation cell. The very next day, having already been exhausted by the prison conditions and by undernourishment, we were sent straight to the quarry. Work norms were not individually set, but determined rather by the performance of the entire brigade....

The guards often beat the prisoners up. Once in 1976, two prisoners escaped from the camp. The guards however found them hiding in a hay stack and stabbed them to death with their bayonets. The guards later boasted of their deed.

The prisoners at this camp were worked to exhaustion. But there were those, the religious prisoners, whose visual presence was a source of strength for the others. There were many of them. They prayed openly and maintained an image of unbroken serenity even when they were thrown into the isolation cell or denied their privileges. Two such men were Boris Plyuta, a Pentecostal, and Semen Korzhanets, a Baptist. Their courage proved to be of enormous help to us (End of LB's statement) [3].

Locations of many prison camps and facilities are documented in that 1980 book. The book is most likely out of print. Perhaps a copy might be tracked down by contacting the organization, Voice of the Martyrs, founded by the Romanian Pastor Richard Wurmbrand.

Romania, in its former dictatorial communist police state, was not far behind the Soviet Union in the regulation and oppression of Christianity. The State's treatment of those who followed Biblical mandates as exemplified by Jesus Christ was often harsh.

Richard Wurmbrand in his book *Tortured for Christ*, describes many historical atrocities committed by the communists against Christians in Romania and Russia during the 1950s and 60s, during a period known as the Time of Terror. It is recommended that the reader also consider reading Wurmbrand's book to gain some understanding, to a small degree, of what many Christians endured in Eastern Europe under early communist domination. A few examples taken from his work follow.

> Christians were tortured by their communist captors in cruel and unusual ways. Christian men were hung upside down on ropes and beaten, they were placed in refrigerated cells with little clothing. They were brought to the point of death by freezing, taken out warmed up and then placed in refrigeration again, this practice was repeated over and over. They were burned with hot irons, strapped to tables and beaten with rods and many other horrors. Many were placed upon wooden crosses upon the ground where other prisoners were forced to urinate and defecate upon them [4].

Wurmbrand gives an example of a pastor who endured torture with red hot irons and knives and was badly beaten. Hungry rats were driven into his cell which would try to eat him. He suffered sleep deprivation protecting himself from rats. After two weeks the communist tormentors brought in the man's fourteen-year old son and began to beat the son in front of his father. Upon seeing this, the father, in anguish, was about to submit to the communists. The son cried out to his father, "Don't do me the injustice of having a traitor as a parent. If they kill me, I will die with the words, 'Jesus and my fatherland." [5] This enraged the communists, who then beat the son to death. Wurmbrand writes of many such things in his book. It is not for the faint of heart.

Another example of communist persecution is that of a Romanian pastor who was involved with taking thousands of Russian Bibles into the Soviet Union from Romania for several years during the 1970s. He was captured eventually inside Romania. He had delivered thousands of Christian books and Bibles to Russian Christians. In August of 1980 Dumitru was caught, imprisoned, and interrogated for months. He was beaten every day and repeatedly shocked in an electric chair. Arrests, interrogations, and torture were common to him. In 1983 he was hung by his waist and beaten on three occasions, resulting in broken ribs and deformity to his rib cage. I met Dumitru much later, spoke with him, and interviewed others who stated, "He is the real deal!"

While Romania did not have the Russian KGB, it did have the dreaded and feared Securitate state police, at times acting as, and called, the Secret Police. During the communist dictatorship of Ceausescu, the Securitate was considered to be one of the fiercest communist police agencies in the world. By the end of the 1980s this totalitarian force had grown to an army almost sixty thousand strong, in a country of only ninety-two thousand forty-three square miles with a population of approximately twenty million. Thousands of Romanians had been imprisoned as political prisoners, and hundreds to thousands lost their lives at the hands of the Securitate from 1949 to 1989. Romania had its own gulag where beatings and torture were used to bring people into submission to the communist will. It has been reported that the Securitate even placed assignation contracts out on leading dissidents. In one case, it is alleged that the agency contracted with the notorious Carlos the Jackal to kill Ion M. Pacepa, a high-ranking Romanian Intelligence officer and Romanian dissident who defected to the west. In 1987 Pacepa authored the book *Red Horizons*, which contains a revealing story about the corruption and the secret criminal life of the dictator Nicolae Ceausescu.

According to Pacepa, the Securitate had its own Division of Counterintelligence in the state penal system known as Romanian Service K. It was modeled after a similar section of the Soviet KGB. This unit was known to have done the worst acts against jailed political prisoners to gain intelligence and incriminating evidence. Service K used torture, microphone monitors in cells, and stool pigeon informants to accomplish its goals. But more heinously, some political prisoners were even exterminated via staged suicides, poisons, or radiation exposure. It was in the spring of 1970 that Service K added radioactive isotopes obtained from the KGB to its inventory of death. Ceausescu called the radioactive materials "Radu," and he personally ordered it to be administered to some of his personal political enemies. It was reported that the dosage used was just enough to inflict lethal cancers [6].

The Romanian Securitate counter intelligence units were structured into primarily three levels. The first level operated against Jews, ethnic Germans, the Hungarian minority, and the religious. A second section classified as a Top Secret Unit answered to the Ministry of the Interior, which also controlled and regulated the state collective farms and enterprises. A third level which was classified as Top Secret of High

Interest answered more directly to Ceausescu and the highest ranking designated officials used in special projects.

During the 1980s the Securitate was continuing its efforts to destroy any form of opposition to Ceausescu and the communists, which included various denominations of Christianity and the unregistered Underground Church. Tactics used against the Romanian people included forced entry into homes, bugging and wiretapping, monitoring telephone conversations, reading private mail, interception of written and oral communications, house arrests, and imprisonments. The Securitate also utilized rumors, frame-ups, public humiliation, denunciations, censorship, beatings, and torture as tools to control the public. The tactics were similar to those used by the Czechoslovakian StB, the Stasi of East Germany, and the Soviet KGB, although at times the intensity of political repression varied within countries and within the will of the Soviet KGB. It truly was a different time for the citizens of Eastern Europe during that era.

The people of Eastern Europe were under the thumb of the various Secret Police agencies which enforced communist rule. Dissent from the Communist Party philosophy was tolerated in varying degrees by the enforcers within each country. Many Christians found themselves at odds with communist philosophies and power brokers just because of practicing their belief in God, suffering as a result. Although many of those Believers courageously did not view their plight as a circumstance to be spurned, they did suffer for faithfully continuing to serve the Lord.

The courageous ones of this account are those who followed their religious convictions about Christ in spite of oppression and persecutions. They did not deny Him and continued to press on through hardships. Many of those Christians stood firm in their faith, not loving their own lives as much as Jesus Christ. Many were part of what became known as the Underground Church. Even though following Christ may have meant assignment to the worst jobs, loss of property, loss of family, loss of homes, public humiliation, prison, beatings, torture, or perhaps even death, they still chose to believe in and follow Jesus Christ.

During the Communist Era in Eastern Europe, following WWII until 1989, there were well over four dozen Humanitarian NGOs (Non-Government Organizations) of various sizes and spheres of influence working out of Austria, Germany, Holland, Sweden, Switzerland, and the U.S. Those groups labored to support the religious dissentients found to be in opposition to atheistic communism, just because they believed in God and followed Him.

There were volunteers from the U.S., Canada, Holland, Switzerland, Sweden, West Germany, and other countries who acted on what they knew about the political oppression of the Christian dissidents and Underground Church in Eastern Europe. There were those who worked discreetly via official channels and those who worked by unofficial means to aid those living under the rule of communist dictatorships.

This is a personal memoir of involvement to help the Christian community and Underground Church suffering under communism behind the Iron Curtain. I learned many lessons from those believers about the meaning of the word "dedication," as we were often convicted and challenged because of their courageous shining examples of faithful service.

[Authors note: More insight verifying the plight of the people of Eastern Europe during the Communist Era may be gained by reading *The Black Book of Communism* written by Karel Bartosek, chapter 20, pages 394-456, and the book *Tortured for Christ* by Richard Wurmbrand, listed in Appendix III, The Recommended Reading List.]

Toward the Curtain

On a beautiful July 4th in the early 1980s I was driving southeast on a German autobahn, traveling with my teammates, Bill Larson from Montana and Vance Goldman, a rancher also from that Rocky Mountain state. Bill, a former businessman, had stopped selling real estate to embark on this trip. Vance had been studying Russian for the past two years to use the language as a tool to help the dissidents of Eastern Europe. During that time one may have been led to believe religious persecution of Christians was something from ancient times, when Christians were thrown to lions in the Roman Coliseum or burned at the stake in Europe. A causal traveler in Eastern Europe who was unaware might have assumed Christian persecution was just an exaggeration of circumstances. But that view was not the full reality of life for dedicated Christians on the east side of the Iron Curtain. That was our destination for the following day. We were headed for Czechoslovakia, where on the other side of that political barrier, people were often persecuted because of actively practicing their Christian faith.

I had been behind the wheel of the van for the previous few hours, driving southeast on the Budesrepublik Deutschland Autobahn {3} headed toward Czechoslovakia near Nurnberg, going southeast toward Regensburg. It was close to time to rotate drivers at our next fuel stop. Vance was to take the wheel and Bill would be navigator. I would move to the back of the van and get settled in order to get some rest and maybe catch some Z's. We were rotating drivers after every few hours to keep everyone fresh. We stopped, fueled up, and checked the oil, water and vehicle road worthiness, because we were transporting a heavy load of books in the light van we were driving. Vance took over and I rotated to the back to kick back.

After some chit chat with my traveling buddies, I started trying to rest. Bill and Vance were up front practicing their German on each other, although not loudly. I was resting in the rear of the van, with my mind starting to wonder about events that may lay before us the next day and about its significance. We would be crossing into Eastern Europe at a checkpoint crossing from West Germany into Czechoslovakia. Checkpoint Flomava was where the border guards would most likely ask us if we had "weapons, pornography, religious literature or Bibles." I considered it interesting that communists considered a Bible to be contraband equal to drugs, pornography, and weapons. But I had border crossings under my belt where guards had asked that very question. So, it would come as no surprise. I'd been studying some about the communist view of religion, as well. That socio-economic philosophy denied the reality of the God of the Bible, becoming a god unto itself. Its own philosophy or state religion of atheism, if you will, determined what truth was. What was morally right or wrong was determined by the State, not the writings taken from the Bible or religious literature.

While kicking back in the rear of the van, watching the scenic German country side stream by, I continued to meditate on some of those things. My mental wondering turned to thoughts about the Holocaust. *How did such a horrible thing as that happen in this beautiful place? How and why did that happen here?* I concluded that National Socialism (Nazism) and Global Socialism (Communism) weren't far removed from one another, in reality. Perhaps, in some ways Nazism was worse, but Soviet communism had also left a large stain of blood on human history. Dictators Hitler, Stalin and Mao became god-like authorities unto themselves, using State socialism to establish their control over the citizens. The people were used as "worker bees" and "the useful idiots," as Lenin called them, to do their bidding. They vilified and preyed upon those who opposed them. They were true despotic rulers who used propaganda and mind control to manipulate the masses. Lenin was a firm believer in using fear to control the masses. God was and is an inconvenience for communists. Believing in a higher power leads to moral accountability. Morality was what the Nazis had proclaimed it to be, as well. The godless political ideologies of Communism and Nazism really didn't seem far removed from one another to me. In my simple meditations, riding in the back of that van, it just seemed that both Communism and Nazism were just political systems where socialism is used by demigods to gain control and power over people. National Socialism and Global Socialism thrive on propaganda, using fear to control others. I guess the same could be said for some religious dogmas.

As I looked out at the lush countryside while absorbed in my thoughts, the serenity of the German landscape was captivating. Yet, not a full generation ago, gross horrors brought about by the Nazis had occurred in that beautiful country. The horrors committed against Jewish people, Christian ministers, priests, and others are well-documented. The lush green German countryside with its rolling hills, thick wooded forests, and the wandering rivers, had once been a place of horror, unrivaled in magnitude in the annuals of human history. How that happened in that beautiful place with its amazing landscape puzzled me.

Man's ill treatment of his fellow man continued to press in on my thoughts, as I remembered Dachau where I had visited with Bill, as part of another team, just a few months before. The Dachau Concentration Camp, a camp operated by the Nazis from 1933 to 1945 was a place where approximately thirty-two thousand people were recorded to have died from substandard conditions, starvation, torture, experimentation, and disease. It was estimated by many that the numbers greatly exceed the thirty-one thousand plus deaths recorded by the Germans. Some sources indicate the number to be as high as two hundred thousand [19].

What is factually known about the camp is that it was the second concentration camp opened by the Nazis. Previously, it had been a former ammunition factory. But in 1933 it was identified by Heinrich Himmler as a place to be converted into a facility for internment. In addition to the thousands of Jewish prisoners, many religious and political prisoners were imprisoned there as well. Those were individuals who had been listed as "Enemies of the State." Many were clergymen or political prisoners of conscience. The Nazis, much like communists, closely monitored the activities of clergymen and church congregations. Many were denounced, arrested, and thrown into the camps, much like the communist regions of Eastern Europe, the USSR, China, and North Korea just over a decade later.

Records at the Dachau historical site indicated there were over two thousand seven hundred clergymen which had been incarcerated at that camp. Approximately ninety-four percent of those were Polish priests, one hundred nine of the clergymen were Protestant ministers, and another twenty-two were Orthodox Priests; they were placed in the camp for their moral stand against the Nazis. Roughly four hundred forty-seven German priests were imprisoned there as well. Records indicate that one hundred twenty priests were used in Malaria experiments and another twenty were used in medical experiments where pus was injected into the victim to see how their bodies reacted to infection.

Some of the totalitarian communist regimes of Eastern Europe from the 1940s through 1980s historically were not that far removed from the Nazi philosophies and actions during the 30s and 40s. Eastern European (EE) communist countries had had their own reigns of terror from the late 1940s to the mid-1950s. Many ministers and Christian leaders were placed in prison and tortured for their convictions which did not adhere to the party line in those communist States. Hundreds and thousands had been put to death in gruesome ways or died at the hands of the communists. During the twentieth century, the total human death toll from communist purges and wars of aggression worldwide exceeds 100 million deaths [8]. Countless time upon time, citizens who did not conform to the communist State dictates received brutal, cruel, harsh, and inhumane treatment. This has also been one of the greatest travesties of human history. The rise to power of the communists in various countries was vicious and bloody. A mental recap of testimonials from men like Richard Wurmbrandt and others that I had read, plus recollection about the communist purges under Stalin in the USSR, Mao in China, and Pol Pot in Cambodia, made it easy for me to come to the conclusion that Nazism and Communism really weren't so different.

Looking out the window of the van my thoughts briefly snapped back to the present moment as I looked down toward the river we were driving along and noticed a team of four guys who were sculling in a shallow draft fast boat. They were moving along quickly in that smooth portion of the Donau River (aka The Danube) as their oars grabbed the water with smooth precision, propelling them rapidly through the water. It looked like fun. The team looked well-disciplined as they pulled in unison on the oars, putting in team effort; but it looked like something I would enjoy. I would have liked to be trying it myself.

But on the following day, the team I was on would be entering a Police State where it would have secret police agents who monitored visitors' movements, like ours. We would be required to check in with authorities every night at a camp ground or hotel, so our travel could be tracked by the communists. We were only hours away from entering Czechoslovakia with our contraband cargo of Bibles. We would be smuggling them through the check point and then covertly getting them into the hands of contacts within the Underground Church in Eastern Europe.

I conjectured that if the world was a fair place, we wouldn't soon be attempting what we were about to do. We most likely would have been out doing one of the various things each of us enjoyed—like hiking, riding horses, fishing, hunting, running, bicycling, playing volleyball or football, or even working cattle, or maybe even sculling. I'd done a little rowing in a shallow two-man boat with my Dutch friend, Marius, on canals in Holland not many days before. Seeing those Germans in that boat drew me to it. Yet helping the believers, often considered as enemies of the State to the communists, was a big motivator for each of us on that team. It was more important to each of us than just seeking out our own pleasures, trying to accumulate stuff, or build our own kingdoms. We each felt the need to make an effort to help those living under communist oppression. We were three ordinary guys who responded to a call. We had almost a thousand Bibles and books on board, some clothes, and a little food for those with whom we would contact.

The Believers who insisted on following the tenants of their faith were considered ignorant by communists and a "less-than" social class deserving little respect – an under-class where social discrimination was part of the mistreatment against them. As non-communists, they were unable to secure the good jobs. Those were reserved for good party members. Therefore, the Christians were often poor even by Eastern European standards. The Believers not only endured physical persecutions but often suffered socio-economic discrimination as well.

As I sat in the back of the van listening to the road noise, watching the scenery go by as we rumbled east, I started thinking about my family back home who would be celebrating the 4th of July in a few hours. I thought about Dad who had served as an MP during the Korean War and his brother who served with the Marines. They grew up in the rolling hills of East Texas where they both became excellent horsemen and marksmen. They learned to ride at early ages and used to play tag on horseback. They had fun as young men on my grandparents' small family farm where they worked and played hard. It was there where they learned to shoot using a .22 rifle and became pretty good marksmen, too. My dad's younger brother, Kurt, had told me about the marksmanship skills of his two older brothers: "Dee and your dad where pretty good shots. Dee could strike a match with that .22, then with a second shot put it out. Then he'd hand it to your dad, your dad would shoot off the match head." I asked my dad about it. He replied, "I never could strike that match, but Dee could. All I could do was knock off the head."

I thought about the times my dad and uncle had together as young men. Dad often told stories about the adventures they enjoyed as they grew up. Then I reflected that I had never met Dad's brother because he lost his life fighting in the Korean War. He served as a Browning Automatic Rifleman, aka "BAR-tender" with the 1st Marine Division. He was posthumously awarded the Silver Star. My dad would say my uncle did what GIs or Marines used to call an "Audie Murphy" or "John Wayne." Dad's brother charged forward with his B.A.R under heavy enemy fire facing strong odds and repelled a large group of the enemy combatants, who had overrun most of his unit's outpost. Audie Murphy was considered as the highest decorated soldier during War World II. Veterans would speak of him in admiration, and dad spoke of Audie Murphy and his brother with admiration. My uncle lost his life at the end of that battle.

Freedom does have a price tag. It cost Dad's brother his life, fighting with fellow Marines to hold ground on a mountain ridge in Korea. His son had to grow up never having his dad, and our Grandma suffered grief over that loss all her days. My uncles and aunt lost a brother they dearly loved, which still touches them to this day, especially around Memorial Day. Dad will not watch a war movie or documentary about that war. It makes him think of his brother. When thinking of the uncle I never knew and the loss suffered by my dad, grandparents, aunts, uncles and all who loved him, I think of the scripture, "Greater love hath no man than this that he lay down his life for his friends." (John15:13 NASB). My uncle died fighting with, and for, his fellow Marines so the Korean people could know freedoms, including religious freedom. It could be said my dad's brother lost his life fighting for others.

As we rolled east on that holiday, I continued to think about my dad who served during the Korean War as well. Although he did not go overseas, part of his service time included serving with a Company of army MPs to provide security during nuclear testing at Frenchman's Gulch, in the Nevada Nuclear Proving testing grounds. He was stationed there during a few of the nuclear bomb tests during his time there. However, when his company had to charge ground zero after a nuclear detonation, Dad was on family bereavement leave to attend his brother's funeral. However, I learned later, Dad did witness about four or five nuclear tests during his temporary duty (TDY) assignment in Nevada. But according to him, he was several miles away.

GIs who participated in those nuclear experiments are now known as Atomic Vets. A few of those Vets who marched toward nuclear explosion ground zero came down with some forms of cancers years later. So whether it is on foreign soil or service at home to guard and protect what American's have enjoyed, freedom has not been free. There is a price to maintain freedom, guard it, and preserve it. The same can be said about spiritual freedom. It must be guarded. Also, it takes effort to guard our spiritual condition. We must routinely pray, read the Bible, have Christian fellowship, and stay away from harmful addictions to grow spiritually. We need to put forth effort to avoid sins to know the Lord and experience more of His love, joy, and peace.

As our team continued east, I continued to muse, *Hmm, it's the Fourth of July*, and I wondered what the folks back home would be doing for the holiday. *Would they be having hot dogs, hamburgers or BBQ steaks? Man, a good hamburger would be great about now!* I thought. The thought stimulated the salivary juices. It had been a couple of months since I'd had one and figured it could be awhile before I might have another, so I started fantasizing about how good a burger would taste. I realized I needed to take my mind off it. It just made me hungry. So I started pondering what my cousins would be doing for the 4th. I wondered if some would be going to a car race, or maybe head to a rodeo or a softball game. I believed they would be having a good time doing something they enjoyed. I wondered if they were going to go to a fireworks show or have their own at home. *What would Dad and Mom be up to? Would they be spending it with friends from church or family?* Then I started thinking about what they would be eating...back to food again! It must have been growing toward "chow" time.

I started missing home some, and felt a bit nostalgic. I thought more about cousins, wondering how they were doing. Then I started thinking about riding horses, fishing and hunting in the coastal mountains and Central Valley of California, and hanging in parts of Texas with them. Yeah, freedom ... the folks back home would be celebrating it, and soon our team would be crossing into a country where there was no such holiday. Hopefully, we would not be having to stay longer than our itinerary was planned.

What a special gift we'd been given in the U.S.! The Christians in Eastern Europe and the USSR didn't have the freedoms we had been blessed with. I knew there were those in Eastern Europe who longed for it. I had visited with some who had asked what it was like living in the U.S. After speaking with some about it in response to their curiosity, I didn't talk much about the subject. I wanted to be sensitive to their circumstances, not wanting to pour salt in open wounds, so to speak. I tried to keep the conversations on other topics. A few shared with me how they prayed for America that we would remain free and the church would stay strong. I knew many wished to have their own Bibles and the ability to attend a home-based Bible study without worrying about being followed and then interrogated by police. Many dreamed about being able to have open discussions about God or just being able to fellowship with foreign visitors in their homes without repercussions from the State. There were those who hoped to teach their children about Jesus without being reported to a teacher for committing a crime against the State.

People in Czechoslovakia couldn't even own a typewriter unless it was registered with the police. Christians and Jewish folks had to be cautious about their speech involving God or religion lest it cause unwanted attention, which could result in a knock on the door from the secret police. I had read accounts and personally talked with some who had experienced that knock on the door.

As I thought of home, I hoped the folks would have a good time celebrating the 4th, realizing how truly special it is. Yet not one family member had a clue where I was right then, much less what our team would be doing the next morning. We had to take special precautions and not divulge our mission to anyone. It was a covert activity. We needed to be discreet, use the bit of training we had, and rely upon the Lord. Only trip planners knew approximately where we would be. A few support staff would know the country where we were headed. Four or five knew our itinerary and who our contacts were to be, but that was about it. None of those on staff were to talk about what they did know, not even to family or close, trusted friends. "Loose lips sink ships," as they say.

When thinking about the Fourth of July and pondering what was to come, I had some consolation knowing that the next day we would be attempting to take in a type of freedom to the people of Czechoslovakia—the freedom of the soul and spirit. Jesus said, "You shall know the truth and the truth will make you free." We would be taking in one of the most important of freedoms. I considered that which impacts the mind and heart of a man or woman to be the beginning of freedom. People can be in bondage not only to political ideologies, but to many various addictions as well. So I realized what we were doing was taking in a different type of freedom—hopefully, something which would be personally liberating to the recipients and provide hope.

My thoughts continued to drift: *If communism (or any ideology for that matter) was so great, why were manipulation, coercion, brutality and force necessary to maintain it? Why was it that people from the Eastern European countries were required by the government to believe the party line? And why were people coerced by the State to be adherents to a certain doctrine of thinking?* A State religion seemed to be an equal of sorts which had to be maintained by coercion. Even strict conditional permission to travel abroad had to be granted from the State on a case by case basis. Why was that? The people who left would most likely choose not to return seemed to be the answer. That's what seemed to be the case in my way of thinking anyway. In my view, I believed God's view of liberty to be one which included individual free will and choice. When coercion, intimidation and abuse are used to control people, it demonstrates the weakness of the dogma, ideology or individual attempting to rule and control others. Many organized religious beliefs have done the same at various times in history too. Not being ignorant to the fact that many religious leaders have used political systems to oppress people, I thought about the arrogance and selfishness of man. Those religious leaders who have resorted to such things must not really have come to know the God of the Universe, His ways and views about liberty, love, and individual responsibility, or they would not have oppressed those to whom they were given charge. Yes, we were taking in a bit of freedom and hope in the psychological and spiritual sense to the Eastern Europeans. I was not extremely apprehensive at that time about what lay ahead for us the next day, but I definitely was contemplating the possible results if we were caught smuggling religious literature at the border checkpoint. I continued to try to get some sleep in the back of that van, but couldn't. I started thinking about the past year and recounting events which led up to that point in time on that mission with Bill and Vance.

Reflections

The previous year had been an interesting time. I had been working as a veterinary technician for Neal, who was not only a good veterinarian but a God-fearing and dedicated Christian. He was a very intelligent guy who graduated toward the top of his veterinary class. He loved to talk about Christian service while at work, too. He was not shy about engaging in conversation about the things of God during our work days. He was hard-working, dedicated to the profession, and had high ethics.

Neal and I would be in route to deliver a calf, preforming surgery on a cow, or tending to the health of a farm animal and find ourselves in a conversation about Jesus, the Bible or Christian service. He was active in his church and involved in a Bible study fellowship on Friday evenings. He would talk about it while we worked. It was good to work with a man who loved God and all His creatures, big and small—a type of James Harriot with a big world view. I enjoyed the conversations about faith and service with him.

During the summer, Neal had invited me to attend one of those Friday night Bible study meetings. I normally attended a denominational church on Sundays but thought checking out that non-denominational fellowship group might be interesting. He had talked a lot about it; so one Friday evening I decided to check it out and really enjoyed it. I met some Christian folks who were not dogmatic about religious denominational doctrines, just people who loved God and each other. The people in the small group were engaging and friendly, not overly religious. It was a relaxed, casual balanced atmosphere. We sang worship songs, read out of the Bible, and had a time of discussion about a scriptural theme. The focus on the scriptural text and the purposes of God in our lives, not just religious dogma, was encouraging. I met a guy named Walt there, a man full of zeal and love for God above all else, who believed in treating others justly, even at cost to himself. He was a combat veteran who had spent time as a LLRP (Long Range Reconnaissance Patrol) in Vietnam. He was a man of moral and physical courage, truly a good team leader. He had received a Silver Star for carrying out wounded soldiers to safety when under fire. He had learned a lot during his time in the jungles of Vietnam and also in his time in the Christian ministry. I felt fortunate to spend time with him and learn from his experiences. He became a friend I respect and look up to (and have for many years now).

After several weeks of going to that Friday night fellowship group, I decided to check out a regular Sunday service at the church. I liked it and eventually ended up attending services there. I didn't miss a Sunday if I could help it. I looked forward to church.

Near the end of the following winter, I took a few days off work and went to visit an old college buddy. I hadn't seen my friend, Mike, in over a year. During the visit he gave me a book about life after death. He was a bit of a cowboy and a bull rider and had been voted "Most Inspirational" on his Junior College football team. He had a big heart and a spirit of encouragement. Although he had been raised in the Catholic Church, been an altar boy, and been taught about God as a kid by his mom, he was not a man of personal faith in Jesus Christ at the time. He thought I would like the book. I left his place, went camping, took the book, read it and the Bible, which captivated a lot of my time for the next couple of days. It was not only a relaxing time out fishing, but a spiritual one too—a time of personal reflection, a real Tom Sawyer time. I did some bait fishing and read, checking my bobber over the top of the book. I caught a few catfish, but God caught more of my heart. Those couple of days spent studying and meditating on spiritual things reinforced thoughts I had been having about God and Christian service. The book *Beyond Death's Doors* by Dr. Maurice Rawlings MD validated things proclaimed in the Bible about eternity for me.

That time challenged me, yet also further strengthened my faith to a point where I wanted my life to count for something other than a paycheck, chasing cows, and just attempting to accumulate stuff. By the end of that trip to the lake I knew I wanted to work to fulfill the purposes of God in my life. I felt a sense of confirmation about my faith and knew I wanted to serve God with my life and not waste it. A path of service which I had not yet seen was beginning to be laid out before me. The Lord was knocking on the door of my heart for greater commitment to His will and purposes. I didn't have a clue about the path upon which I was about to embark.

As that short mini-vacation neared its end, I had lunch with Dale, a former roommate and friend of Neal's. He invited me to a meeting with students that Friday night not far from the local campus. There was a guest speaker from an organization connected with Open Doors International. He was to share about the persecution of Christians in Eastern Europe.

Open Doors was an organization founded by Brother Andrew, a Dutchman who worked to support and encourage Believers persecuted and oppressed by the communists. Andrew had also authored the book, *God's Smuggler,* which was his testimonial about supporting the Underground Church in Eastern Europe. Couriers with Open Doors smuggled in Bibles, books, food, clothes, printing equipment, and various other supplies to the Underground Church and religious dissidents in that part of the world.

I had personally heard Andrew speak my senior year in high school and had also read his book, *God's Smuggler.* It had intrigued me then. I had even sent some small financial donations to his organization a few times during my college years. I thought it would be interesting to check out that Friday night meeting where someone would be speaking about Eastern Europe.

As the speaker, Les Samuels with Eastern European Bible Mission, shared about the Underground Church, I was once again stirred about Christians' circumstances. During the question and answer session after the presentation, I asked a lot of questions. A nagging desire to do more kept tugging at me, which continued after the meeting. The passion to do something regarding the injustices I heard about continued to grow. Doing something about the issues Eastern European believers were dealing with became a priority for me. I was not content with knowing about their circumstances and just telling others. I wanted to do something about it. After that meeting, I began thinking about what I could do to help the Christians suffering under the yoke of communism.

Days later, while thinking about the circumstances of the Eastern Europeans, I was reading through the gospel of Matthew. The passages in Chapter 16, verses 24 – 26, seemed to leap off the page at me. There Jesus was saying to His disciples:

"If anyone wishes to come after me, let him deny himself, and take up his cross, and follow Me. For whoever wishes to save his life shall lose it; but whoever loses his life for my sake shall find it. For what shall a man be profited, if he gains the whole world and forfeits his soul? Or what shall a man give in exchange for his life?" (NASB)

It seemed like God was speaking out of the scriptures to me: "Are you willing to serve me? It could cost you, but are you willing?" Long story short, after no small amount of prayer and counsel with friends, I decided to apply with the Open Doors affiliate, Eastern European Bible Mission, and then see where it led.

I contacted them and requested an application. A few days after having applied I was again reading in Matthew. This time in Chapter 25, verses 35 - 40:

"For I was hungry and you gave Me something to eat; I was thirsty, and you gave Me something to drink; I was a stranger, and you invited Me in; naked, and you clothed Me; I was sick and you visited Me; I was in prison, and you came to Me." Then the righteous will answer Him, saying, "Lord, when did we see You hungry, and feed You, or thirsty and give You a drink? And when did we see You a stranger, and invite You in, or naked, and cloth you? And when did we see you sick, or in prison, and come to you?" And the King will answer and say to them, "Truly I say to you, to the extent that you did it to one of these brothers of mine, even the least of them, you did it to Me." (NASB)

That scripture spoke to me. It seemed to be a confirmation that I was on the right track. My acceptance with the organization was in the hands of the Lord, but having applied was definitely the right move. The outcome was in God's hands.

Brother Andrew, the founder of Open Doors had been taking Bibles, books, and supplies to support the Underground Church since the late 1950s. Andrew had been a commando in the Dutch army during the Dutch-Indonesian war of the late 1940s. He had stepped on a landmine during that conflict and was severely wounded. He walked with a limp for several years. But after committing his life to the Lord and studying theology in Bible College, his foot was healed. He felt called to serve the people of Eastern Europe. The book, *God's Smuggler*, about Brother Andrew's service to the persecuted church is a dynamic story. He was lead to help those suffering political and religious persecution behind the Iron Curtain and then globally. His organization still serves persecuted Christians around the world today.

Hank Paulson, also a Dutchman and a friend and associate of Brother Andrew, was the European Director of Open Doors - Eastern European Bible Mission (EEBM), a Dutch-American organization, known in Holland as The Answer Foundation. In the late 1970s to 1980, EEBM was part of Open Doors. As I understood it, in the business world or in a government agency it would have been called a Division of Open Doors. Hank had been serving the Underground Church and religious dissidents for some time. He was part of the European Operations branch of Open Doors. He had been taking Bibles, books, and supplies behind the Iron Curtain since the early 1970s. He later authored the book, *Beyond the Wall*, about the plight of Believers living in Eastern Europe. I decided to send an application to be part of his team headquartered in Holland.

The application was a lengthy five pages. It seemed like one of the longest job applications I had ever filled out. I prayed and asked that God's will be done in the matter. The application was thorough enough for any disqualifying factors to come into play, but none did.

After the mission completed verification of my application information and performed their own background check, I received an acceptance letter with enclosed instructional information and assignments. Additionally, I studied a little German, some Russian history, and information about believing dissidents in Eastern Europe. Also, I studied leadership and cultural studies topics. I would be on my way to Europe in a few weeks and needed to learn a lot during the interim.

One Saturday, Walt, his bother-in law David, and I attended a lecture by Richard Wurmbrand, the exiled Romanian pastor who had been imprisoned for 14 years and tortured for his faith in God. Wurmbrand's lecture was informative and challenging. But one thing which impacted me as much as his words was the fact that he had to do his presentation sitting down. That was because his feet had been severely damaged by communist interrogators who had used clubs and rods on his feet when they beat him. Wurmbrand was the author of the book *Tortured for Christ*, which I had read and have a copy to this day.

In addition to hearing Wurmbrand speak during that season, I was reminded on several occasions of a statement made by a missionary pilot who was killed during to trying to help others. He was trying to help the South American *Auca* Indian tribe. The missionary pilot, Jim Elliott, once said before his life was taken in the jungles of South America, "He is no fool who gives up what he cannot keep in order to gain what he can never lose." That thought came to me often while thinking about what I was stepping into.

One day not long before leaving for Europe I went hiking in some San Gabriel Mountains overlooking the Los Angeles area. I spent some time in prayer and reading a little New Testament I had taken along. I started feeling a bit overly religiously zealous, you might say, and became a little too proud about what I was going to do. After a time on the maintain side, I headed back to my apartment and began thinking, *I'm gonna go help those poor people suffering in Eastern Europe. Yeah, I'm going to go do something special for God.* My pride started to swell and along with it my hat size, as I thought about what **I** was going to do to help those who were suffering.

Later that evening after making it back to my apartment, I walked over to the Bible sitting on my study desk; I opened it to the book of Hebrews. My gaze fell on Hebrews 12:3-4:

> "For consider Him who has endured such hostility by sinners against Himself, so that you may not grow weary and lose heart. ...YOU HAVE NOT YET RESISTED TO THE POINT OF SHEDDING BLOOD IN YOUR STRIVING AGAINST SIN."

I knew that many in Eastern Europe had. Woah! You could've knocked me over with a feather! Was I humbled! I had been feeling like I was something special for a little while, and God jumped on that really fast. I was quickly reminded that those I thought that **I** was going to help were some who had shed blood and been placed in prisons for nothing more than giving away a Bible, attending a House Church meeting, or being involved in unpermitted Christian activities. Many had been beaten and some had died, having been martyred for the Gospel in a quest for religious freedom to worship God as they chose. Who was I to get puffed up? There is no room in service and team work for self-indulgence. Confidence in the Lord, yes…self-indulgent ego, no! The Lord had corrected me. But it was the good correction of a loving Father to a son—not harsh, but clear.

August 30th was no ordinary day. It started out early as a nice, sunny, warm day at the folks' house and ended at a busy airport terminal with me trying to catch a flight out to New York, then to Brussels. That day was the beginning of a new season in life wherein my world view would be impacted for the rest of my days. Briefly, before leaving to Europe, I again was reminded of the quote by the missionary Jim Elliott, "He is no fool who gives up what he cannot keep, in order to gain what he can never lose."

Making It to Europe

Labor Day weekend at the airport was a "zoo"! Due to circumstances, I was flying standby but couldn't catch a flight out—just too many people. I missed the first go around for the "on-call." I knew I couldn't be wasting time still stuck in an airport stateside, so I coughed up extra money to fly with American Airlines to New York, but they didn't have space until a little later that day. I prayed and ask the Lord for some help. A few minutes after prayer, American Airlines announced that anyone heading to New York could catch a connecting flight to New York by flying on a charter flight into Washington DC and then to New York. It left within the hour. As busy as it was that weekend, I imagine many others were praying to catch a flight out to the east coast too. But that announcement was certainly an answer to prayer for me. *Hey, anything that would get me outta there to New York!* I caught that ride and ended up flying with a soccer team. Being that it was a chartered flight, they had steak for dinner on the flight. Well, I ended up with steak, too. I certainly did enjoy the meal with them! I hadn't eaten much in a while and was I ready for some good chow!

    I finally made it to DC and then caught the connecting flight to JFK that night. I spent the next day in JFK trying to catch a standby flight out. What a newbie! Here it was Labor Day weekend, and I was flying standby trying to catch a flight out of New York to Brussels. It was a long day to say the least. But I did get to meet some interesting folks. I hung out for a short time with some German guys, then met some European girls headed to the Continent.

    I was in New York trying to catch a flight out, but had a bit of a snag as my luggage had gotten lost from the flights between California and

New York. Yet, I still needed to catch a plane as I worked through the luggage issue. I tried other carriers, but they were booked too. It was wait, or pay an arm and a leg; and I needed to watch my cash. Well, while in line waiting for a carrier, a cute girl from Jerusalem sat down by me. Anna was a student at UCLA and had been called back up for duty in the Israeli Air Force. Next to her came a good looking blond girl from France. Sylvia was just returning home after being in Virginia for a while. Both of them were pretty nice looking and friendly. Things were looking up. Hanging out with them sure beat the German guys any day of the week! Then there was a guy from L,A, who showed up and happened to be an author headed to Europe to do research on a book he was writing about Church history.

While dealing with the boredom of killing time sitting at that check-in area, I sat there, read some, and visited with the two girls. After a while, the girls and I went to lunch together while the guy from L.A. held our spot in line. It was a good time. When we got back, we learned the guy from L.A. was writing about the history of the church in Europe. I didn't share with them the purpose of my trip. I just told them I was doing some traveling in Europe. We had a good visit which was fun and helped kill the boredom of sitting around in an airport. The Israeli girl and I shared dinner together a few hours later. So, all in all, being stranded in JFK was not a total wash. I got to hang out with some girls and an interesting author writing about Christian history.

I finally caught a flight out. I said goodbye to the girls and to the author from L.A. Anna gave me her address in Jerusalem and asked me to come for a visit, and then gave me a friendly kiss goodbye on the cheek. Sylvia also gave me her address and an invitation for a visit, which I knew would not materialize but would have enjoyed. Finally, I was on a jet flying over the "big puddle," and I arrived in Brussels late the next morning. As luck would have it, my luggage got lost again. So there I was in Brussels with no luggage. I seriously wondered about the flying standby stuff. I never did it again.

All things worked out. There was a cute brunette in her early to mid-twenties whose luggage had gotten lost, too. We had seen each other on the same flight. We hit it off as we visited waiting for our luggage that never came. While we filled out missing luggage forms, she helped me with translation as she spoke French, having just had come back home to Belgium from the U.S. She was from Brussels and her mom was picking her up at the airport. Thus far, the Europeans had been friendly, and the girls were great. The Belgian girl talked to her mom about giving me a ride to the train station. That was way better than taking the bus. Public transportation would have cost money and time, too; so of course I didn't refuse the ride, although I did turn down an offer to go home with them. I really was appreciating the friendliness of the European girls I had met. But I had business at hand, and priorities were priorities. When we arrived at the train station, she walked me up to the ticket counter and pointed out were I needed to go and gave me a kiss goodbye on the cheek. She and her mom were good people. I thought I would have enjoyed spending some time with her, but I did need to continue north fast.

I needed to get to the mission base as soon as I could. I went up to the train ticket counter. The guy at the counter was speaking French, and I couldn't communicate with him (another hiccup!). I said a little prayer under my breath. About then, a dark-haired guy was running toward my location. I thought he was a local. He was coming in a big hurry, headed toward the ticket counter. I decided to speak to him and said some of the only French words I could remember:

"Parle vue Angla?"

He responded in clear English with "Yeah, I'm from Berkley, man."

"Great, I'm from California too," I said. "Hey, can you help me with buying a train ticket? I'm having a language problem." I told him I was headed to southern Holland.

He responded with "Yeah man, that's the same train I'm takin'. Ya want first class or coach? I'm in a hurry, the next train leaves in about 5 minutes. We've gotta hurry."

"Coach," I replied.

He translated to the cashier, we got our tickets, and started running to catch the train. We made it to the train just seconds before it was to leave. He yelled out, "You get on that car. I'm in first class," as he kept running. "OK thanks!" I yelled back, as I stepped into the rail car. That's the last time I ever saw the guy. The doors closed shortly after. He didn't know it, but he had just been an answer to a prayer.

Finally, I was on the home stretch to Mission Base headquarters, and taking in the view of the beautiful lush countryside of northern Belgium then southern Holland, which passed by outside the train window. The ride included views of pastoral countryside with forests interspersed along the way. This part of Europe was one of the greenest places I had ever seen, next to east Texas. It would give most places in the southwest U.S. where I had traveled a run for their money, as far as beauty. But it still didn't top the majesty of Yosemite Valley, the splendor of the giant Sequoia redwoods, or the grandness of the California Central Coast. But it was certainly beautiful. I eventually made it to the Central Train Station in Roosendaal. As I got off the train, I finally got to set my feet on Dutch ground—happy, but almost couldn't believe I had finally arrived in the Netherlands.

As instructed, after getting off the train I found a phone booth, put my Dutch quarter in the phone and dialed the mission. Then the cotton-picking phone ate my quarter. OK, having little hiccups is a good way to get immersed into foreign travel. *What was next?* I thought. A quick look up the way revealed a bank outlet in the train station. I was in luck. I went in, exchanged money, and was back in business. That was my first time at a currency exchange—nothing like learning through experience. Finally, I got the mission on the phone and spoke to a guy who said with a Dutch accent, "We're glad to hear from you. We've been expecting you. Someone will be coming to pick you up at the station." I liked the sound of that for sure.

He told me there would be a couple of guys in a brown Ford Escort to pick me up. "OK, thank you," I replied. I began questioning as I hung up, *What does a Ford Escort look like?* There weren't many of those back in my neighborhood and I couldn't recollect what the body style looked like. I thought, *OK, it's gonna be little, and it's gonna be brown, and there will be more than one guy in it.*

Out to the front of the train station I went, wondering how those guys were going to recognize me. There were a lot of people around, and I didn't have any luggage. I was thinking, *Without any luggage I didn't exactly look like a new arrival.* So, I decided to sit down on the steps off to the side, in an out-of-the-way location, assuming that would not be ordinary. I'll stand out and they'll pick up on it, if they're paying attention. I started reading the little pocket New Testament, which I had with me. Where did I start reading? The book of James, one of my favorites! I turned to the first chapter, and wouldn't you know it! My eyes fell on 1:2 which says, "Greetings, my brethren, count it all joy when you fall into various trials, knowing that the testing of your faith produces patience." I began to smile, thinking, *Lord you really do have a sense of humor.*

After a bit of a wait, three guys showed up in a little brown car. I thought that it must be my ride. I walked out to the edge of the road. The driver asked my name; I replied. A guy in the back seat said, "Hey, Lawrence?" "Yep, that's me, and am I glad to see you guys! You can call me Larry." "Where's your luggage?" the driver asked. I was just happy to see them, knowing the Lord knew what was going on with my luggage, and He'd work it out. I had filed a lost luggage claim at the airport and knew it would show up somewhere. "I don't have any idea, but the Lord does. It'll work out. It's a long story!" As I got in, the driver said, "I'm John." The others piped up, "I'm Bill," and "I'm Mike," said the third guy. "Good to meet you guys," I responded. After I got in we did the usual, "Where you from? What do you do?" discussion. As we visited on our ride out to The Company Farm, I shared about losing the luggage, the girls, and the adventure getting there.

Even with the jet lag and being tired from the trip, I enjoyed the ride to the base as I soaked up the views of the cultivated fields of wheat, potatoes, sugar beets, and lush green farmland, crisscrossed with canals and dikes. What a beautiful country! We eventually arrived at the mission compound known as The Farm. It was a secluded little farm approximately a kilometer outside of a small Dutch farming town. The Farm compound area appeared to be about two to three acres in size, supporting a large two story farm house connected to a huge barn and a couple of out buildings surrounded by trees and a large wheat field. John, the driver showed me around and introduced me to folks, including Hank Paulson, the Director. I explained the circumstances of my delayed arrival to him. He was gracious about it and asked the escort driver to show me the locations of things I was interested in at that time – a shower and food. John took me to where I'd be bunking and showed me the locations of the kitchen and restroom facilities. He was a hospitable guy, a former army radioman from San Diego. I was assigned my quarters, which ended up being in the loft of an out building shared with six other guys.

That night I didn't sleep well due to jet lag. My body had not adjusted to the time difference yet. I got up at about 4 a.m., snuck out, went down stairs and read my Bible by flash light. A guy from California named Phil got up at about 5:00. He couldn't sleep either. He had just flown in a day or two before from San Diego. We had a short visit. He shared that he attended the same church in San Diego as John and served there as an usher. We were both experiencing some jet lag.

35

I was not put to work that first day. They gave us time to adjust. Phil and I hiked down a country road and walked out to a dike holding back the waters of a large river. We checked out the local environment around where we would be based, working, and living for a while. We made it out to the river after walking by several small farm houses on some dikes, passing by some potato farms and along the edge of a wheat field. The river was pretty wide, and turned out to be a tributary off the Rhine, with waters headed out to the North Sea located in an area known as Zeeland. It was a scenic place. It turned out that where we were based was eight feet below sea level. It had been good to take the walk just to get the blood circulating through the body again, get out and scope out the local area, especially after so much time in terminals and on aircraft.

Phil had built houses as a construction worker in California. I had done some oilfield construction work, so we hit it off OK and compared jobs. He had taken time away from his job for the work to be done in Europe. He was motivated to help the Believers in Eastern Europe. We walked along and talked about our home cities, jobs, and the circumstances of the Eastern Europeans. We discussed the local Dutch economy, potato, and wheat farms along the way. It seemed as though potatoes, wheat, and sugar beets were what was mostly grown on the farms in the area. We learned later that potatoes, wheat, and sugar beets turned out to be major export crops from the Netherlands. The Dutch were very resourceful and frugal with no land space wasted. Sheep were on the side of grassy dikes, which had been developed for grazing space. If there was not a road or a canal through the landscape, there was a crop of wheat, potatoes, sugar beets or something grazing on it. It was really green. Having grown up in the California Central Valley where ten inches of rain a year is a wet year, it was great to see the lush productive countryside.

The next day I was put to work by a Dutch guy named Cees, putting a thick dark wood sealer in between the layered planks on a barn. "Tarring a barn," I called it. It rained quite a bit there so the wood siding needed to be sealed every few years. It was a bit methodical, but not hard work. After three days, I'd still not heard word on my luggage, and my clothes were getting a little stale. Finally, the next day the airline company office in Brussels called. My luggage had decided to make its appearance in Europe. On the following Saturday, I hopped a ride down to the city with JJ and a girl who were headed home taking a flight out. Linda,

JJ, and Phil attended a church in San Diego, whose pastor had been involved traveling into Eastern Europe himself. Their local church had been substantially involved with supporting the Underground Church. I was happy to be headed to Brussels with those Californians to pick up my clothes.

Sunday, September 6th, a group of us loaded into a van and went to church service, my first in Holland. It was a non-denominational Dutch church, not the typical reformed church service. They had brass and strings as part of the worship ensemble. They played great music and had good prayer times, with a fiery Dutch pastor whose name was Hank. The people were friendly and treated us Americans well, I enjoyed the service. I met a Dutch guy there named Albert who lived in the village near where we were based. He loved Americans, as many Dutch families did. He remembered what Americans had done in World War II, helping to liberate Holland from Nazi occupation. He was a good guy with a big heart.

That following week another American guy, Dave, and I finished "tarring" the barn and sealing the wood. On September 9th I was put to work with a group which included Mike, Phil, JJ, Bill, Will from Virginia, and Dave from New York removing old equipment, junk, debris, and old fencing out of the inside of a large, aging barn, which looked like one of those country barns in a Norman Rockwell painting.

On September 11th we continued our work inside the old barn which had been constructed in the 1930s. After cleaning out the debris and junk, we started with sledge hammer work breaking out a long old brick cow manger and feed troughs. A crew of about six of us worked on it.

That evening, after we had busted out portions of the lengthy brick manger with sledge hammers and moved the brick by wheel barrow, we had some dinner, cleaned up, then went into town and watched the movie, *Pilgrim's Progress*, at the EGR church. The movie based upon the John Bunyan 1678 novel was about the spiritual journey of Christian from the City of Destruction (this world) to the Celestial City (Heaven). While the movie was not a Hollywood blockbuster adventure flick or thriller, it was full of spiritual truths in allegorical form. It was stuff for us to reflect about while in our own spiritual journeys.

The following day, on September 12th, we resumed busting out the brick manger and flooring and hauling bricks out to a pile on the compound grounds. After we got the bricks busted out, which took some time, we started digging, leveling the ground, then setting forms to pour a concrete slab for a new portion of barn floor. My oilfield roustabout experience framing and pouring concrete pump jack pads was helpful for that chore. We leveled and framed the area with footing forms. Later in the week we poured a good-sized slab for a portion of the barn flooring. The barn was fairly large and could hold several vehicles inside. Having new level floors for storage and work areas was a significant improvement for that old barn. Additionally, that sleepy looking old barn housed a small warehouse and two workshops inside. One of the work rooms was a small print shop, which was an area where I would eventually end up spending a lot of time. There was also a small shop, which led to a book warehouse on a second level that housed thousands of Bibles and Christian books. The adjoining general office was attached to a nice large two-story Dutch farm house. It was a sleepy looking barn and farm house on the outside, but a significant work was going on inside.

One could have equated the Dutchman directing our work, Cees, to an Operations 1st Sergeant. He was a former Dutch army commando and had been a mechanic for Mercedes-Benz. He was a diverse and talented "fix it" man. He also was a great photographer and dark room specialist. He loved to play the trumpet during lunch time breaks, too. He wasn't a bad trumpet player either. We enjoyed listening to him play as we relaxed during our lunch breaks.

While working with Phil the contractor, John the former army radioman, Mike the Marine, Bill the realtor, Dave and Will from New York, and Virginia, a comradery developed as we worked. We were refurbishing and remodeling the interior of the old barn. I began to like the style of the former Marine and began to gravitate some toward him. I have always appreciated those who served in the military. Bill, Dave, and John were good guys, too, whom I was growing to appreciate. They were all a dedicated hard working bunch of guys. They were good workers, too, and knew how to do it. Phil the contractor and Mike the Marine (if there is such a thing) paired up well. Mike had also received a degree in Civil Engineering and liked to build things. Their combined building skills helped with establishing project priorities and methods. As we worked, we talked about the Bible and the circumstances of the Eastern European Christians. There was a common sense of purpose about our support role for the Eastern European Believers. The labor and the developing friendship and comradery was good. The physical labor with men who didn't mind doing it was great. As we worked and talked, we wondered aloud when our training for going in country would begin and where each of us might be headed.

Mike and John got along well, as they were both former military communications specialists. Mike, the former Marine, was a squared away guy and had served part of his tour in Korea. Then he went on to college and received a degree from Virginia Tech. He was an intelligent Virginia gentleman with a quiet warrior spirit. John had been an Army radioman, was discerning, enjoyed studying the Bible, and was very involved with his church in California. Bill, a former real estate salesman from Montana loved to run ten K races, cross country ski and hike in the Rocky Mountains of Montana, was not pretentious, and had a dry sense of humor. Dave was from New York and had worked in rescue missions. He was a kind, humble man.

One might say I was a "windshield" cowboy, where the tools of the trade had been a pickup truck instead of a horse, a quick release rope instead of a lariat, ear tags instead of branding irons. and multi-dose vaccination guns as opposed to six shooters. I had been around horses some, ridden a few, and had been around and worked more than a small amount of cattle, "critters" (domestic animals, horses, cattle, farm animals), and wildlife. I had also worked as a roustabout in the oilfields to earn college money. I enjoyed target shooting, hunting, and traveling. I really appreciated the guys I worked with, and they didn't seem to mind my talking about cattle and working in the "oil patch."

In the evenings after work some of us would head out from The Farm to a little Dutch village about ten kilometers away, with a couple guys running and two or three of us riding bikes. We would leave the farm on an outing to enjoy the Dutch countryside and head out to get some ice cream or "friets mit maonasse" (French fries with a yellowish sauce similar to mayonnaise but with more flavor). The snacks were an enjoyable treat, as was the fellowship with the guys and the few girls who worked as support staff. Some of them were scheduled to travel on teams as well. The girls lived at a downtown apartment which also at rare times doubled as a safe house, so to speak. They would head back to it at the end of the day. Their flat served not only as housing for the girls, but had been used in its capacity for some Eastern European religious dissidents and U.S. church leaders. Beth, Lucy, Mickey, and Roda were dedicated to help the Eastern Europeans. They would travel into the East with other girls.

On the last Saturday in September, I took a break from the activities around the base and went to the Dutch National War and Resistance Museum at Overloon. The open-air WWII museum was located south of the city of Nijmegen, a place where one of the largest but less known tank battles of WWII happened on Dutch soil. My Dutch friend Albert, who drove us to the museum, and I spent a couple of hours walking around the 35-acre museum site looking at the tanks, armored vehicles and artillery pieces.

I looked at an M4 Sherman tank, which had had its turret half blown off during combat when it had been part of the US 7th Armored Division. Then I examined a destroyed German Panther V, which was from the German 107th Panzer Brigade, also taken out in the battle. Standing by those implements of armor, thinking of their size and power, then comparing the fragileness of the occupants, I reflected about the gruesome deaths of the crew members in those machines of war. Then I thought about the horrors of war.

There was also the presence of a British Cromwell Mk IV and a British Churchill Mk V tank at the site which testified of the terrors in that region during September and October of 1944. As we looked at all the various implements of war used in combat, it helped us have a greater appreciation for the intensity of what had happened there thirty-six years earlier. The Dutch village of Overloon had been completely destroyed by the fighting which occurred in that region of Holland from September 30 until October 16, 1944. During that battle, approximately two thousand five hundred combatants lost their lives in horrific ways.

The battle at Overloon occurred on the heels of Operation Market Garden, the largest airborne assault operation of WWII. As I walked through that place, I thought of scenes out of the 1977 movie, *A Bridge too Far*, which I had seen when in college just a few years earlier with my friend Mike. The movie about Operation Market Garden* contained history from World War II fought in that very region. I walked around that unique open air museum amazed that I was looking at the actual pieces of military equipment and standing on the very ground which were part of the battle which I had seen portrayed in that movie.

Operation Market Garden had been a battle plan put forth by British General Montgomery to airdrop troops from the U.S. 82nd Airborne Division, the U.S. 101st Airborne, the British 1st Airborne, and the Polish Independent Parachute Brigade into various locations in Holland. Their objectives were to secure bridges in the south of Holland near Eindhoven, at Nijmegen and Arnhem, with those units then reinforced by armored Divisions. It was an attempt by Allied armies to secure positions in Holland and across the Rhine, then push east into the heart of Germany, hopefully ending the War by Christmas. However, it did not to come to fruition, as the bridge at Arnhem crossing over the Rhine was not captured and held. Military officials considered the operation a failure as a result. But when I think of it, I'm reminded that a portion of Holland was liberated from the Nazis even then. There were several tactical successes with ground gained due to the effort. I didn't think of it as a total loss.

Standing next to the M4 Sherman tank, not far from Overloon, with its turret blown half-off, while reading the names of the crewmen killed in it was a poignant moment though. I thought about the brutal deaths of the American tankers who died to liberate Holland from totalitarian Nazism. But I felt that they did not die in vain. I considered the sacrifice of those guys, not much younger than I at the time, and the thousands of others who died fighting for the soil I was standing on. I talked with Albert about those who perished in Operation Market Garden and those killed at Overloon in the effort to liberate Holland from the Nazis.

While we walked and looked at those machines of war, we talked about World War II. During our visit, while walking around that battlefield, my thoughts turned east where I would be headed in several days. I considered the Soviet Armies who had fought the Nazis in the east, who came not so much as liberators but more like conquerors. Instead of liberating Eastern Europe, they replaced one totalitarian system with another. After WWII, Soviet communists insured that communist governments were set up in the Eastern Europe countries that the Soviet armies had conquered.

A quote found in one of the brochures from the Overloon Museum said "Remember, what was threatened yesterday may be endangered again today or tomorrow. Preserve it and remain alert! May God help us towards that end." It had its own impact, after seeing what I'd seen that day. It was again a reminder that freedom does have a price, and part of that price is eternal vigilance against the forces which seek to control and enslave others.

*(Note: The 1977 movie, *A Bridge Too Far*, produced by United Artists is a powerful presentation about Operation Market Garden and contains visual reenactments of history which may be of interest to the reader.)

Bibles for Romanians and Russians

October 1st began with a change from maintenance and construction work around the base for three of us. We started a time of briefings and training to be part of a three-man team for a mission into Romania. Our team of three was composed of Bill, Will, and me, with Bill Larson from Montana as our team leader.

We began study of country information, including maps, itineraries, contact addresses and personal information. Also, we received briefings and training about driving conditions in Eastern Europe, currency exchange, city information, border crossing and counter interrogation training. Though limited, it was far better than going cold turkey. All contact and itinerary information was committed to memory, as absolutely nothing on paper would be carried with us. We were given some city and country highway maps to take with us and that was it. Each man was assigned a specific task and specific contact information. One was the finance guy, one assigned to vehicle maintenance and responsibilities, and another had trip itinerary and contact information. Each team member was assigned a job, and each of us was responsible for various parts of the mission. I ended up with vehicle responsibilities, which included daily maintenance, keeping track of fuel and mileage and, in addition, some contact information. Will became the finance guy and would also have information on a contact; and Bill was our team leader, shouldering all of it. He had a trip to Czechoslovakia under his belt and had some experience in Eastern Europe, which would be helpful. Our routes had to be planned and memorized. Every aspect of the trip was committed to memory. Contact familiarization needed to be without flaw; there would be no calling for help. We would not be taking anything written down or marked-on maps. We quizzed and tested each other. It was kind of like cramming for midterm exams. Our team was to transport a cargo of five hundred Russian Bibles and just short of the same amount of Romanian Bibles, some Hungarian Bible commentaries, plus some clothes, all hidden in a large dark blue Peugeot van which resembled some we would see in Romania, although this one would be tagged with French plates.

In the early morning hours of October 6th after a double check of each other's luggage, making sure our teammates had not inadvertently left something in their stuff like an identifying t-shirt or hat, names on paper, home town or personal information, we loaded up our stuff. We conducted a final vehicle check then "saddled up." Bill fired up the van and drove us off base. Bill, Will, and I left the familiar Dutch farm headed south toward Belgium where we would then take a swing east toward Germany near Antwerp. Then we would head south east toward Stuttgart after making it to Germany. The next day would be onto Salzburg, Austria. Then we would head toward Hungary and from there the primary destination for our cargo and our mission, Bucharest, Romania. Our first stop, other than for fuel was scheduled for Stuttgart, Germany, where we were to link up with a German sister organization, Licht im Oosten (Light in the East), which did literature work in Eastern Europe, as well. We would be dropping off some Czech Bibles for them and stay the night at their compound.

It was raining the morning we left the base, typical Dutch weather, as we left Holland headed south toward Antwerp. It continued to rain as we entered Belgium. From there east toward Germany and on into Koln it continued to be wet and rainy. We arrived in Stuttgart late that night. It was still raining after a full day and hundreds of miles of driving. We dropped off the cases of Czech Bibles to Licht im Oosten and spent the night at their compound. It was nice to sleep in the beds they provided and have a brief time of fellowship with our German compatriots. The next morning, we were engaged mostly in small talk about the U.S. and Germany, as we could not share about our mission and they could not share a lot either. After a good continental breakfast, we headed on toward Munich.

When north of Munich, we took a break from the autobahn and did a short tour of Dachau, the former Nazi Concentration Camp, as it was allowed for on our itinerary. It was a very sobering experience for all three of us. We saw the ovens where thousands had been cremated after being worked to death or executed. We saw the blood ditches where firing squads had executed the innocent and the grave sites labeled "Thousands Unknown"—truly evidence of previous horrors committed by the Nazis. The SS goon squads which operated this camp and the dozens of other concentration camps brought murderous devastation upon Jews, Christians, and European citizens on the continent during the 1940s. They murdered thousands at that camp.

We left Dachau in a somber, reflective mood and headed away from there onto Munich, and from Munich, onto Salzburg, Austria. Austria was beautiful with awesome vistas; it reminded me of the 1965 musical, *The Sound of Music*. The Alps where amazing, splendid, and rugged. The high Alpine peaks and lush mountain meadows were awe-inspiring. It was truly like being in a scene out of the movie which starred Julie Andrews. It was good to see the beauty of the Creation after the heaviness of Dachau.

That scenery was truly a boost after experiencing the somberness of the former concentration camp. Having hiked in the Sierra Nevadas myself, and Bill having hiked in the Rockies, we enjoyed the views as we talked about some of our camping and hiking experiences stateside. I shared with them a couple of bear stories, of encounters in the back country of Yosemite National Park. Bill talked about hiking and running ten K races in the Rockies. Will told us about some good fishing trips in the hills of Virginia.

As we traveled south into Austria, we traveled into the Pinzgau Region of Salzburg. There I appreciated seeing some of the original breeding grounds of Pinzgauer Cattle, a European breed being imported into the U.S. as an exotic-beef cattle breed. Its early development had been traced back to Alpine Herdsmen somewhere around 500 AD in the Salzburg Providence of Austria. I enjoyed sharing with my teammates about the then newer exotic breed being utilized in the U.S. for beef production, although I don't know if they appreciated it as much. As the expression goes, "I talked their ears off," telling them about the breed of cattle. They were good sports about it, seeming to appreciate the download of information about the animals. That night we found a spot to park our van and bedded down on the outskirts of Salzburg.

The following day, we left Salzburg and headed east down the length of Austria to Wein (Vienna). We arrived that afternoon, but could only spend a couple of hours in the city. It was a beautiful place. The architecture was amazing. Vienna was a place where music, art, and the creative genius of many artisans have flourished over the past several centuries. It is considered one of the more beautiful cities in the world. It is a city known as a leader in the arts. It is also a city where many international agencies and organizations are headquartered, since it was a cultural center of Western Europe and just across the Danube from Bratislava, Czechoslovakia (the capitol of Slovakia). It was also reputed to be a city where espionage activity between communist Eastern Europe and the west was common. So, we would need to watch what we talked about when in public and be guarded in our conversations, even in that western city. We definitely would not talk about our mission, but just appreciate the history and architecture of the place.

We spent a short time in the old section of the city. But playing tourist was part of the cover for our mission, which we could talk about at the Hungarian and Romanian Border checkpoints. The architecture of Vienna was inspiring as had been the Austrian Alps. We enjoyed the views of the Cathedrals with their Gothic spires as they stirred appreciation for their design and construction. The rain and our restricted time element prevented us from spending time to absorb a lot of architectural magnificence which we would've liked to soak up at bit more. But we did stop for a short time to check out Saint Stephan's Cathedral, quite a piece of architectural constructive creativity. However, we did not stay long as we needed to get back on the road. The architecture and engineering of that structure was pretty interesting, as well as were many others in the city, especially considering that many of the Gothic structures were built in the twelfth and thirteenth centuries prior to the use of modern day power tools, lifts and cranes. Vienna, during the twelfth century, had been a center of German culture in Central Europe. Up until the 20th century it was the largest German speaking city in Europe. During the 1980s it had a population of just under two million, so it took some time to get out of the city due to traffic congestion issues.

We finally got out of Vienna and then headed southeast toward a little place called Laxenburg. We found a campground on the edge of town, where we were able to locate a decent camping spot; but the weather was still raining and wet, so we had to stay in the van. After the night's sleep, we left Laxenburg the next morning and headed to Hungary. We were not far from our first border crossing into a communist regime and would cross into the land of "goulash" at Checkpoint Sopron. It was there where we would pass through the Iron Curtain. Fortunately, although a communist country, Hungary was considered the least repressive of the autocratic regimes on the other side of The Wall and the best of the communist countries to live in. But having contraband materials would still mean big trouble if we were caught, including the loss of our mission objectives for Romania.

On the morning of the 9th we were up early, hoping for a let-up in the rain. No such luck! That morning we were still catching the wet stuff, the third day of it. It had been raining ever since we left Holland. After our team meeting, including prayer time about the crossing, we headed toward the checkpoint. This was not the famous Checkpoint Charlie of Berlin, but this checkpoint had its own intimidating "No-Man's Land" with mine fields, barbed wire, machine guns, and guard towers which greeted us. We were at the point of no return. After leaving the Austrian side of the border and passing through the "No Man's Land," we could see the rolled barbed wire and machine gun positions growing ever larger and intimidating as we drew near. I started thinking how this thing might go down for us. A little apprehension started swelling up inside as the heart rate began to increase. It was definitely something to deal with, but I could not afford to let any nervousness show. I had to stay as cool as possible and leave the results to the Lord. We crossed through the "No Man's Land" and pulled up at the end of the line of several vehicles waiting for our turn. Guards walked down the line of cars toward us carrying AK47s slung over the shoulder. One approached our van, walked up to the driver's window, and asked for our papers. Bill handed over our passports. Then guards directed us to park, go inside a building to obtain visas, and pay a "per deim," where we had to cough up a fee for each day we would be in the country. We were inside to process papers for what seemed like an hour; but in reality, it was less. After paying the per diem money, we were issued our visas. We went back to the van; then it was time for a vehicle search before we would be allowed to enter. Vehicles in front of us and behind us were being waved over to the side into a special area, stopped, and searched for contraband; some were gutted and stripped down. One was on blocks, jacked up with wheels off. It came to our turn. Praying to ourselves, we hoped that we would not be waved into the special inspection bays. We knew if that happened, we could be busted. The potential existed for our mission to be over before we even got started.

Border guards with the ever-present AK-47 motioned us to pull forward; of course, we immediately complied, and who wouldn't? I was wondering if we would be waved into one of those special inspection stalls. They had us stop, but they did not wave us off to the side for an in-depth search, which in some cases meant the beginning of a partial or thorough vehicle disassembly. I was certainly grateful we weren't selected for one of those inspection bays. The guards performed a lite visual check of our van, did a final check of our stamped passports and visas, then waved us forward to pass on through the exit barrier. Felt a "Hallelujah" swelling up inside wanting to bust out, but knew I better keep my mouth shut. The crossing had gone well and was an answer to prayer. They barely even searched our van, thank the Lord! We had over a thousand Bibles on board for the Romanians and Russians, which were considered contraband materials. Getting caught obviously would not have been cool. Each of us thanked the Lord quietly to himself for the safe crossing. We had prayed that the guards wouldn't find anything or see what they should not see. Thankfully, they didn't! We made it through Checkpoint Sopron and crossed into Hungary. Border crossing number one was successful, but nothing to get giddy about. There was a sense of relief about our first success, but we were definitely not over confident, as we were now in communist controlled territory with a van load of contraband Bibles. We were on the other side of the Iron Curtain in a place where we had illegal religious literature. Thankfully, Hungry was considered the most open place in the East Bloc to live at that time. Although it was the least repressive of the Eastern European countries, it was still under Soviet domination and the cold war between East and West was ongoing.

We were where they had the home field advantage with security police and informers, and we didn't even speak the language. Thankfully, Hungary did not have the same Secret Police army that its citizens had suffered under from 1948 to 1956. The AVO (Allamvedelmi Osztaly), State Protection Department, as it was known, had been extremely brutal on its people. Its harsh treatment of the people was a primary reason for the Hungarian Revolt against the communist government in 1956. After the revolt, the AVO was somewhat reformed and became known as the AVH, State Protection Authority, which was eventually disbanded in 1961 after further reforms in the nation. Hungary was the only communist country in Eastern Europe without its own formal secret police army. However, the nation did have an element within the Ministry of the Interior known as Sub-Department D, which was involved in dealing with what were called "enemies of the State." Those enemies were considered to be in the churches, culture, the humanities and the arts. So, while not as intense as the other East Bloc countries, Hungary did have an element of thought police operating in the country[19]. We wouldn't have to worry about an army of secret police like we would need to in Romania, but we could not consider ourselves free from potential scrutiny either.

As we drove into the country, we knew that persecution of Christians was not as intense as in Romania, but we would still need to exercise caution. While the country was the least repressive we were, after all, behind the Iron Curtain—in a place under the control and thumb of the Soviets, a place monitored by the KGB. Romania, where we were headed, was to be the place where we would meet our first two contacts in a couple of days. And it was known as one of the more oppressive Stalinist styled regimes in the world. It was ranked by some as 5th behind North Korea, Albania, China and the USSR. Our border crossing into Hungary was practice for our crossing into Romania.

As we headed for Gyor, Hungary, I was thankful for our success through the first checkpoint, but knew that what had just transpired was border crossing number one with tougher ones to come as we headed further east. The crossing into Romania would be more intense with greater potential for being busted. We would shortly be crossing into the territory of the dictator, Nicolae Ceausescu. We were continuing to prepare ourselves spiritually and psychologically for what may lay before us in that oppressive land. But we certainly weren't disappointed about the outcome of the Hungarian crossing. All in all, so far things were going well. Each of us thanked the Lord in our own way and were grateful for the outcome!

But it was not a time to be cavalier. We were just getting started. We couldn't afford to be over confident. We needed to stay focused on the mission, stay loose, yet likewise not get uptight or work up unnecessary fear. Being either too relaxed or uptight could cause us to make mistakes. We needed to try to enjoy the journey, so to speak. Yet we needed to continue to stay focused on our purpose, exercising discernment and discretion. The three of us were continuing our cohesiveness as a team through the experience. As I was considering the way the crossing went, we broke into discussion about the rain, as it was still drizzling; the weather wasn't exactly the best, but at least it wasn't pouring.

After making it through the checkpoint, we continued on for a few kilometers and started looking for a decent place to pull over and check the vehicle, as we had passed the ten-kilometer mark. As we drove along, we saw several military patrols off in the woods on each side of the road. We could see soldiers patrolling through the scattered forested areas in two man teams armed with assault rifles. I couldn't tell if they were Russian or Hungarian. It was an interesting experience. We had a moment of levity when we saw that the first military vehicle we encountered was an East Bloc army truck broken down along the roadside with the hood up. A soldier was trying, unsuccessfully, to get it started. That brought smiles to us—not laughter, just smiles. We knew better than to laugh. Well, at least we could out run that one.

Bill, who was driving, spoke up at just over ten kilometers as we entered a curve in the road and said, "We need to pull over and check the engine." That was a prearranged code for us to pull over, get out, and quietly check for tracking devices under the wheel wells, fenders, bumpers and under the car – places the guards had searched while having a conversation about the vehicle. After we made it around the curve, Bill pulled over and stopped alongside the roadway. Will and I jumped out and started checking for tracking devices which a guard may have placed on the vehicle while we were obtaining visas. We were also watching for any vehicle which may round the corner, then stop or drive on by us, and then pull over. Maybe a border police agent tail may have been assigned to us.

We were in a bit of a precarious position with Russian and Hungarian troops in the area, as well as police. Troop concentrations were much greater within this first few kilometers from the border. We saw a lot of troops off in the woods in small patrols. We would need to be "as wise as serpents and innocent as doves." No longer operating within the freedoms we were used to in the West, we needed to exercise caution in what we did and said. After we made our own vehicle inspection, we headed on toward Gyor traveling Highway {84} in route to Budapest. The road was two lanes wide and not in the best condition, not an autobahn for sure. After traveling through Germany and Austria, driving there was like we had driven though a time warp. It made me think of things I had read about the Great Depression of the 1930s and Dad's stories about it. Visually, it didn't look like we were very far removed from the 1940s. Older, smaller cars, and carts or wagons pulled by draft animals on the highways were a common sight.

As we drove further into the country, we began seeing more troop transports and several East German (DDR) Trabants. Those little cars were powered by a two-cycle motor and sounded like a Yamaha motorcycle. They would not have passed a California Smog Emissions Test either! They often smoked like a little freight train, were very small and compact, and made a VW bug look like a Limo.

We began to see cars called Skodas from Czechoslovakia. On occasion, some Ladas, a Soviet knock-off of the Fiat, would show up passing by us. In fact, it looked like the communists borrowed the blue prints from an Italian Fiat factory to make the things. Funny thing was they seemed to be mostly black or dark blue with some being an off-white color. The Skodas seemed to be mostly either green, red, or a faded creamy off-white. Occasionally a Skoda might show up in the rearview mirror wanting to pass. Usually they were the same body types, just different colors. Some just looked older than others—the creative, automotive genius of state-run factories. It seemed most Trabants were gray, off-white, or rust red. When we got stuck driving up hills behind a Trabant, I thought the people inside were going to have to get out and push the little cars to make it up the inclines. Did those two-cycle engines ever belch the smoke when headed up a grade!

Somewhere west of Gyor, we were driving northeast and came up behind an army convoy driving up an incline. We had to pass in between the trucks to get around it. There we were, first following, then driving among a military convoy full of armed troops; and we had a load of about a thousand Russian and Romanian Bibles with us! It was not a good time to have car trouble or be pulled over by their version of MPs (Military Police). It seemed like we were in a bit of a vulnerable spot. But everything worked out fine as we moved among through the convoy and passed it without incident.

We pulled into Gyor, a city of over one hundred thousand people, halfway between Vienna and Budapest in the northwest part of Hungary and a place where three rivers converge. As we arrived on the outskirts of the city, we saw troops all over the place walking and milling around. Most were enlisted men hanging around their trucks, some armed with AK-47s. Some troops were sitting in the back of their transports. The trucks looked to be the equivalent to the U.S. deuce and a half trucks. The soldiers' uniforms were a lighter green than U.S. soldiers' OD uniform and were not in a woodland style camo pattern. The sight of all the troops was yet another reminder that things between Eastern Europe and Western Europe were in a state of political tension, as troops faced off on opposite sides of the Iron Curtain. But right then, we were on the east side of that wall. The government of the nation was dominated by the Soviets, as the attempted Hungarian revolt in 1956 had failed. The Russians who had invaded with tanks and armored divisions squashed it and maintained a significant presence. So even though Hungary was a more open communist country, we were under no illusions as to who was behind the power there.

Leaving Gyor, we headed on to Budapest, through the Hungarian countryside. It was good looking countryside. We hit Budapest in the afternoon. Budapest, was a beautiful city; I loved the views. The architecture of the buildings was great. The city located on the Danube River is one of the most beautiful cities in Eastern Europe. "Buda" on one side of the Danube and "Pest" on the other, the city was known as the "Paris of Eastern Europe." As we drove through the city, we tried to follow the driving rules the best we could. We didn't need to be stupid and get pulled over for a driving infraction so a Hungarian cop could fine us on the spot. They didn't need much of an excuse for pulling over vehicles from Western Europe.

The architectural styles were not quite like what I'd seen before, similar to Brussels, a little like Vienna but slightly different. It was hard not to be distracted while driving in the heavy traffic by the structures. But we needed to keep moving. There was not a lot of time to play tourist. We headed southeast out of Budapest on Route {5} toward a little place called Kecskemet. Then we headed on toward Szeged, a university city in southeast Hungary, not far from the Romanian border. It was approximately a forty-five kilometer (twenty-seven miles) drive to the Romanian Border from there on Highway {43}. We would make camp that night and then complete the drive to the border crossing into Romania the next morning. We had to find a place to camp and check in with the Hungarian authorities before it got too late. Every place we stayed was recorded on our visas by the State authorities so they could track movements of foreign visitors.

We finally found a campground. It was still raining, mostly light sprinkles, with intermittent heavier rains. We'd been talking about a lot of stuff, football, fishing, hiking in the Rockies and Sierras, cattle, real estate, theology, the Bible, and of course girls. We messed with each other about who would be the first guy to meet his Eastern European sweetheart. We joked around that one of us might end up with a Bulgarian weight lifter type. We dubbed the fantasy girl "Olga." Now, Olga was "all woman" who could sweep a guy off his feet and carry him home to Mom, or bounce him off a wall (laughs and smiles). But really, the girls were mostly good-looking and could have been a real distraction.

Bill was a character with a good sense of humor, although a bit dry. Just when he was telling what I thought was a serious yarn, it would turn out to be a joke, which fit his dry wit. He could have made a good poker player if so inclined. When Will or I said something he thought was funny, after a slight chuckle, he'd reply slowly with a bit a drawl, "Ya know, ... ya... really are a ...wise...guy...!" He had an excellent memory, like a steel trap, I thought. He could quote the entire book of James, five chapters in length. I asked him to quote a passage and he replied, "Which version do you want it in, King James, New American Standard or New International?" We would choose and he quoted it, word for word, which certainly impressed me. He was a good team leader who treated us with respect, was humble and not arrogant. He was not a glory hound or self-absorbed. He put others before himself. I imagine he would not have been in that type of service had he been.

We finally arrived at a campground outside of Szeged, Hungary, after dark. It was still drizzling rain. We checked in at the gate where there was a cute little dark haired Hungarian girl working as the gate house attendant. She was no Bulgarian weight lifter for sure. Bill started talking about how cute he thought that girl was. As we checked in, he talked with her briefly. She gave us directions toward our camping spot. Then after finding our space, while setting up camp, Bill commented, "That girl, ... is as cute as a bug's ear! I think I'll go back and talk with her." "How cute is a bug's ear anyway?" Will and I asked simultaneously. After getting set up at our camp site, Bill decided to do just that. Well, being the good friend that I was, of course, I volunteered to go with him and help out. It could be interesting, maybe some fun.

On the way to the gate house, we walked by a flower bed. Bill picked a red flower to give the girl, as part of his ice breaker. We got up to the gate and spoke to the cute gatehouse attendant. Bill gave her the flower and started chatting with her, having a nice visit. And, of course, she just loved Americans! As Bill was enjoying the conversation with the sweet Hungarian girl, up walked an Army officer. I'd say probably a Major judging from his uniform and age. He had booze on his breath, smelled, and looked like he had a few too many to drink. He started talking to the girl, cutting in on Bill. We didn't know what he was saying but it looked and sounded serious from his tone and the way he looked at us. He continued talking to her. We figured he was asking about us. Maybe he was out for some romance with the girl or maybe information about us. We never knew. He seemed a little too serious and interested in who we were as he kept looking our direction. Discretion said it was time to split in case the officer started asking too many questions. *Tough break, Bill. You didn't get that cute Hungarian's contact info*, I thought. That was our first unofficial Hungarian cross cultural visit, short and brief. We certainly didn't get to learn much about the country from her. The next day was going to be a full day; it was time to grab some grub then rack out.

We said some prayers that night for the coming border crossing into Ceausescu's Romania the next morning. According to some political analysts, Romania ranked as one of the more oppressive Stalinist styled communist regimes in the world. Estimated to be about number five, with North Korea, Albania, Red China and the Soviet Union preceding it in human rights violations and persecution of Christians. Ceausescu had traveled to Red China and North Korea in the early 70's and became friends and allies with Mao and Kim Il Sung of Korea. After Ceausescu's visit to North Korea, he began to increase the development of his own form of a dictatorial personality cult, a lot like Kim's. Social and economic oppression and persecution of Christians and Jews was part of the political climate. Individualism, religious behavior or activism like preaching, initiative and creative thinking, were monitored and punished. Lack of conformity to the communist party line could lead to job loss and "reeducation," loss of a home, prison, and/or a prison camp, where torture may await the non-conformist, free thinker.

Next day we were up early, ate breakfast and packed up our gear. Bill, as team leader, issued an important pre-border crossing directive. "Well guys, it's about time to change underwear, don't ya think? Will, you change with Lawrence and I'll change with you." We laughed. It had been three or four days since any of us had a shower. The camper-type baths we had been taking—wash cloth and a pot sponge baths—weren't the best, but better than nothing. The three of us were getting a little grody, although I'd gone a lot longer without a shower when hiking in the Sierras, and so had Bill hiking in the Rockies. But we were starting to ripen some.

The next morning one of the guys read a scripture out of the little New Testament we had along. Then we had a time of prayer. In the back of my mind was the thought that perhaps this could be the last time we prayed together for a while. The time was approaching for our border crossing into one of the more oppressive communist regimes on the planet. *Would we be caught? Would we be interrogated, then put in prison? Or kicked out of the country having lost our personal belongings and, most importantly, the Bibles and that specialized vehicle which had transported thousands of Bibles and books into Eastern Europe?* If that were to happen we would not only have lost our cargo, but declared "persona non grata," never able to return.

The question loomed quietly, I believe, in all of our thoughts. We were not full of brazen bravado. We knew our position, but we were committed. There were others depending on us. We had already made that choice long before we left Holland. We knew that for us, if caught, it most likely only meant confiscation of our vehicle and all of our goods except the clothes on our backs, and being kicked out of the country. Maybe a few hours of interrogation, a few days, or maybe weeks in prison. Then after being kicked out and never allowed to return, we would have been "black-listed," so to speak. I had read of one team that had to spend a few months in prison just the year before. But that was not even close to comparable to what some Christians had had to endure in prisons or concentration camps just because they were Believers.

We rolled eastward on Hwy {43} toward Checkpoint Nadlac, a primary border checkpoint entering into Romania from Hungary. Once again, we stopped about ten "Klics" prior to the border, did a final vehicle check for loose papers or anything out of the ordinary which could alert border guards. We made sure things were secured and squared away. But perhaps more important we had some prayer time. (When in those circumstances prayer could be considered akin to calling in for smoke rounds to cover your position.) We read some scriptures, maybe our last as a team for a while. Psalms 25, 27, and 91 were some of my favorites. After reading the little team Bible was hidden. The border crossing loomed before us. We proceeded on toward the Hungarian exit. The Hungarian exit inspection went well with no issues. But when we saw the expressions of the border guards' faces, they appeared curious and a somewhat puzzled. Which I interpreted to be, *Why would you want to go to Romania?* The guards checked inside the vehicle; then they waved us through, knowing what lay before us at the Romanian checkpoint.

So far we were doing OK, but inside my gut I was tense as we drew nearer to the Romanian checkpoint. After we crossed out of Hungary, we passed through the intimidating no man's land with mine fields, fences, tank traps, barbed wire, machine gun positions and border guards with Romanian AK47s, not to mention the guards with patrol dogs. It was a bit intimidating. As we motored slowly into Checkpoint Nadlac, it was still drizzling rain, overcast, dreary looking and cool. We didn't see many vehicles. Only a very few Eastern European passenger cars and a couple of Mercedes trucks pulled off to the side. The trucks seem to be of Eastern European origin. There were not nearly as many people headed into Romania as there had been when we headed into Hungary the day before. We were motioned forward by a guard with his AK and pulled up beside a guard house. A guard out front came up and spoke to us, asking for our papers, we assumed, as we couldn't understand him. There was a communication issue. Bill was driving and spoke to him in German; we handed him our passports. He realized we didn't understand and then motioned for us to get out of the vehicle and wait. We complied, waited, and waited.

After a while another border guard who was younger and seemingly had higher rank came out of the building to greet us. He could speak fairly decent English, although it was accented and choppy. He welcomed us with a friendly smile. Then began questioning us, asking why we were visiting Romania. What was our business in Romania? Did we know anyone in Romania? How long we would be staying? Where would we be traveling in Romania? (It was against the law for us as westerners to visit any Romanian citizen in their personal home without first obtaining permission and clearance from the government.) Then he turned and asked me the question of questions, "Do you have weapons, pornography or religious literature?" I don't think I'll ever forget the moment nor the question. My heart rate quickened as I responded trying not to appear anxious, but with too much of a curt reply in my mind said, "All we have is food, bread, clothes, and personal items!" I considered that the Bibles were spiritual food and bread for the soul. I hoped the Lord was extending grace for that approach. The guard said, "OK, thank you." Then he continued with polite professionalism, as he asked if he could search our vehicle.

Well, we certainly were not going to say "No" to guy who had us surrounded by soldiers with AK 47s, but at least he asked nicely, and he wasn't rude or arrogant about it. He got into the van and started going through our stuff, cabinets, foot lockers, storage compartments, etc. My heart rate had not slowed, as I wondered if the guard might start ripping things apart and discover the Bibles we had hidden. We had seen the aftermath of that one Hungarian checkpoint when entering there. We stood by and watched, each of us praying quietly in our soul. We were at a critical moment with our load of Bibles in the middle of a checkpoint search. It was hard not to be a little uptight; but I needed to internalize it, give it to God, and try not to worry. I knew we were in God's hands, but my human nature was acting up. I was nervous, wondering what would happen next.

The senior guard, after going through our stuff, the closets, cabinets and storage areas of the van got out seemingly satisfied. He didn't find anything out of order, thank the Lord. But we were not out of there yet. After we had answered his questions and he had conducted his search, he gave us the clearance to obtain a visa. Then we went inside and coughed up money to pay the per diem charge for the number of days we would be in country. That seemed to be one of the primary reasons the Romanian communists allowed westerners into their country, for the tourist dollars and revenue generated.

It was an interesting question the guard had asked me about religious literature, weapons, and pornography. There in that "Workers' Paradise," they equated Bibles and religious literature to weapons and pornography. Then on top of that, they charged us a fee just to let us inside. One might think they thought this was a resort in a tropical paradise or exotic location. However, I noticed people were not backed up at the gate to get in.

A few trucks coming in were waved over to be searched. After we were questioned, the search of our van and then the issuance of our visas ensued. After we passed muster, we were waved forward and allowed to enter into Romania. Thank the Lord, we had made it through Checkpoint Nadlec successfully! The vehicle had been searched and the Bibles remained hidden and undiscovered! The words, "Praise the Lord," rolled quietly off my lips as we exited no man's land, but, of course, didn't dare utter a word too loudly. Not now at least. We didn't say much at all at that point. We saved talking about the experience until we made it past the ten kilometer point inside the country. When past that marker, we would once again conduct our own vehicle inspection, searching for bugs while watching for tails coming up a distance behind us. We had made it through with our cargo of Bibles, which would touch far more than just a thousand lives. They were part of God's provision for many living behind The Wall... words of hope and light for people living in a dark place of oppression.

Protecting the Christians whom we were there to help was, of course, a top priority. It was important that we maintain situational awareness, be alert to being followed and guard our ways. We didn't need to be stupid and bring undue attention to ourselves by being haphazard in our behavior. A scripture I considered at times was Matthew 10:16 where Jesus spoke to His disciples saying, "Behold I send you out as sheep in the midst of wolves. Therefore, be as wise as serpents and harmless as doves." That was one of those times. As we continued on in the country, we drove slightly past the ten kilometers when soon Bill said, "We need to check the oil."

He stopped and all three of us got out and started checking under the tire wells, bumpers, frame, etc., inspecting the places the guards had searched, just in case they decided to leave something with us. We did not say much; we just had a dialogue about the road worthiness of the van. All was well, the vehicle was clean with no bugs or tracking devices, as far as we could tell. We resumed our trek and as we drove down the road, we start talking more freely again among ourselves.

We traveled east on Route {7} about forty-seven kilometers prior to arriving at Arad, a place which is close to the third largest city in Romania. It was an important and large metropolitan area but not our target city. We were headed on from there to Bucharest. It was in Bucharest where we had two separate contacts which would be the recipients of the Russian and Romanian Bibles. Our first contact was part of an underground network which smuggled Russian Bibles into the Soviet Union. Carman was part of the Lord's Army, an underground evangelistic break off from the Romanian Orthodox Church. We would be meeting up with him the following day; then later we would meet with our second contact to arrange for a drop off of Romanian Bibles for the Believers there. But those things would not be taking place for a couple of days.

Traveling on from Arad we headed south to Timisoara on route {69}, from where we would head toward Bucharest. As we traveled deeper into the country, we noticed we weren't seeing as many Skodas or Trabants like we had seen in Hungary. The cars we saw were by and large the Romanian national car, the Dacia, another communist "wonder" car. I couldn't help but have a sarcastic thought about the vehicular accomplishments of the communist party. I think I made a comment to my two traveling buddies. The communist national vehicles were failing to impress this country boy. I thought, *Give me a Chevy, a Ford or a Dodge any day of the week, hands down! Absolutely no comparison!* Even a Pinto or Vega beat those things, not to say anything bad about those little cars. Some people liked those, but personally I preferred having the choice of muscle cars or pickup trucks. I appreciated the car shows, race cars, and races back home.

While driving through the countryside, we were having to drive alertly and dodge Mercedes trucks and gypsy covered wagons pulled by horses, which the trucks were passing. One of the primary differences in the gypsy wagons and the covered wagons seen in the American western movies, were the rubber car tires, instead of the wooden spoked wheels from the 1880s. Driving in Romania presented its own hazardous experience. It was then I realized why we were required to have driver's training and had been warned about driving in Eastern Europe. We would round a bend in the narrow winding road suddenly coming upon a slow moving gypsy caravan of two to four wagons headed toward us being passed by a truck or a Dacia. It was not uncommon. The Romanians driving the cars didn't seem to be too concerned about oncoming traffic either. They would pass vehicles with close oncoming traffic taking their "half" out of the middle of the road. So, we would hit the brakes or the right shoulder of the road…sometimes a bit of both! All of this happened in wet, rainy weather road conditions with limited visibility, sometimes on slick cobblestone roads or streets. The cobblestone roads in or near the villages were the worst. After some of those near collisions, you could hear big sighs of relief from one of us or all three simultaneously. Sometimes we would start to breathe again after subconsciously holding our breath. We squeezed through near-miss situations multiple times.

The guy acting as navigator might yell at the driver, "Hey, watch out!!" while the driver was dodging and swerving. Or maybe it was the third guy exclaiming, "Look out for that crazy guy!" "Did you see that?" was more of an exclamation than a question. Sometimes we got stuck driving behind gypsy caravans, and it seemed like there were a lot of those occasions. Just when you thought it was safe to pass and make your move, something would pop up from a dip in the road ahead like a Dacia, a Skoda, Lada, truck or covered wagon. Perhaps it would be a car passing a wagon coming toward us. Drivers of small cars would pass on narrow winding two lane roads, again taking their half out of the middle. The driving experience definitely presented its own type of excitement. Sometimes the driving hazard would just be the lone ox cart being pulled by a draft cow or a wagon pulled by a horse. We'd come around a curve in the road and a wagon or tractor loaded down with riders would be staring us in the face, moving along slowly right in front of us—not a dull trip! After a while, we got somewhat used to it and adapted, but at times it could be a challenge to just flow with it! We figured they didn't have many drivers' training classes like back in the U.S. Perhaps they just forgot what they learned. Maybe they were just absent on the days that defensive driving was taught. But then again, what kind of drivers' training is needed for a horse and wagon?

We headed south from Timisoara on route {6} toward Drobeta Turnu-Severin. More gypsy caravans as we approached the Southern Carpathians. It started getting later in the day on us. Somewhere near a place called Lugoj we start looking for places to camp and stay the night. We were unsuccessful.

We came upon an old wood sided building that looked a little like an old log cabin, but slightly bigger, nestled down in a river gorge with the river running behind it down off to our right. There were a lot of trucks parked across the road on a large dirt lot and on fields around the cabin. It appeared to be a truck stop, Romanian style. It was a truck stop cafe with a huge parking lot with European Mercedes and Peugeot styled Romanian trucks on it. Someone on the team had the idea maybe it might be a good place to get some food. We were all hungry and due for some chow. We needed to eat, but I was feeling hesitant about going into the place. It was a gut feeling which proved to be right. It seemed risky, but we went inside to check it out. One could cut through the smoky, grease filled air with a knife and fork and probably eat some of it too; it was so thick. We stood out in the place like a sore thumb in that crowd of Eastern European truckers. I was ready to "exnay" the joint. Bill and Will agreed without much hesitation. We stood out way too much. We were supposed to be running low key, and that was not the way to be doing it. I felt like we had neon signs hanging around our necks, which said "Stupid westerners, easy target." It seemed as though every trucker in the place had his eye on us, and I don't believe I was being paranoid. There might have been an informer in that roadside truck stop. Probably there was—most likely, more than one. There usually was Securitate secret police in many public gathering places, hotels or motels, and restaurants. Well, deciding to have chow in that place was not the smartest idea. It didn't hurt my feelings that our team leader felt like having dinner in our camping van, which was a better idea.

We headed back to the vehicle and began looking for a countryside location to set up camp and get some sleep. We found a place on the high side of the road by some big rig trucks, eighteen wheeler types, which were parked there. We snuggled the van in between a big rig truck and the base of a hillside.

The old café truckers' stop had reminded me of something out of an old Dracula movie. While we made our dinner, we talked and joked around about camping not far from the Transylvania Alps. We wondered out load how far ole' Count Dracula's Castle was from us:

> *You think he might show up for dinner?*
> *No, he doesn't want any of our blood.*
> *Yeah, he wouldn't like yours anyway.*
> *Hey, let's eat!*
> *What's in this stuff we're eating anyway?*

That night was interesting; we ended up having parked on the downhill side of a train track. We hadn't seen the tracks about fifty yards above us due to the heavy growth of brush and weeds on the hill above us. The tracks which were only yards higher than us brought the freight trains pretty close. When trying to sleep, I thought most of Romania's rail freight must have traveled at night down those very tracks that night of the week. I didn't get the best sleep; it seemed like just every time I dozed off a freight train passed by on the rails above us. They kept the other guys up, too; but we made jokes about it and maintained good humor, all things considered.

The next morning we had breakfast, a team meeting, and prayed for travel protection from crazy drivers, informers and secret police. We also asked the Lord to hold back the rain while we were in Bucharest, so that we would not damage our system or get the Bibles we were carrying wet. We would be arriving late that afternoon or early evening, and it was still raining. We were concerned about the tolerances of our system and getting mud, small gravel or muddy water into the grooves and hinges. Things had to mesh within less than a millimeter; the tolerances were very close. A large grain of sand or small pebble could cause problems with the system during closure. We didn't need any mud to get into the vehicle which could contribute to system jams. We also hoped for good weather when delivering the Bibles—didn't want any of them getting wet from rain which could have been a possibility.

That morning as we pulled away from our camping spot not far from the truck stop, we saw that the water level in the river had risen somewhat. The unpaved road looked even worse in the morning light. I for one was really glad that we hadn't camped down in that spot. Happily, we were safely leaving there and "On the Road Again," as Willie Nelson might have sung out.

We were headed southeast on Route {6} traveling toward the Danube River at Drobeta Turnu-Severin. From there we would be at Craiova and then on to Bucharest. We drove through a mountain pass to a place called Orsova with it still raining. As we dropped down into that Danube River gorge, the rains began to lift and the clouds were pushed back by beautiful rays of sunshine. Up ahead were blue skies, filled with white tall beautiful cumulus clouds. That morning in the Danube river valley, it was the nicest, sunny weather I'd seen since leaving California nearly six weeks earlier! I felt like singing; but I decided to save Bill and Will from the agony so I didn't.

The Danube looked awesome. What a beautiful sight! At Orsova it widened considerably. It was sparkling blue with rays of new morning sunshine dancing on the water. Looking at the sight I understood why it is often called the beautiful Blue Danube, and the *Straus Waltz* can be so meaningful. I used to hear it on the radio. My mom had an appreciation for classical music, and the song was played occasionally on a local radio station she enjoyed. It was cool to see the real deal on such a beautiful morning. We saw the low, tree-covered mountains of Yugoslavia over on the far bank of the river. It was turning into a good day.

As we continued southeast along the river beyond that point, we began to notice guard towers along the water line below us. The towers had guards with field glasses and were equipped with machine guns and search lights, which were manned by Romanian soldiers. It seemed that they were spaced apart every few hundred yards. We didn't think it was just to keep the Yugoslavs out either, but served the dual purpose of keeping the Romanians in as well. It was just another reminder of the "friendly" communist regime. No wonder there weren't too many people from the west rushing to get into the place. We would be in Bucharest in a few in hours and wondered what conditions would be like there.

As we drove northeast to Craiova, continuing to dodge gypsy caravans and trucks, we left the Danube behind us. Craiova, was a southern industrial city where cars and engines were made in the state-run factories. They made some of the little Dacias there. From Craiova we pressed onto Bucharest. We finally made it there in the late afternoon.

Bucharest, our destination, was known as the "Little Paris of the East" from about 1881 until the Second World War. It was reputed to be at its peak, holding the reputation up until World War I. It continued to barely hang onto the reputation until the outbreak of World War II. During World War II the city sustained significant damage from allied bombing raids resulting in damage to multiple cultural and historical buildings. After World War Two, communism gained power with the support of the occupying Soviet Union. Bucharest was reported to be in recovery from the damage caused by the impact of the war. It certainly appeared that recovery was taking a really long time. The infrastructure seemed to need a lot of work. I attributed the condition of the city to communist policies, as cities in Western Europe who had likewise been significantly damaged by the war had been repaired, upgraded and in modern condition well before that time.

Upon arrival to Bucharest one of the first things we noticed in addition to the poor conditions of the infrastructure were the numbers of two man teams of police carrying AK47 machine guns, patrolling the neighborhoods on foot. I guess we wouldn't have to worry too much about being mugged—just other things, like the secret police and informers.

A lot of the streets were cobblestone or brick, with pot holes and/or low ripples and ridges. The road conditions were hard on the suspension of our vehicle, especially since it was loaded with the extra weight of a thousand Bibles and books. Riding on some of the roads felt more like we were in a boat rather than in a van. But this wasn't new to us; we'd already encountered some wavy cobblestone roads in some Hungarian villages and early on in Romania. It was just that it was a larger and allegedly more modern city, so there were a lot more of those than expected. It seemed as though the war and the earthquake disaster had not afflicted the city as much as Nicolae Ceausescu's socialist collectivization polices. Ceausescu had had many historical buildings, museums and churches demolished and removed, replacing them with his vision of more modern State structures, housing complexes or manufacturing and production facilities, which he considered communist progress. But progress in the city seemed behind the times and appeared to be slow moving.

While driving through the city, we decided it was prudent to locate our contact's neighborhood as one of the first orders of business so we could reconnoiter the area while we had some daylight. We knew that we could not drive directly to his home or even near it. Visiting a Romanian Christian would not be like going for a visit to someone's house after church on a Sunday in the US. We would need to be discreet and park at another location several blocks away with only two of us walking to his house. We couldn't risk getting him into trouble with the Securitate and/or us getting arrested for being stupid by parking near his house, or bringing attention to ourselves by three of us walking together. As previously mentioned, foreign visitors had to have permission from the communist government to visit a Romanian national, and the authorities would want to know the purpose of any visit. Just trying to get permission of course would "flag" the person to be visited; then they would be marked and most likely interrogated by the communist police authorities.

We found the contact's neighborhood in order to scope out the area, then do a recon, and plan a safe walking route to his place. Afterward, we needed to kill a little time, so that we would have the cover of darkness on our walk to his home. We decided to go out to eat. Our growling stomachs helped us make that decision. But our decision-making was being influenced by remembering the smoky truck stop the night before and seeing some of the local diners which reminded us of it. Plus, with the presence of multiple uniformed Securitate with their AKs in some areas, we decided to head for the touristy Intercontinental Hotel. That may have been a mistake, but hindsight is 20/20 as they say. The Intercontinental was located in the downtown part of the city near a park where tourists hung out. We figured it would be a decent place to blend in and the cuisine wouldn't be too bad. It was located off Intr. Zalomit and Strada Brezoianu Ion near Strasa Republicll b-dul Gheorghe Gheorghiu-dej street. The area had a lot of little stores and shops and there was a lot of foot traffic. It was a good tourist trap where we would fit in fairly well with the crowd. The possibility of encountering Secret Police in the area increased as well, but that was always a gamble when in a country with sixty thousand Securitate officers—a risk, but a trade-off. It was important that we visit some tourist locations. After all, that was our cover story, and it was a touristy place where souvenirs could be purchased and seen by guards at the border exit.

When we entered the restaurant at the Intercontinental, we began to feel somewhat uneasy. We began to smell a rat. As the head waiter escorted us to our table, he leaned toward us and whispered, "U wanna chenga munee?" The guy was wanting us to do a blackmarket money deal. He could have been a regular two-bit criminal or on the secret police informant payroll. Either way, it was bad news. We responded with "No thanks!" Then he followed with another question asking in a low tone, "U heb anee ceegarettas?" We responded again with, "No, we don't," with a somewhat more direct tone. He said, "Okaaay! Eberyting bee Okaay. Eberyting bee alrit."

He seated us, then called for the waiter. We noticed there were not a lot of customers in the place, and it was the beginning of the dinner hour, which was another thing that caused our suspicions to grow. We asked for the dinner menu. The waiter whose English was not so good had a communications problem (or maybe we did). Bill tried German. English seemed to work better. But there was still a bit of a problem. We asked what they had available for dinner. "Vie heb cheehan, an cheekan wit, patatos an, wie heb beafshtech wit patatos, an vie heb gordon boo mit patatoe. Whaa ou lech?" responded the waiter.

As we continued trying to order, he seemed to have difficulty understanding us. He became slightly frustrated, so he called for help from a waitress. A fair-skinned girl with wavy dark hair, wearing a native costume (black pleated skirt with floral print and a frilly, white blouse) came to the table with a friendly smile and showed us a menu. Her English wasn't much better than the waiter's. She tended to focus on me as I was sitting by myself. Bill and Will were on the opposite side of the table across from me. She got in close, leaning over me. She came on a little strong and very friendly. I was somewhat guarded, but did enjoy the attention, remaining friendly as I ordered. "Can I have the Cordon Blue, please?" She stayed friendly, close to my right arm, touching my shoulder and bending in low in front of me, getting close.

She definitely was showing me some extra attention; I'd be lying if I said I didn't enjoy it, but I knew it could be bad news. Was she attractive? *Yes.* Was she friendly? *Yes.* Did she see American dollars as she flirted with me? *Absolutely!* So, wisdom said, "Be careful." I also ordered what I thought was orange juice. She left and returned with a pale yellowish milky orange-looking fluid with little black flecks in it and a smile on her face. It sure didn't look like orange juice to me, or juice I wanted to drink anyway. It looked like a glass of very weakly mixed tang with brownish rust flecks in it. I decide it was time to order something else. "Can I have a Coke or Pepsi please?" She left and returned with a glass with nothing but Coke in it, no ice. The glass didn't seem that cold to the touch. I asked for ice. She left, came back smiling and proud, with one cube of ice in the glass of coke. I guess we Americans are spoiled. Thinking I must be looking like one of those picky Americans to her by now, I hung with it. I didn't want to create a stir. Although if she did think I was one of those ugly Americans, she certainly didn't act like it.

My two teammates were enjoying themselves, watching the entertainment created by my exchanges with the girl and laughing some. They ribbed and teased me when the waitress left our table with comments like, "Hey man she really likes you. She is into you." "Looked like you were leading her on," the other one said. "Hey, you shouldn't lead the poor girl on," poked the other. I retorted something akin to, "Lead her on, you guys? I'm just being friendly." "Yeah, Yeah," from them, with light guffaws which ensued.

A little later when I asked the waiter for some help, he leaned toward me and told me that the waitress was getting off work soon, implying I should come back and pick her up. I guess I was being too friendly after all. I thought the waiter had been trying to do a money exchange deal when we walked in the business. Next, he was trying to hook me up with this girl! What a place! I knew that many men have been snared by the friendly smile and wiles of a woman to their undoing. It was like offering up a T-Bone steak laced with arsenic. I was not interested. The guys messed with me for a while about my interaction with the cute brunette and got some laughs out of it. I thought we may have paid too much for dinner in more ways than one.

Leaving the restaurant, we decided to walk down the street, play typical tourist and check out some of the local shops along the street. I noticed some shorter guy about 5'5" with stoop shoulders and a hunched back, wearing a black coat and dark trousers, following us. Every time we stopped at a shop window doing a "lookie-loo" this guy would stop at the next shop or two down and stare in the window. He started working his way up toward us gradually, eventually getting up close after about three window shopping stops. He had "marked" us. He worked up his nerve, then walked up close behind us, and asked in a whispered low tone, "Wanna chenga muwnee?" The guy could have been secret police, an informant, or trying to get a little piece of his own black market action. He was bad news regardless. "No, we are not interested," Will responded. The guy asked again in the form of a statement, "No chenga muwnee." The three of us immediately and simultaneously responded with a direct "No!" Then we decided it was time to split from the area and head back to our van, the "blue whale." We made it back to the vehicle, while checking that we weren't being followed when in route.

We left the area and decided to head over toward our contact's neighborhood and reconnoiter that area, also taking an indirect driving route, checking our six o'clock position, making sure we were not followed. We needed to explore the lay of the land so to speak. We also needed to find a place to park our ride for the night. We were in a search mode.

It was dark and the streets were dimly lit. Brown-outs were not an uncommon thing in Bucharest. The street signs were located on the corner sides of the older brick buildings not easily seen, much less read. They were not out on a sign post on a street corner like in the U.S., but we managed. We finally made it to the neighborhood where our contact lived. Arriving in the contact's neighborhood, we noticed several soldiers walking around not far from his home and a team of two cops, which appeared to be uniformed Securitate, patrolling the area with AK47s. So, this is what life is like in a police state, I thought. We were not in the best circumstances. Uniformed Securitate were all over the area where our contact lived. Close to his home there was a lot of patrol activity. Bill decided we should hold off until the next morning...no argument from me. It was Saturday night. We figured our contact more than likely would attend church the next day, so we would make it an early morning visit.

The next order of business was to find ourselves a place to stop and get some sleep. We didn't find any camping grounds in the city using our maps and did not see any campground signs while driving. We weren't feeling very comfortable about hotels either. We knew that would be a place where our room could be bugged or we might pick up a secret police tail. We knew from our training that the Securitate (secret police) would hang out in hotel lobbies and many of the hotels rooms were bugged. I had a friend who actually discovered a listening device once in a Russian hotel where he was staying. After our episode at the Intercontinental, we decided to avoid the hotels. We ended up finding a parking area at the back of a sports stadium and decided to spend the night in the van there. We drove around the area and happened to stumble on two blue vans backed into a little indented parking area notched off the main street, with bushes on each side. They had a profile and color similar to ours. There was just enough space for one more. We decided that it should be us. We backed in beside them. From the street it looked like a small fleet of three blue vans. We kept the lights off, the curtains closed, and stayed dark, quiet and low key. We kept our voices low and to a minimum. We had a dark camp that night, and hoped throughout the night not to have a knock on the door from the local Polizei.

Early Sunday morning, Bill and I checked out the map and the location of our contact. Bill believed he had a good route planned to our contact's home. We had a little discussion about it. I didn't agree; but he was the leader, so off we went on foot. Will stayed behind with the van, lay low in the vehicle, kept curtains drawn, and prayed for us. That was the worst job I think; staying behind tested a guy's patience. Plus, the vulnerability was every bit as real.

Bill and I headed out covering some distance after about twenty minutes. I wasn't seeing street signs that looked familiar to the route we had planned on the map. It seemed like we had made a wrong turn somewhere, for we could not find the right street. Bill had an epiphany when we saw a cop walking the beat across the street and down a block headed our direction. We were in the wrong place at the wrong time. The three of us were the only ones on the street that morning—the cop, on one side, Bill and I on the other. It was a residential area, and we as westerners most likely should not have been there. We didn't know anyone in Romania either, right? At least we weren't supposed too. So, what would western tourists be doing in a residential area early on a Sunday morning? It would be a legitimate question for a cop to ask. I was not feeling comfortable. Being inconspicuous was something we tried to attempt, but sometimes it didn't take much to stand out. Bill had blond hair, blue eyes; I had brown hair and blue eyes. The biggest percentage of Romanians have very dark brown or black hair and dark brown or black eyes. We didn't have Romanian features, didn't fit in the best, even dressed down. Luckily it was cooler weather so we had on jackets and long pants which covered most of our lighter complexion; Bill also had on a Navy blue, dock-workers style knit cap, which I'd loaned him. He discreetly pulled as much as he could lower over his blond hair to cover it, as the cop continued to approach drawing within about fifty to sixty yards, continuing to close the gap between us. At that point, he didn't seem interested in us, but he could have been being discreet himself. Bill and I hadn't been talking much because we didn't need our English to be heard by anyone. We had been walking for a little while, so we must've been well over a mile away from the vehicle. Bill decided it was time for a change in plan and direction. He had no disagreement from me. We turned right at the next street corner and slipped away to the right from the cop and headed back to the van for reorientation.

We made it back to the vehicle, having burned up some time since we left and not having made contact. We looked at the map again, got our bearings a little better and struck out in the other direction. We found ourselves at Brother Carman's house within probably ten minutes after having taken another route. As we approached his home, we did not see any sign of police or any one out on the street which could have ended up as a potential informant. Going in early on a Sunday morning turned out to be a good thing. It was all quiet in the neighborhood. We didn't see a soul. We spotted the address on the side of a small home with a very small front yard. We went through a gate into the yard, up some steps, and lightly knocked on the door of the address we had memorized. An older man opened the door. His appearance fit the description we had been given. We spoke softly in a whisper and said, "We bring greetings from the West." "Come in, come in," was the quick reply. He seemed happily enthused to see us. I knew we were certainly glad to see him. He quickly and quietly ushered us inside. It was good to be inside his house! He seemed as happy to see us, as we were to see him.

His Romanian-accented English was easy to understand, and he was pretty fluent. On top of that, he was open, warm and hospitable. After establishing rapport, he offered us coffee and asked if we'd eaten. We took him up on the offer for coffee. He seemed as though to be a long lost great uncle whom I'd never met. He was like a father figure—old and seasoned in the ways of the world, yet full of the peace of the Lord or like a kind, older brother. His warmth, kindness and hospitality were truly genuine. He was a good man.

He had us sit down at a small kitchen table and served us some Turkish coffee in a clear glass. The coffee grounds must have been close to an inch thick on the bottom of that clear glass cup. The Turkish coffee was strong! I wasn't a big coffee drinker; I would drink it occasionally out on a cold work site in the oilfields, a farm or a ranch, but could take it or leave it. Here I was presented with a cup, I conjectured to myself, in which the grounds would hold up a spoon. Guess he saw me grimace slightly, so he offered some cream. *Nice man!* I took him up on it. I made the mistake of stirring the cream a little too vigorously. It became a speckled cup of light brown coffee. But with his hospitality, I was going to drink that coffee no matter what. I did, but wished I'd had a strainer on my teeth! I sipped it slowly.

We had a good visit with our new friend and new ally, Brother Carman. He was a generous, kind man eager to spend time with us. I shared with him about having heard the Romanian dissident pastor, Richard Wurmbrand, speak in California. It turned out that Carman had been a personal friend of Wurmbrand and former cell mate of his when doing his own prison time in the Romanian gulag. Carman was interested to hear about his old friend.

Wurmbrand, the former Romanian Pastor, had been released from the gulag and was able to get out of Romania after fourteen years of imprisonment. He immigrated to the US, where he became a prolific author, writing several books about his Romanian prison experiences. Some of the titles included *Tortured for Christ, With God in Solitary Confinement, 100 Prison Meditations, If Prison Walls Could Speak, Alone with God,* and others. He became the founder of an organization which would come to be known as The Voice of the Martyrs. I had been fortunate enough to hear him speak just a few weeks prior to heading for Europe. Wurmbrand had to sit when he lectured, as his feet were badly damaged from the beatings he had received while in prison. Prison guards had strapped him to a table and beat his feet with clubs and metal rods. His feet would become swollen and painful when he stood for any length of time, sharing his story with a church or university group.

Brother Carman wanted to know more about the welfare of his former cellmate and friend, Wurmbrand, and how he was doing. He and I talked about his old friend. Bill patiently listened with interest as Carman and I continued in dialogue.

As we sat there visiting at Carman's table sipping on coffee, I asked our new friend with whom we were now allies the question: "What is living in Romania as a Christian like for you?" He responded after pondering the question and said, "Well, it is kind of like living on top of a volcano. You never know when it will explode," implying life is peaceful with only some rumblings, and then the authorities would explode on them. Then, he paused and after a few seconds commented, "You know the government treats us like a hedge. They let us grow up for a while, and then they come along and trim us back!" implying arrests, confiscations, imprisonments and torture. Then he leaned toward me in his chair. A little smile creased his face, his eyes sparkled, and he said in a confident, yet humble way, "But you know, trimming the bush keeps it healthy." What a statement to be made in that environment! What could be said as a reply to his comment? I groped for a comment. All I can say is that it was humbling. I think Bill may have made the next comment, as I responded, "Yes, I would think so."

I remained silent, briefly contemplating the statements we had just heard. Thoughts about that conversation still touch me. As we continued the visit with Carman, he shared with us that he had been in prison for the Gospel on three separate occasions, totaling four and a half years. Additionally, he had been called in for questioning several times by the police. He made another statement which was also a bit humbling. He said, "You know, I've been questioned so many times by the police, I'm almost on a first name basis with them," as he smiled. Then he said, "Yes, last time they arrested me, I asked them, 'What kind of new tricks are you going to teach me this time?'" again implying beatings or torture. He did not make that statement in a proud or arrogant manner. It was more matter of fact, but he conveyed it in such a way that it was a badge of honor for him. As he sat there, he smiled and shared his story and coffee with us.

Sitting with such a man and visiting with him in his home, having to avoid detection by secret police and uniformed Securitate just to be there with him, was impacting my worldview. Other things certainly became less important than what was happening at that very moment. What had transpired the previous several weeks just to get there melted into the sea of oblivion. There Bill and I were, sitting at the table of one who could truly be called a man of God and a hero in his own right. It felt like I was sitting with the Apostle Paul, one who had suffered imprisonment and torture for the sake of the Gospel. Yet he was not a bitter man. He was a man full of kindness, love and some humor. There was certainly no guile, arrogance or pride in the man who sat in front of us. In First Peter 4:1-2 the Bible say:

> "Therefore, since Christ suffered for us in the flesh, arm yourselves also with the same mind, for he who has suffered in the flesh has ceased from sin, that he no longer should live the rest of his time in the flesh for the lusts of men, but for the will of God."

Here sat a man who had truly learned the lessons of forgiving and loving his enemies...a man who did not live just to serve his own self, but to serve the Lord and others. He was the real deal! We were being blessed by him. We came to help, we thought; but we were the ones who were encouraged and challenged in our walk with God.

He shared with us not only out of his experiences and provisions, but out of his heart. "You know toward the end of World War II," he said, "we were hoping that the Americans would come and rescue us after the Nazi occupation. We did not want the Russian communists to come. We kept hoping over the years that America would still come to our aid. We pray often for America and the churches in America. We pray that America will be strong and that the church will be strong and remain free."

During the conversation he told us he was a member of an underground movement called The Lord's Army, an unregistered evangelistic underground group splintered off the Romanian Orthodox Church. After about forty-five minutes to an hour of visiting, we made arrangements for another meeting that afternoon at a park. It was to be for setting up details of the literature drop with him and a Brother Georgi, who was part of Carman's network. They both distributed Bibles into Russia and throughout Romania. We were scheduled to drop off our cargo for the Russian Believers to him. Brother Carman would contact Georgi after we left. He would then meet us again at the park. "You know this park?" as he gave us the name, told us where it was located, and showed us on a sketch map he quickly drew. "I will meet you there," he said and set a time for 5 p.m. in the afternoon. We knew it would greatly increase the risk to him for us to visit at his home more than once. Prying eyes or informers could see something and report it to the police. That experience was definitely not like visiting friends for coffee after church on a Sunday in the U.S.

We left and made it back to the vehicle without incident. Will greeted us with a big smile, happy to see us. It was good to see him too! Bill and I shared the things we had just experienced, but we needed to move and get out of there, which we did. We also needed to set up a meeting with contact number two, which was scheduled to be a contact for Will. We planned for him to meet with his contact in the early afternoon. Montana and I dropped off Will at a predetermined location and headed off to play tourists at an Industrial Fair in the center of the city. We made arrangements to meet up with him at a certain location at 3 p.m., giving him time for his meet with Brother Alexi. Then, Bill and I would meet Carman at the park. It would be a busy afternoon.

We dropped Will off at a predetermined drop point we had established on our map of Bucharest, and verified another location set up as a rendezvous point. Bill and I later hooked up with him back at the van, after our time playing tourist. Bill and I waited for Will at our rendezvous point. He had successfully found and met with Brother Alexi. They had set up a meeting time and place for the following night. We were scheduled to meet Alexi at a park. Will filled us in on the details for the drop which was for the following night at 8:30 with Alexi. He would meet us at the park, then lead us to a literature drop location where we would unload four hundred fifty Bibles to the Romanians.

Next it was time for Bill and I to meet Carman at the park that he had pointed out. We found it on our map, drove our vehicle to a location a few blocks away, and began our walk to meet him, ever alert for police patrols, suspicious people, or out of place activities in the area. Montana and I showed up in the park at 5 p.m. as scheduled. We saw Carman approach us from the shadows of a tree-lined residential street, opposite the park from us. He was wearing a long gray overcoat and a dark French artisan style cap. He walked calmly toward us from out of the shadow of some trees. We did not see anyone following or watching him. Everything looked good for the meeting with him up to that point. As we met up, Brother Carman took hold of my arm like a long-lost uncle. We began a leisurely stroll through the park walking side by side, his arm in mine. It reminded me of a movie scene. Bill remained behind us a few steps and was watching out for uniformed or secret police, as Carman explained the details for the rendezvous and literature drop for us with him and Georgi. Everything was good to go; he had set a drop for that night. We were to meet up at a roadside pull-out on a highway he designated a few kilometers outside of Bucharest at exactly 10 p.m. Carman was very clear and precise, giving us exact instructions on location. He emphasized the time and gave us a vehicle description, made sure we understood, and emphasized the importance of being exactly on time. He had a humble, yet very professional demeanor. We were to meet them at a roadside pullout outside of Bucharest in the countryside, on a primary route he named headed northwest. He said he would see us later that night, broke off from us, and headed in another direction. The meeting in the park was over. We headed back to the van to hook up with Will, making sure we were not being followed. As we neared the edge of the park, I dropped to a knee to tie my shoe, which enabled Bill to check our six o'clock position, looking over my head as he faced me to see if we were being observed or followed. He scanned the area behind us. My partner checked the area as he appeared to be talking with me, looking for any sign of someone which may have seemed out of place, acting suspicious, suddenly changing the gait of their walk, coming to an abrupt stop, or having an erratic change of direction. We knew there were a lot of Secret Police and informers in Romania and caution couldn't be thrown to the wind. Individuals who stopped or appeared to hesitate when we stopped and anyone staring or taking an extra-long look may have been cause for us to take another alternative route back to our van. Anyone on a park bench looking over the top of a newspaper with an extra-long gaze would trigger suspicion. I finished tying my shoe and everything seemed good. Bill did not detect an obvious informer or agent. We believed we were not being watched or followed.

We made it back to the van unhindered, but remained diligent in our situational awareness. It was a balancing act to keep watch, stay aware and alert and simultaneously not get nervous (or at least having the appearance of nervousness), even if we felt that way in our gut. We needed to be cool, smooth, and confident. We placed our confidence in the Lord, which was very helpful. Will actually was very good-humored, had a quick easy smile, seemed to be happy a lot and very calm. Even if he wasn't, he never did show it. He was easy going and a great traveling partner. Bill continued to maintain his dry wit and kept a calm composure and cracked one-liner jokes. It was good to be with these great guys in these circumstances.

For our next order of business, we needed to find a good location to get into the vehicle's hidden compartments. We had to find a reasonably safe spot to park, then open the system, retrieve the Bibles, and place them in the on-board plastic trash bags. We kept the curtains drawn, making sure no one was close. One man would be the lookout for anyone coming near the vehicle, while the other two guys got into the system via the hidden entry point. We found a good spot, pulled over, opened the system under the cabinets, began pulling out Bibles and placing them in trash bags which we had hidden with them when loading the Bibles back in the Netherlands. Five Hundred Bibles resulted in a lot of trash bags one third full of Bibles, when we finally got our load in the bags after pulling them from beneath the floor a few at a time. We had a good-sized pile of Bibles in bags on the van floor when finished. We placed our jackets and sleeping bags over the top of them, as a small precautionary covering in case we might be stopped by police when in route to our rendezvous with Carman and Georgi.

We arrived at the roadside location given by Carman at about 9:50 p.m., a few minutes early. The rest stop was definitely not like you see along freeways in the U.S. It was nothing more than a wide shoulder pullout at the edge of the road, slightly wider than the vehicle. It had two trees and one trash can about the size of a fifty-gallon barrel.

It was a busy highway with only one lane in each direction. It was a road leading into Bucharest from a northern city, with cars coming from both directions every few seconds. Oncoming headlights from every car lit us up. We could be easily seen, and we were in plain view from anyone driving by. We really didn't need the Securitate to drive by, or anyone to spot us and turn us in during the literature hand-off. We felt vulnerable, and didn't feel too comfortable with the location. But we confirmed that it was the designated place and it was there that we would remain until our contacts arrived. If they were a no-show, we would wait longer. Then we would have to develop a plan B. Once again, we prayed and asked the Lord for covering protection. We had been doing a lot of that. As I looked up at the beautiful night sky while waiting on the Romanians, I saw the stars hanging over head and thought of the greatness and beauty of the creation. A passage in Isaiah captured the moment.

"Comfort, O comfort My people says your God." (Isaiah 40:1)

"Do you not know? Have you not heard? Has it not been declared to you from the beginning? Have you not understood from the foundations of the earth? It is He who sits above the circle of the earth. And its inhabitants are like grasshoppers. Who stretches out the heavens like a curtain and spreads them out like a tent to dwell in? He it is who reduces rulers to nothing, who makes the judges of the earth meaningless. (Isaiah 40: 21-23)

"To whom then will you liken Me That I would be his equal?" Says the Holy One. "Lift up your eyes on high and see who has created these stars. The One who leads forth their host by number. He calls them all by name; because of the greatness of His might and the strength of His power, not one of them is missing. (Isaiah 40: 25-26)

"Do you not know? Have you not heard? The everlasting God, the Lord, the Creator of the ends of the earth does not become weary or tired. His understanding is inscrutable. He gives strength to the weary, and to him who lacks might He increases power. Though youths grow weary and tired, and vigorous young men stumble badly, Yet, those who wait upon the Lord Will gain new strength; They will mount up with wings as eagles; they will run and not get tired, they will walk and not become weary." (Isaiah 40: 28-31)

Interestingly, just seconds before 10 p.m., the traffic stopped coming from either direction. The number of cars on the country highway reduced to zero. No cars or trucks were coming from either direction. A quiet stillness and peace seemed to come over us. Suddenly, Georgi and Carman drove up and pulled in front of us, in a Dacia, of course. They arrived at exactly 10 p.m. When they pulled up, it seemed as though an invisible dome of peace descended over the location. I felt a great sense of relief as peace and confidence rolled over me. Carman and Georgi got out and came over to the right side front door. Bill positioned himself up at the front door. Will was past the midway point of the van up toward the front, and I was at the back. I started throwing bags of Bibles forward to Will. He tossed them to Bill at the front door, who threw them out to the Romanians. They packed the Bibles into the trunk and back seat of the little Dacia. All I could say was, "Praise the Lord!" as I threw bags of Bibles forward. Working quickly and quietly throwing those bags to Will, we were off-loaded in short order.

While throwing the bags full of Bibles forward, and saying under my breath "Praise the Lord," I thought of the story of a navy Chaplin in World War II which legend says yelled, "Praise the Lord and pass the ammunition!" as his ship was under attack from the Japanese. That event occurred while he was helping a bunch of sailors and gunners' mates, giving them words of encouragement. Patting them on the back, yelling out and throwing ammo forward, he shouted out to the sailors, "Praise the Lord and pass the ammunition!" It became legend, and a song was written about it during that era. I thought it interesting that decades later alongside a highway in Romania, that I was reminded of the phrase in that song. Those same words were giving me encouragement as well, while I threw bags of Bibles forward. The Bibles we were passing on to the Romanians held words of life, comfort, and hope for Russian Christians living under the heavy-handed persecution of the communists. Truly words from the Bible have amazing power to lift the soul, bring peace, hope, comfort, and consolation—ammunition for the human soul as we fight the battles of this life, if you will.

After the Romanians' Dacia was loaded, we had a special gift for Brother Carman. It was a *Strong's, Exhaustive Concordance of the Bible with Hebrew and Greek Dictionaries*. He was a student of the Bible and greatly appreciated the study aid. No Christian bookstores were in the country. Nor any bookstore for that matter which contained such Biblical study aids. Even if a person had large sums of cash they would be hard-pressed to find such a thing in that country. Additionally, we passed him some Excedrin pain reliever for his sister who suffered pain from significant arthritis. They didn't have many effective pain meds. He informed us that about all they could get was aspirin and it was of poor quality. Carman and Georgi each gave us three big bear hugs and a kiss on each cheek, bidding, "Thank you and God bless you! God bless and be with you." They jumped into the little Dacia and off they sped. I look forward to seeing Carman in eternity someday. It will be a special reunion.

Moments after they were gone oncoming headlights headed toward us as traffic again resumed, once again heading toward us from each direction. We were in awe as we drove away. The Lord had made a special provision by seeming to stop traffic and bringing a sense of peace too us. He covered us. We had just delivered a load of comfort to Christians who knew what it was like to suffer for Jesus Christ. We made it back to the city and found our camping place back at the sports arena once again.

Next day we killed time as tourists. It was a beautiful sunny day with no rain. We relaxed a little and took a walk in a park which had a small amusement area and some little kiosk shops. We saw more two man teams of Romanian Securitate "goose-step" through the streets while on patrol with AKs. It seemed like those guys were everywhere.

That evening we found a good spot to park the van, get into the system, and access the four hundred fifty Romanian Bibles. It was the same procedure as the previous night. We found a low traffic area near a park, closed the curtains in the van, opened the system, placed Bibles in trash bags, and covered them with clothing and sleeping bags. Next, we found our prearranged rendezvous point for linking up with Alexi at the edge of a park. We were at the meeting spot in the park parking lot before he arrived. Alexi showed up in his Dacia at 8:30 sharp, walked over, and asked us to follow him. He led and we followed as he performed several block to block, right, left, right zig-zag evasive turns through the city. We got somewhat disoriented from our location. I yelled out at one point to Will, "Don't lose that guy!" Will was having to do some pretty good driving to stay up with Alexi, as he hurriedly drove down the streets, darting through angled intersections at times. We came very close to running some red lights. Alexi was driving his little Dacia pretty fast, as we maneuvered through the city. He led us through multiple neighborhoods making various right and left hand turns. All three of us were up at the front shouting: "Don't lose him! Stay on his bumper! It's time to drive like a Romaniac. Watch out for Politzi! Does anyone see any street signs? Where are we headed? What did that sign say? Where are we on the map?"

One of us helped the driver keep track of Aexi, while calling out street names to the other, who was trying to track where we were on a map. The street signs were posted on the corner sides of the buildings and not easy to see with the dim city lights and the "brown outs" of some neighborhoods. We were able to at least ID the general part of the city where we were located. Eventually we turned onto a narrow dark tree- lined residential street with dim lighting, and even darker shadows cast from trees and buildings. On our left was a solid concrete fence wall which seemed to be about six and a half to seven feet high. Alexi slowed to almost a stop and moved toward the right side of the road. He tapped his brake lights a couple of times. We stopped briefly. Will rolled down the window, and we heard a whistle signal from a lookout. Up ahead about twenty feet and to our left at about a forty-five degree angle a couple of big solid wooden gates in the wall opened up revealing a courtyard. Alexi waved us to the left and motioned for us to drive through the gates. We did; he drove away. We pulled into the courtyard, and two people closed the large solid wooden gates behind us immediately after we drove through the opening. There was a signal given and immediately a squad-size group of people appeared from a building in front of us, behind bushes to our right and out of the shadows from the right front. Alexi's team descended upon us like a small swarm of bees and formed a line headed away from the door of our van toward the building in front of us. After stopping the van, we took up our own stations with one of us at the back of the van, one in the middle, and one at the door as we began to toss bags of Bibles out to the Romanians. We started quickly throwing the Bibles out the van to this human chain of Romanian Christians. They tossed the bags up the line to one another, heading up some steps and into a building at the trailing edge of the courtyard. About the time we had off- loaded roughly one third of our cargo, one of the lookouts signaled with a whistle. The lookouts had spotted someone outside of the wall walking in our direction not far away. We immediately froze and ducked low in the van; those in the court yard melted into the shadows. It could've been a Securitate patrol or an informant who would turn us in. It was getting late; perhaps it was just a civilian out for a walk, but it could still be a good communist who would report us. Perhaps it was one of the patrols like the many we had seen earlier. Regardless it was not a time to make any noise. We stayed low in the van. No one moved as we lay low, not saying a word. Apprehension filled the air; all I could seem to hear was some of my own slightly labored breathing. Then someone walked past us just on the other side of the gate. The rustling sound from the plastic bags and low noise when caught would have been a dead giveaway that something was going on behind that wall. A cough or a sneeze could mean bad news. No one moved; not a sound was made. We were motionless for several minutes. Then an all-clear signal was given with another whistle coming from the lookout. We quickly resumed throwing the Bibles to the Romanians who had reassembled from out of the shadows into a throwing line. As we tossed the bags out the door of the van, we saw them being thrown from one person to the next where they disappeared up the steps and inside the building in front of us. After a few minutes of heaving bags our cargo of Bibles was completely off-loaded. The three of us quickly and quietly got out of the van. Bear hugs were quietly and quickly exchanged among all of us, Romanians and Americans. Expressions of thanks and gratitude were whispered, "Thank you Brothers, God bless you." We replied, individually, "Thank you! God be with you!" All hugs, greetings and thanks were quietly exchanged within a couple of minutes. The three of us jumped back into the van, and waited for the all-clear signal to start the motor and leave. The lookouts gave the all-clear, the gates opened, we fired up the van, and backed out. Then we headed out of the area. That was it for drop number two. We were done with our deliveries in Bucharest for Romanian and Russian Christians. But we were far from home; and if caught with an empty system, we could be accused of smuggling drugs or guns.

After having delivered the Bibles and having driven away about three or four city blocks, it started to rain again! The weather had been good the entire time we had been in the city for three days. We had made our contacts, opened our system, and taken care of our business in the city. I made the observation, "Hey isn't it interesting we prayed for no rain while here. Now we're done, and it starts raining." Will commented, "You think that was God!" It appeared our prayers for good weather while in Bucharest had been answered—so far, so good. Next order of business, we needed to figure out where we were in the city and head out of there. It was back to the sports arena to park and bed down. Then we would head out of town the next morning. We had a some books for a Hungarian pastor left in the van, to be delivered to a village outside a place called Nyiregyhaza in northeast Hungary. We were to pick up a manuscript of a Bible commentary there for printing in the West, as well.

Two successful contacts had been made. Bibles were successfully delivered, but we were still in country and not out of the woods by any stretch of the imagination. We had the books to deliver to our contact in Hungary and we would pick up a manuscript there. We still had to keep our guard up. We could not become over confident, leading to carelessness of speech or actions. We still had things to attend to and be concerned about. It could have been just as bad or perhaps worse to get caught with a near empty system, as one full of Bibles. The Romanian authorities could have accused us of smuggling and other things, and could have wanted to interrogate us more strongly to find out who our Romanian contacts had been. If caught, we could have still done jail time and/or paid heavy fines. Even worse, the authorities could have confiscated all our money, the vehicle, and all that we had. We could still be kicked out of the country with "Persona Non Grata" status and leave with only the clothes on our back, never allowed to return, which would be the least of the issue.

We were ready to hightail it out of the country the next morning and head up to Hungary. It was a two-day drive to our Hungarian contact's village.

Although Hungary was not as oppressive as Romania, it was still a communist regime with a degree of repression. Literature was censored, as was the mail. Christian literature was not readily available in bookstores. Hungary was allied with the USSR and part of the Warsaw Pac nations with a Soviet military presence in the country. KGB agents and a small force of trained secret police also operated there. Its political policies were still influenced by Moscow and the Communist Central Committee under Leonid Brezhnev. We knew too that it was under Brezhnev's influence and that the 1968 Czech "Prague Spring" was crushed by Soviet tanks and military which invaded Czechoslovakia. That lesson was not lost on the Hungarians or their neighbors to the south, either. These southern neighbors had also had their own freedom movement crushed by the Soviets in 1956 when Nikita Khrushchev, Brezhnev's predecessor, invaded Hungary. We would be headed back into a Moscow-controlled satellite country. We had only a few books for a Pastor in the northeast part of the country. We were to pick up a manuscript for printing in Holland. After printing in the West, other teams could bring back the book into the country in volume. We would also find out what books and supplies were needed by them. Then we would report the information to the Dutch and American planners back at the base. This, of course, was key in planning future missions.

Next day, October 14th, we headed north out of Bucharest on Route

{1} toward Ploesti and the Romanian oilfields. That part of Romania had been part of some interesting history. The area was one of the major oil producing areas in Europe and it was there, in 1857, the world's first large oil refinery was put into service. Additionally, those Romanian oilfields were of great value to the NAZIs during World War II. Hitler needed them for his war machine. Romania was occupied by the German army who seized the oilfields and refineries around Ploesti. The region supplied approximately thirty-five percent of the petroleum for Axis armies during the war.

In order to reduce the oil supply for the German military, bomber Squadrons from the U.S. 8th and 9th Air Force flying B-24 Liberators bombed nine refineries north of Ploesti on August 1, 1943. The bombing raid was known as Operation Tidal Wave. It was one of the costliest bombing raids of the war because German anti-aircraft batteries had anticipated the coming raid, were prepared, and lying in wait. Extremely heavy losses were inflicted on the U.S. bomber air crews. One hundred seventy-eight bombers took part in the raid. The majority of them didn't make it back home. Many of the refineries around Ploesti were damaged, but not significantly enough to halt processing and production for any significant length of time. Repairs were made and production was resumed just weeks after the raid. It was not considered a success. It has been known in U.S. Air Force history as "Black Sunday".

While driving through the Ploesti area, we saw older looking oil pumping units, also known as pump jacks in Texas. Most of them looked pretty worn, rusting with peeling paint, and dried oil and dirt accumulation on the units. The units had the appearance of not only being older technologically, but deteriorating as well. They did not look nearly as good as the ones I had seen in the Texas and California oilfields. The Romanian refineries we saw were fenced and the fences were topped with barbed wire. There were guards walking the perimeter fences with AKs slung over the shoulder. Guard tower positions could be seen at some locations as well. I'd certainly never seen anything like that around a U.S. oil refinery. It was as though they were in a mode ready for a war or sabotage.

We continued north on Route {1} toward Brasov and then up toward Targu Mures on Route {13}, headed northwest to a place called Turda. Turda had its own place mentioned in history, as it is known for the Battle of Turda during World War II. It was at this city that German troops allied with the Hungarian Second Armored Division fought against Soviet and Romanian troops in a defensive action. The Russians and Romanians prevailed after a month-long battle. It was the biggest battle in Transylvania and Romania during World War II. In addition to that battle, Turda was also known for having a big salt mine. The salt mine dates back as having been used in Roman times. We transited through the area in our travel from Turda northwest toward Cluj Napoca.

On the road toward Cluj, once again we encountered a lot of gypsy wagons and caravans along the way. It was a unique driving experience. Having left the Ploesti sometime earlier, we continued the journey into the Transylvanian Alps moving on to Cluj, which at one time was known as the Grand Principality of the Transylvania region. It is the second largest city in Romania superseded only by Bucharest. The narrow, winding road along the route was full of the road hazards of gypsy caravans, horse or ox-drawn farm wagons that we were getting used to seeing. The presence of the gypsy wagons and ox-drawn carts reminded me of my dad's stories of the Great Depression of the 1930s. It was like being transported back in time some forty years. Ever mindful that we were still deep in communist territory in a vehicle with specialized compartments used for smuggling, we did not need to be involved in a vehicle accident with a gypsy wagon. The empty compartments carried just as much risk factor as the full ones. It could have been disastrous in more ways than one. So as my dad, the former MP, would have reminded us about keeping our mind on our business: "Cross our 't's and dot our 'i's…Watch 'em and dodge 'em."

Once again on the way out of the country, exiting by another route, we met or passed tractors loaded down with people, moving slowly down what was called a highway. Interestingly, people hitchhiking along the road would wave down a tractor to catch a ride. We saw tractor drivers pull over on more than one occasion stop and give hitchhikers a ride. It gave new meaning to the word "Hitchhiker." I'm sure that tractor ride was better than walking.

We continued along on road surfaces which turned from asphalt into cobblestone or brick. Usually the small villages had roads which were worn and full of potholes or had big dips with pushed up ridges and ruts. Wavy ruts best describes these ridges. The condition of those roads had evolved into natural speed bumps, which really slowed us down. It cost us decent travel time. As the day was drawing to a close and beginning to get late, we found a decent roadside pullout and pulled over to eat and get some shut-eye. We camped just off the road, not far from Cluj. Wouldn't you know it...there was another train track near the place we had stopped! Our sleep continued to be interrupted time and again, as not far off in the distance a train would go by with the roar of the engine, the noisy sound of the cars on the tracks, and the reoccurring whistle blowing. But even with the road hazards and trains, the country side had a lot of good looking forested low mountains and green pastures. So far our trip had been more than well worth it not only for its beauty but also for the Bibles we had delivered, which would be blessings bringing encouragement to many people.

On October 15th we headed toward Oradea to make our border crossing west of the city. We were ready to get out of the country. Our mission was close to being accomplished, and we had had all we wanted of the drab, dank buildings draped with red flags, banners with Hammers and Sickles, and large billboard pictures of Nicolae Ceausescu hanging from buildings. We were about ready for some color and culture of the west and nicely designed buildings including the colorful advertising brought about by free enterprise. The political and economic oppression of the people in Romania seemed to create an atmosphere where one could literally feel the heaviness hanging over the land. This seemed to have been brought about by the policies of the communists. But this was the way of life for the Romanians who knew no different; so many could be manipulated by the dictator Ceausescu.

Once again, before the border crossing we stopped to check the van and took the usual precautions, inspecting our vehicle, making sure the system was secured, and said some prayers before reaching the checkpoint. We approached the border crossing just west of a place called Bors. As we drew nearer we saw the barbed wire, no man's land, mine field, tank traps and machine gun towers which stood high before us. When we arrived, the guards armed with AK47s of course were curious about us and questioned where we had been traveling and staying in Romania, as they examined our papers. They gave us some extra attention compared to previous crossings and became more interested in the van and us. They had some discussion about our visas and papers. They also brought out measuring sticks and started examining the bottom side of the vehicle, measuring distances from the bottom of the frame to the floor of the vehicle. An older more experienced ranking officer came out and took charge. He tended to grunt, was gruff, and had a serious demeanor, not friendly at all. I was beginning to wonder if they might start tearing our vehicle apart or how much more serious this border inspection was going to get. After four of them had congregated around our blue Peugeot van and looked it over, checking us out, they had a bit of a discussion among themselves. They were closely examining our vehicle. But then the senior officer seemed to have a change of mind. Perhaps he decided we were just some dumb tourists or the Lord changed his mind about us. Whatever transpired inside Him, the Lord used it and he let us go. He gave us back our passports, and the guards motioned for us to leave. They waved us forward toward no man's land. We did not question but gratefully complied, believing the prayers we had said had been heard. We passed by the guard towers, through the mine field, and no man's land. Being at that checkpoint was a bit of an intense time, but the Lord had intervened for us. We drove forward past the barbed wire and mine fields and were pretty relieved when we drove out of Romania and into Hungary. It was good to be out of there and at the Hungarian border checkpoint. Yet we still had to undergo the scrutiny of the Hungarian guards. The Hungarians preformed a search of the vehicle, but it was not as extensive as the Romanian search had been. We told the border guards that we were headed to Budapest, then back to Western Europe. They issued us our Hungarian visas and let us pass; we were there for less than 45 minutes. We weren't planning on heading back to Romania any time soon. Being in Hungary was a relief compared to Romania, but it was still a place where religious activities were monitored. My toothache even eased up some after we crossed the border.

We headed west on Route {42}, made it to a small village where we intersected with Route {4}, headed north to Debrecen, and then continued north east to Nyiregyhaza. Our third contact lived in a small village at the outskirts of the city. We managed to find his home to meet with him. The communists of Hungary were not as hard on Christians as the Romanian communists had been, so at the pastor's insistence, we agreed to attend his small Methodist Church that Wednesday night. We were asked to bring greetings from the West, which was about all I did and I didn't feel very good about it. Public speaking was not something I enjoyed, especially in those circumstances. My greeting to the congregants was very short as I introduced Bill, who was from a

Methodist background. He shared a good word of encouragement. The church was smaller and more traditional, composed mostly of people.

After the service, a twenty-something or younger guy came up to us and told us about an unregistered house church in Budapest which met in an apartment complex on Thursday nights. He gave us the address and told us it was a group of Believers full of the Spirit, in revival, and recommended that we visit there. Our team talked it over after we got back to the van and decided we would go for it, to hopefully learn more about conditions for Christians there and make a new contact for the mission. We would be in Budapest to meet up with a contact anyway. We found a campground that night and camped northeast of town. We camped less than twenty-four miles from the Soviet Union.

On October 16th we headed west back to Budapest, the "Paris of Eastern Europe," although some in Romania might disagree with that statement. We were to meet with and establish a new contact in Budapest as one of our objectives. Bill and Will attempted to meet with the new contact that evening, but it proved fruitless. I took a walk down by the Danube River while I waited for them.

The walk along the Danube was relaxing, especially after the previous several days. There was a large majestic palace on the opposite bank of the river. The reflection of the golden rays of the setting sun illuminated the structure with shafts of orange and golden light, causing it to take on a golden hew. It was a stimulating view that I absorbed while waiting for my teammates, especially after the heaviness experienced in Romania. It was a beautiful location for me to reflect on the trip up until that time. What an impact the past several days had made on my life and hopefully would make in the lives of others in the future!

That evening, although Bill and Will had an unsuccessful contact attempt, our trip into Budapest was not a complete loss. We were able to attend the Underground Church house meeting the guy in Nyiregyhaza had told us about. It took place in a hacienda styled type of structure with a large living area. The guy had given us good directions and information. Furniture had been pushed aside and the room had been set up with folding chairs. It seemed like there were about seventy or eighty people packed into a room where twenty would be a crowd. The time was great. We actually got to hear a sermon in English. It just so happened that an evangelist from Spain was in the area, but none of the Hungarians knew how to speak Spanish. There was, however, someone with the Spaniard who could translate into English. Many of the Hungarians could speak English so the sermon was conducted in three languages. The Spanish guy preached in Spanish; we heard it in the English translation; then someone translated it from the English into Hungarian. It was a long, but interesting sermon and service. We were warmly received as well. Bill was asked to share a testimony again and speak to the Hungarian Christians. Once again, he did a good job. After the service we found a place to camp that night and slept fairly well, although it was near a train track again, which had its fair share of freighters go by during the night. Staying by the train tracks was becoming a big joke to us or on us you could say.

The next morning, we left the beauty of Budapest behind us, headed for Gyor and our last Border Crossing check point at Checkpoint Sopron. We made it out of the country late that morning with a smooth crossing back into Austria, without much scrutiny. Although we still observed strict protocols of conversation until we were ten kilometers into Austria, we anticipated every kilometer! As we drove past the ten K mark, it was shouts of "Praise the Lord!" and "Hallelujah!" We broke into a chorus of "God Bless America." If a person has not experienced it, you just don't know how good it feels. While we were elated to be back in Western Europe; we also were bothered by what we had seen and heard east of the Iron Curtain. Truly we had mixed emotions: thankful to be out, yet sad for those who couldn't leave and had to live under the conditions which we had observed first hand.

We were still two days away from The Company Farm and began the trek westward down the length of Austria. We thanked the Lord for His protective hand of mercy while we were behind the Iron Curtain. I thank Him to this day, when I think about it.

We headed westward across Austria and camped outside of Salzburg a few kilometers. We headed on up toward Switzerland the next day, then cut north on through Germany and back up to Holland.

October 20th marked the last leg of the mission. We were up early, made it to the checkpoint crossing the border from Germany into Holland. The Dutch border guards were very curious about us and our vehicle; it was not the quick, easy crossing we had expected. The Dutch looked us over and asked several questions; it was not a quick wave through. They could have given us a shake down and may have discovered an empty system. Whereby we could have been accused of drug smuggling, and the vehicle could have been confiscated. Thankfully, we made it through the checkpoint unhindered. Then we headed on to the base where we arrived at 7:07 p.m. Praise the Lord...we had made it safely back home! We could finally "let our hair down," speak freely with our team mates, and share what we had experienced. The crew at The Base greeted us with enthusiasm and a lot of hugs. It was certainly good to be back in the Netherlands. We praised Almighty God for all of the travel mercies, protection, and safety that He had poured out on us and our contacts. They would live forever in our hearts and minds. I often think of Carman and wonder about the outcome of his life, as I wondered about the other Romanians I had met. I also wonder if we Americans realize what a special blessing the First Amendment has been for us.

The next day oral and written debriefings began. We started on trip reports, vehicle reports, costs, and financial accounting. Reports on meetings with contacts and border crossing events were documented. Particular behaviors or interests of border guards were put in reports. We continued working on reports for two days, then cleaned the vehicle, and worked on getting it ready for the next team. All reports and vehicle cleanup were completed on October 23rd — mission accomplished! We could truly say the Lord had been with us, blessed us, and provided protection.

October 24th, I began working on Hungarian Bible Study Books with Dave from New York. He was a humble man with a good heart and deep love for the Lord. He was a man of no guile who gave of himself to others. I enjoyed working with him.

On November 8th I read the book of 1st Samuel, learning some good lessons about King David. Dave and I rescued a cat stuck up in a tree abouttwenty-five5 feet off the ground, on the first lower limb. As far as we could determine, it had been stuck up there all day or perhaps some the night before. It was crying out loudly, and it was a really windy day, too. I climbed up to the second rung from the top of a twenty-foot ladder just leaning against the tree, trying to rescue that cat. I extended my arms up to the cat and was still a couple of feet short reaching her. I kept calling her to me, but she was scared and wouldn't come toward me. After a while on the ladder in the high winds, I started planning on heading back to the ground myself. She must have sensed that I was leaving, so she jumped for my arm and hit my forearm, while I was looking down to begin my descent. I steadied myself by grabbing the tree to regain my balance. In dismay, I watched the poor cat plummet to ground. But surprisingly when she hit, she landed on her feet and did not seem to be injured. The little tabby, excitedly in almost a run, wove herself around Dave's legs as he held the ladder for my descent. I made it down OK, and the cat was one happy kitty when I got down. I'd seen dogs jump on people happy to see them, but the cat kept running back and forth between Dave and myself. We kept petting the cat and stroking it while we checked it for injury. There was a bit of a spiritual lesson in that cat rescue for me. I reflected that God wants us to come to Him to be saved and rescued. But often controlled by our fears, we are afraid to come to Him. He wants to save us from the plights we face. For our own welfare we need to come to Him and follow His ways, most especially when he extends His outstretched arms to us.

November 9th included a church service at EGR which I enjoyed, then a Baptism service at a local indoor recreational swimming pool. Seventeen were baptized. Christine, one of our Dutch friends, was baptized. After the baptism service Dave and I visited Christine and Marius, Christine's brother. We had a good visit with them. Christine was an attractive blonde Dutch school teacher and Marius was an inquisitive college student with a lot of theologically based questions. I enjoyed spending time with both of them. They were open and friendly and treated Dave and I well. They were good people and later became good friends.

November 10th-12th was spent working with Phil and Cees installing a security alarm system for a section of the base compound. I read the book *Ben Israel* by Arthur Katz that evening. Dave prepared to head out for work in Israel. He was to be working on a Kibbutz helping Israelis. During November, Mike and John shipped out. John went to England to work with YWAM (Youth with a Mission). Mike, Bill and Will returned to the States. Mike and Bill began speaking tours about persecution of Christians behind the Iron Curtain. Will returned to his waiting fiancé whom he was soon to marry. He was looking forward to their new life together.

December 5th - 7th was Saint Nicholas Day week in Holland. I spent Saint Nichols Day evening with Cees and his family. Cees' wife, Nel, had knitted a pair of wool socks for me. It was nice of her; I had not expected anything and it was a real surprise. One of the cool things about it was that she had a spinning wheel and had spun and made the yarn out of wool herself. It made the gift that much more special indeed. I was able to visit with two other Dutch friends. Cees had cautioned us against close friendships with the local Dutch, and it was a word of wisdom. The mission didn't need locals becoming too curious and intrusive into activities at the base. I went to their locations; they didn't come to mine. Mission activities and trips were not discussed. We only conversed about stuff in the U.S. and in Holland and had discussions about personal interests, theology, life in Holland and the U.S.

From December 11th-15th, the weather was cold and windy. I had "KP" duties that week—inside chores after outside construction work. Phil and I put up new wood siding on an exterior side wall on the barn. It had been constructed in the 1930s, and the wood was beginning to decay. We were able to complete one side of the barn using 1" x 12" x 10' planks. The barn with the various workshop areas, print shop, and car garage had been overdue for some new wood on the sides. It was good to finish the job on the north side, stop working out in the cold wind, and start working in the print shop again.

During WWII the German army had commandeered this property where our Dutch operations base was located four decades later. The Germans had built an artillery platoon there. Those Germans became involved in an artillery battle with Canadian forces during Operation Market Garden, but no Canadian artillery rounds hit the house or barn. I believe some rounds did hit on the property, but thankfully none of the Canadian shells hit that farm house or barn. I found it interesting that years later the facilities were used as an operational support base for taking supplies to the Underground Church.

When making plans for a return to the States, I was approached by Cees to consider returning to work full time with the mission. Hank Paulson, the mission Director, also met with me and requested that I return to Holland to work with the mission fulltime in an internship for another year to eighteen months. I considered the requests a compliment and an answer to prayer. I could not forget the past few weeks and those people that I had met. The work was a worthy effort, one in which I was happy to participate. I did not want to just return to a regular daily grind in the U.S. at that time. The past few weeks had been life changing.

Books for Czechoslovakian, Hungarian, and Russian Believers

December 19th found me headed for home to the good ole U.S.A. I had a life changing experience which changed me forever. I left Holland just before Christmas with mixed emotions. I wanted to return home and see family, but I really wanted to be in Holland to continue the work as well. I had made some good friends which had become like family. When I returned home to the U.S., most folks I encountered had been continuing with their regular daily routines of life. They did not seem to understand the depth of what others were having to endure under communist rule in Eastern Europe. I didn't seem to be able to communicate too well with them what I had seen and heard. My heart became more burdened for America and some of the spiritual condition of the nation.

"Lord, please help our country its people and leaders," was my prayer. "Please send spiritual renewal and revival to the land. Lord may the US remain free, not just for ourselves, but for others around the world as well so the Gospel can be spread. Let America continue to be a place of refuge and hope, a beacon from where light and the freedom of democracy would continue to permeate dark places on the planet."

I was reminded about comments from an Eastern European Christian: "We pray for you in America, that the Church in the United States will remain free and that you will be strong." I was concerned for America but knew I wanted to be back working in Europe for those who were enduring the oppression of communism.

I spent the first part of January in California. The rest of the month and February were spent in New Mexico and Texas, visiting and working with cousins in the Texas oilfields and sharing about my experiences. I spoke at a Church youth group meeting in New Mexico. I traveled to California with a cousin in late February. In March I spoke at five churches in California. I received a letter from the mission asking me to return to Holland as soon as possible. A major project was waiting so I flew out on March 22nd. I landed at Schipol Airport in Amsterdam on March 23rd, happy to be back in Holland working with the mission team in the Netherlands, feeling a sense of purpose in the work. Upon reentering the Netherlands, I got stopped at the airport in Amsterdam, was detained by Dutch police, and questioned. It was interesting, but had a good outcome. They were concerned about what I would be doing in Holland and how long I would stay there. I gave them a name and phone number to call. After a call to my contact at the base, the Dutch authorities released me to head on to the mission base.

Soon after getting settled back in at The Company Farm, Cees had me working on a special printing project. I started printing forty thousand Hungarian Bible commentaries and some leadership training books. After printing those, they would need to be collated, assembled, and have a cover placed on them. So there was enough work ahead to keep me busy for a while. Cees also had me to help him construct a dark room for developing photos to be used in publication work, including the organization newsletter, "Focus" magazine. The dark room would also be used for development of photo plates to be used on the offset printer I operated. Cees and I worked on several printing projects. We also worked on vehicle projects by sanding, painting, and repairing our small fleet of specially prepared vehicles, cars, vans, and a couple of trailers with hidden compartments and specialized access systems. I certainly didn't get bored working with Cees; he always seemed to have one project or another which needed to be done. We did everything from printing jobs to minor construction jobs to helping with vehicle maintenance or turning the soil and preparing it for a new garden from where we would grow a few of our own vegetables. After a few weeks John Murphy from Iowa returned to the mission. It was really good to see him again and have him back to work. We enjoyed working together on special projects assigned by Cees.

In late spring Mike Lee returned from his speaking tour in the U.S. Then, in June, Bill Larson returned from speaking engagements

Stateside, as well. It was really good to see those guys. The four of us had a special kinship; I really appreciated those guys. Bill was a good friend and fun to hang out with; his dry humor was full of entertaining surprises. Mike was not only a squared away Marine but also a southern gentleman dedicated to the work we were doing. John was an honorable man of good character who held a special place of respect and admiration in my heart as well. He was a quiet, hardworking man of exceptional character and trustworthiness who became Cees' special projects assistant for work on special vehicle projects. What a good bunch of guys! We bonded well and were part of a good team. They all became like brothers whom I never had or met. I thought the world of them. Working with them to support the Believers in Eastern Europe gave life purpose and meaning. Cees kept us busy, too, and seemed happy to have us around. There was a lot of interesting activities which went on inside that sleepy looking Dutch Farm house and barn. The next few months were interesting and good; we developed some close friendships.

Early July found me on the road headed toward Czechoslovakia with Bill and Vance. I had been reminiscing about home while headed down the autobahn in Germany. That July 4th the weather was not bad. It was certainly a lot better than it had been when we headed to Romania a few months earlier. Traffic on the German Autobahn Budesrepublik Deutschland {3} going east was busy though. Vance had taken over driving. After my time of rest and reflection, I moved up to riding shotgun in the navigator seat and started visiting with Vance. Bill moved to the back. I was happy to move after my time in the back of the van, thinking about what had led up to this trip with the business man and the rancher. Having been unable to sleep in the rear of the van, I was ready to be in the navigator seat riding shot gun.

The next day, July 5th, would be crossing through the Czechoslovakian no man's land and mine fields where east met west. This would be another border checkpoint like Checkpoint Charlie, but at a different spot through the Iron Curtain. It had its own barbed wire, coiled razor wire and mine fields, lookout towers, machine gun positions, and listening devices. We would soon be crossing into the Warsaw Pac again—Bills third trip, my second, Vance's first. Thinking about the next day which lay before us carried a bit of its own degree of subliminal tension.

It was good to be traveling with Bill again. We drew upon our travels together in Romania, having established not only a friendship but a degree of confidence in each other. Bill was a good traveling partner and team leader. Vance was a good man, too—a rancher and cowboy from Montana, the real deal! I had worked some with cattle myself, but not like him. He was raised on a large working cattle ranch consisting of several thousand acres. They used horses for working cattle. I thought he probably cut his teeth on cow hide! He was an individualistic guy with a big heart and loved animals and people. He had a strong desire to help persecuted Christians for a few years and worked toward that end. He had a lot of self-discipline, too, as he had studied Russian for over two years preparing so he could do what we were attempting. He had a fair degree of fluency in German as well. When I thought of cowboys, I certainly didn't think of one who learned to speak German and Russian just so he could help others suffering in another country. But he was one for sure a different kind of Maverick in his own right.

I felt for him, though. He had experienced a "Dear John" break up with his girl just before he came across the "Big Puddle," the Atlantic Ocean. He had struggled with it at first, but pulled himself together pretty well. I liked the guy. We hit it off pretty well. We talked about working cattle, girls, relationships, and of course theology, Christian persecution, and the Lord. He and Bill got along well, too. Both of them being from Montana, familiar with the Montana Rockies, and both with a fair degree of fluency in German helped. We made a good team.

We had already committed all of our contact information to memory as necessary and had our various assignments for this trip memorized. We had our team pocket New Testament which we shared and rotated daily. The guy that lead devotions for the morning was the keeper of the little Bible; after devotions he handed it off to the next guy, who was responsible for securing it all that day and then leading devotions the next morning. We did not take personal Bibles and we were discreet with the New Testament we had; in other words we hid it! It would have been foolish to risk the well-being of those we were going to help by being "marked" by border guards for tracking, just because we wanted to have a Bible. That would not only have been selfish but just plain stupid.

Our cargo for that trip consisted of a few hundred Russian Bibles, some Slovakian Bibles, some Czech Bibles, and Christian books about the family and leadership, along with a bunch of clothes for Russian dissident Christians. We took an absolute bare minimum of our own clothes (only two changes of clothes, underwear, and socks). We filled our suit cases, ruck sacks, back packs, closets, and storage areas with as many clothes for the Russian Believers as three guys could put in our luggage and the RV closets. We were able to include a pretty sizable amount of clothes, all things considered.

Our network of contacts in the underground church would get the clothes distributed where they needed to go. The locals would take care of distribution. We were scheduled to drop them off with our first contact in eastern Czechoslovakia, where they would be distributed to Russian Christians and also delivered with Russian Bibles. Our contact, I'll call "Daniel," lived in a smaller village in Slovakia, less than sixty kilometers or under thirty-six miles from the USSR. The closer to the USSR, the greater the intensity of Soviet influence...thus more secret police.

We were within a few kilometers of the village where Daniel lived and somewhat early, yet needing the cover of darkness for our meeting up with him. We needed to find a place to lie low. Just after dusk we found ourselves driving down a dirt road into the middle of a wheat field with head lights off. A car showed up from around a curve on the main road about two hundred yards behind us; I did not want them to see the flash of our brake lights as Bill was starting to slow and stop. Bill, who was driving, was about to hit the brakes to stop. "Bill, use the emergency brake!" I called out. Bill stopped the van using the hand brake, saving us from being spotted from the road. After the car passed by, we just sat there in the middle of the wheat field on the other side of the world from the U.S., looking at the stars and counting the time before we could head into the village. About an hour later we were at Daniel's home where we would set up a meeting place and time to deliver a few hundred Russian Bibles, books, and the stash of clothing for the Russian Believers to him. While there, Brother Daniel shared with us about vehicle problems he was having. His car needed a battery before he could haul the Bibles into Russia. Daniel did not speak much German or English, but he did speak Russian. Vance spoke with him in Russian and acted as our interpreter. Vance told us of Daniel's request for money to repair his car. Our team met and discussed his request. After discussion and prayer, we ended up giving him money to cover the cost of a car battery out of our travel funds. That cut into our funds, perhaps a mistake. But as it is said, "Hind sight is 20/20."

The hand-off of books and supplies went well, and we left stuff in his living room. The pile of clothes filled up the length of a couch with a height about three to three and a half feet, including a chair where we were able to stack close to four feet of clothes. I certainly didn't remember we had loaded that many clothes. It was a surprise and a blessing for us everyone. We visited with them for a short time, prayed with them, then wished them Godspeed and left to find a camping spot. We camped about twenty-five miles from the Soviet Union that night. Thankfully it was uneventful.

The next day we headed southwest toward Bratislava, where Bill and I met with an elderly couple. The man spoke only Slovakian and German. Bill's German was far better than mine. Upon arriving at their apartment, when I walked into the home, I felt a wave of peace roll over me like I had not felt since Romania at that roadside pullout months earlier. It had been some time since I had felt peace like that. Their home seemed to have the sanctity of a Church. It was like entering a peaceful harbor in the after a storm. Their home was full of the peace of the Lord. During the visit we mentioned it to them. They confidently replied that they knew they had angels of the Lord watching over and protecting them.

We had communication difficulties with that brother, but it was resolved when we started communicating through Bible stories. Interestingly, I was beginning to understand him in our communication via the scriptures and Bible stories he was telling; yet they were in German, and my German was not the best. We established rapport not by the language of our tongues but by the language of the heart and Spirit. We communicated through the Word and the Spirit. It seemed as though God opened my mind, and I was able to understand him fairly well even though he spoke in German. Even though Bill's German was better than mine, he did not have to interpret much at all. After a time of fellowship over the Word of God we sang with them. Their windows were open, yet they did not live far off the street. We asked them if they were concerned about the singing; we seemed to be more concerned than they were. We asked if they would like to shut the windows. They replied again that their home was protected by the Lord; they did not seem worried about communist police or informers. They trusted in the Lord; their peace and hope were in Him. Bill and I were amazed at their calm confidence.

After a time of fellowship, they loaned Bill and me two empty suit cases for us to bring Bibles back to their apartment. Later that night, after we returned to the campground, we took Bibles out of the van's specialized compartments and filled the suit cases. We then planned our tactical approach for the drop the next day. We set up the literature drop, at their insistence, to be at their home. Bill and Vance dropped me off at the edge of a bus stop parking lot the next afternoon with the two suit cases full of Bibles. We figured it would appear normal to see someone leaving a bus stop area with suitcases. The cases were full of books and a bit heavy for carrying a couple of blocks. The guys had dropped me off in the parking lot. I walked through it and continued a few blocks to the couple's apartment flat. I made sure I wasn't being followed with turning maneuvers. I had to stop a few times and readjust my grip, but the Lord helped with endurance carrying the heavy cases. I arrived at their hacienda style apartment complex and turned into the square, then took a second right and started up steps to their second floor apartment. I heard footsteps steps coming up behind me at a faster pace than I was carrying those suitcases. I did not want to be knocking on the door with someone coming up behind me so I stopped on the stair well. The footsteps were coming up faster than I was making it up the stairs. I sat down the suit cases. I bent over and discreetly untied my shoe before the second person arrived at the same level. I got in fairly close to the wall. Then, watching out of the corner of my eye, I began tying my shoe as the individual went by. A lean, brown-haired man about 5'9" walked past me up the steps. He did not seem to care about me and just kept on walking. Several seconds later, I heard a door shut up the hall above me. Picking up the suitcases, I proceeded to the couple's apartment door, which thankfully was the closest to the stairwell. I knocked very lightly; the woman opened the door and rushed me inside. I felt peace once again as I entered their home. I happened to looked up and saw a Crown of Thorns painted on the ceiling.

The delivery of the suitcases full of Bibles took only seconds; it was fast and smooth. Their suitcases were returned full of Bibles. Hugs, smiles and blessings in German were received. I left bidding them Godspeed; within a New York minute, I was gone. Again, I had felt the peace of the Lord as I had entered that home. It was an island of peace in a stormy sea. The Lord was with those people I knew. Their home truly was a sanctuary. I only spent moments there but they had meaning and impact. Maintaining situational awareness, I left the apartment. I did not see anyone loitering in the complex square or as I turned left out of the complex walking back toward the bus stop where Bill and Vance would pick me up in the van. I made it back to the bus stop with no tails. I got into the van and we took off. We did not see anyone following us as we left the area. Our team headed for Prague.

In route to Prague from Bratislava, just south of Bruno, Vance discovered that his visa was missing from his passport. We stopped and searched the vehicle from top to bottom. He searched his luggage two or three times and his clothes multiple times. We searched the vehicle again and again. Yet, no visa was to be found. We came to the conclusion the authorities at the campground must not have returned his visa when they returned the passport back to him. He did not remember checking the passport when it was returned by the campground authorities. We turned around and drove all the way back to the camp ground outside Bratislava, where we had stayed the night before. It cost us a lot of time, fuel and a little travel money. But that visa was way important. Vance could not leave the country without it. By the time we made it back to the camp ground, there were other people working at the gatehouse. We explained our circumstances; they looked for the visa (at least, they said they did) but returned empty-handed. We checked our camp ground and the footpath from the camp ground to the gatehouse. A visa was not to be found anywhere. The people at the gate house explained we would need to obtain another visa from authorities in Prague. This was turning into a boondoggle. Our hearts dropped. Disappointment does not describe our feelings.

There we were in a communist country with contraband Christian literature on board and told we would need to go into the heart of the government bureaucracy to obtain a new visa for Vance. That was the last thing we wanted to do! But life throws a curve ball at times, and the best laid plans can go south; Murphy's Law always shows up at the unexpected times. We just needed to adjust and adapt. We headed to Prague to find the agency in charge of issuing new visas and complete our mission.

Prague was not only our destination to obtain the new visa for Vance, but also to meet with a Christian family active in literature work who lived not far from the government embassy housing area. Vance was feeling badly about his visa and the next contact was to be his. It would hopefully be an encouragement for him as well as to them. We needed some good stuff to happen for him as he was beating himself up pretty badly.

There were a lot of older larger multi-story beautiful homes in the neighborhood, where our next contact lived. There was also a lot of VB State Police as well as Secret Police in the area. It was a high profile diplomatic area. We were going into the heart of the Lion's Den so to speak, right under the noses of the communist officials. Our contact family had more than a couple of kids, and their home was a large house. After selecting a drop-off point for Vance and then a rendezvous location a couple of miles from the contacts home, Bill and I dropped him off a few blocks from the contact house. Bill and I returned to the rendezvous point and then waited, waited and waited some more; it seemed like a two to three-hour wait.

Vance eventually made it back to us after a lengthy visit with the Czech family. He had a huge smile on his face. He was beaming from ear to ear when he returned to the van. The way he was smiling you would have thought he had just won the Grand Champion prize with an FFA bull he entered at the local county fair. But he had a better story than that for us. His contact family had shared the following story about a miraculous deliverance of the Lord from the State police.

Their home had recently been raided by a large team of police, composed of several officers, who searched their home for a full day. The police had somehow learned that the family was active in Christian literature work. The police raided the home and began a long thorough search of the entire house, going through it from bottom to top searching for Bibles and Christian literature. The house had one room which had been dedicated for literature and Bible storage until they could be distributed. The dad was arrested by police, taken into custody, detained, and interrogated at the police station. He believed he was in deep trouble and that the Bibles in his home had been discovered. He assumed he would be seeing some prison time. He was anxiously wondering when police would start asking, "Where did you get the Bibles?" Surprisingly after all day in the police station, they let him go. They never did ask him where he got the Bibles which were stored in his home. After hours of anxiously waiting, the police just let him go. He was puzzled and thought maybe it was a trap. Somewhat bewildered, he returned home. Upon his return, he asked his wife what had happened.

While police were searching the house, the family members present quietly prayed. They asked the Lord that the hidden Bibles not be discovered. As they anxiously waited and felt the books soon would be found, they assumed they would soon be arrested. But as the search continued, members of the police team assumed that others of their team searched the particular area where the Bibles were hidden. No one ever checked the area where the books were stored. The hiding place was never discovered and searched; all the members of the police team passed by it! The Bibles were never discovered by the VB! Later the family of Christians surmised that the Lord confused the minds of the police. Truly, it appeared that the Lord had messed with the minds of His enemies, just as He had done in times of old written in Old Testament stories. No, this was not the ancient Midianites nor Philistines; but the Lord had certainly covered His people, and His Word was destined to be gifts for many others. The Bibles had not been found by the communists, and Dad was released to go home. The family was reunited and Bibles were distributed!

That family had been protected from an entire team of police who had searched the home for the greater part of a day, but never found a large store of Bibles hidden in their home. It truly was a deliverance. It was fitting that Vance would be the carrier of this news to report back to the mission, where the story would most likely be publicized for reading in the west.

After that literature drop, our next order of business was to take care of the visa issue. When we eventually made it to the agency where Vance would get a new visa, all three of us were interviewed by a government official. We were told it would take three days for a new visa to be issued for Vance. That was not good news. We were supposed to be out of the country the next day. It would cost more money than we had for per diem money for three of us and for three new visas to be issued. Bill and I would need to extend our visas as well. It was not looking good; we were in a bit of a jam. We knew having more money wired would not be good. We couldn't risk calling the mission because phone lines where tapped and monitored.

We had a discussion about our circumstances, resources, money, time, options, etc. During that meeting Vance volunteered to stay behind for two more days. Bill and I didn't like the idea at all and said, "No way!" to it. Breaking up the team, risking Vance's welfare, etc., was too much of a chance. It was a hard decision for us. Bill and I had a more difficult time with it than Vance. He was a cowboy used to camping out on the range; he was game and kept pushing us for it. He said that he had stayed out on the range by himself more than once and that he was up for it.

Our options were limited. As we reexamined our resources, all we had was enough money for fuel to get us back to the Base and one more night. With Vance's insistence, Bill and I began to waffle. Bill gave the green light. We would give Vance a some team money and some food out of our supplies, and he would stay. We set up a rendezvous point, for a meet-up to be at a big oak tree just east of Furth im Wald, the place we had stopped to pray just before crossing into Czechoslovakia. We agreed to meet in two days at the large oak tree near the roadside turnout east of Furth im Wald. That oak tree became our marker for the rendezvous.

Before leaving the city, the three of us spent a little time together at the old town center of Prague. We visited the Charles Bridge which crosses over the Vitava River; it is over five hundred yards long and ten yards wide. It has three towers which guard it and thirty statues along its length, fifteen on each side. The statues are statues of the twelve Apostles and Saints of Moravian historical culture.

There were many artisans along the Bridge stationed at the base of many of the statues with easel and canvas, painting portraits of tourists who would cough up the Czech Kronun for their picture to be painted with a backdrop of Prague behind them. While walking along the Bridge absorbing the sights and sounds, I spotted a yellow and white Czech VB police car entering from the far end of the pedestrian bridge. The vehicle was moving slowly toward us. As it eased its way through the crowd of foot traffic, I noticed that many of the artists far ahead of the VB patrol were discreetly packing up their brushes and easels, then waking away and fading into the crowd. It made for an interesting scene. The VB patrol idled past us. After it moved past us about one hundred fifty feet further it pulled up alongside one of the artisans at the base of one of the statutes and stopped. One of the troopers got out and started talking with the man. Then the driver of the patrol car got out and joined his partner. A short discussion ensued; then the two VB officers grabbed the artist and shoved him into the back of the VB patrol car. "Wow, what was all that about?" I wondered. As the VB patrol drove away, I stepped over to a younger guy not standing far from us who looked to be about our age. He had long hair and appeared to be a bit of a non-conformist. I asked him if he might have an idea what happened between the police and the artist. His reply surprised me. He said, "Here in Czechoslovakia, we have to have a painter's (artist's) license." I asked, "Why is that?" He explained, "Because the State does not want us painting anything bad about it. They inspect our paintings so we do not paint bad pictures about the State." So as well as having to have permits from the local police for typewriters, the citizens had to have permits to do art work.

We knew from our training that regular citizens there could not legally own a typewriter unless permitted by the local police; but this was a first for me, a painter's license! Unbelievable! We were truly operating in a Police State where the government sought to control the ideological thoughts of the people. It emphasized the importance of what we were doing there.

After we left the Charles Bridge we searched for a place to drop off Vance. After checking our maps, we found a decent looking area with a large park with a lot of trees, bushes and shrubs, within a decent walking distance to the government building where Vance would pick up his visa. Bill and I had to drop off him off and head to the checkpoint in order to make it there before our visas expired. We didn't like it, but it was what it was. We had decided it was our best option. Those conditions placed us at a little higher risk at the checkpoint as well because we went in country with three American guys and just two of us were exiting. We wondered if that might result in a more thorough search of the van. If the system was discovered, we could be accused of smuggling drugs or guns. But our position was still much better than his; Vance was at the greatest risk. But hopefully their record keeping at the border wasn't the best, and I doubted they tracked such things or cared that much. I hated dropping him off. But as we let him out at the park, he was smiling and actually seemed happy about it. He liked camping and a good adventure. Bill and I didn't feel the same way. We were concerned about it. But we did know that the Lord had been with us up to this point, and our dependence was on Him. We had improvised a plan, so we stuck with it. Improvise and adapt to overcome was a view we had to put into practice.

We prepared to say our goodbye as we agreed to meet in two days at the tree outside the little German town of Furth im Wald. We said a prayer at the edge of that park, then bid Vance farewell and told him we would see him at the big oak tree. Bill and I headed west that afternoon toward Checkpoint Ceska' Kobice.

Just before we arrived at the checkpoint, I stuffed the team New Testament in the front of my pants under the shirt and behind the belt buckle. I stayed with the van, sitting in the passenger seat, while Bill went inside to present our passports and visas and take care of the paperwork.

All was going fine until a border guard came over to my door and ordered me out of the van. He wanted to search the van, and he asked me to open the van back door. As I stepped out of the van the little New Testament worked loose from behind my belt starting to take a trip down my pants leg. *Oh no, what a way to get busted*, raced through my mind, as the little book headed down the inside of my pants toward the ground. That was way bad! If it were to fall out of my pant leg onto the ground in front of that guard, we would be had! As the guard was walking away from me headed to the rear of the van, I quickly put my hand in my pocket caught the little New Testament by the trailing edge, as it reached the inside edge of my pocket. I pressed it hard against my leg; I had it trapped! But I was in a bit of a pickle. I managed to hold it tightly against my leg while walking slightly stiff-legged behind the guard to the rear doors. The guard ordered me to open the door. I tried to open it with my free left hand. It was locked! The extra set of spare keys was in the very pocket where I had my hand pressing hard against the Bible. I couldn't retrieve the keys for to do so would mean the little New Testament would race down my pants and fall onto the pavement right in front of the guard. The guard repeated, "Open the Door!" I was in a bit of a jam so I quickly told the guard that it was locked and the other guy had the keys. Then I pointed in Bill's direction explaining we would have to wait until he came back. So, I stood there next to the guard, trying to look casual pressing that Bible tightly against my leg, holding it by my fingertips. Standing next to a Czech Border Guard with his AK...*oh what fun that was*! Bill showed up a few minutes later, thankfully. I told him the door was locked and we needed the car keys to unlock and open the door. He flashed a quick look in my direction which was a combination of quizzical and annoyance, implying, "Why didn't you use the extra set of keys, and open it yourself?" Thankfully, he didn't say anything. I asked him again, trying to communicate with my tone of voice and inflections that there was a special need for him to do it. Thankfully, he didn't ask what I did with the other set of keys and played along. Whew! He unlocked the door; the guard stepped up into the van and began his search. We stood there watching; and unknown to Bill, I was standing there pressing that little New Testament hard against my thigh. The guard completed his search without finding anything which alerted him or caused suspicion. He got out and motioned that we could shut the door. After checking papers one last time, he gave the papers back to us and go -ahead for the other guards to let us move forward through the barrier gates, to let us leave. Whew! I walked back to the van passenger side, continuing to press that little Bible hard against my leg and got into the van breathing a deep sigh of relief. Bill sat down behind the steering wheel. I whispered to him as he settled in, "I'll tell you later about the keys." The senior guard motioned for the guards manning the barrier gate to let us pass. We drove through, passed by the barrier gate and the fences of barbed wire, then through the mine field of no man's land. Soon we were out of there and back into the freedom of the West, coming to the West German Border checkpoint. Relief flooded my mind. After we had gotten safely through the West German Checkpoint into West Germany, I quietly explained to Bill what had happened with the little New Testament and the keys. I can't recollect his reply, but he seemed to be reassured.

When we got near Furth im Wald, we saw the big oak tree just east of town, which would be our rendezvous point with Vance in a couple of days. We drove on into town and found a telephone booth. Bill called in to report and explained what happened with the visa to mission leaders back at the Base. He had to tell them we would be arriving back at the Base two days late. I stood by him near the phone booth as he placed the call. I felt for him, yet simultaneously I was glad it wasn't me making that call. He had to explain to them what had happened causing our delayed ETA back to The Farm.

After his call we found a nice little café in the village and ate dinner. We enjoyed that meal but remained concerned for Vance. Then we went back to that big oak for the wait. We ended up camping there for two days waiting. We played a lot of cards and read a lot. In the afternoon of day two, a little European compact car pulled up at our camp site and Vance got out. He had obtained his visa, then hitchhiked out of the country, only needing to catch one ride. Were we really glad to see him! He was in good spirits too! You would have thought that he had just returned from a good camping trip in the Rockies or won a Silver buckle at a rodeo competition. All three of us were literally "happy campers" at that reunion. We mixed up some chow for Vance, ate dinner, then headed west to base camp. It was good to arrive back at The Farm a couple of days later, where a warm welcome awaited us, with a lot of hugs and smiling happy faces. The next few days were full of trip reports and van clean up. We had debriefings and reports to complete; we also had to explain in debriefing and written reports the circumstances surrounding our delayed return.

Down on the Farm

After the return from Czechoslovakia, the remaining part of the summer I worked with Cees and John helping to get other teams out. Additionally, Cees had me working on special projects, including printing study guides, in-house communications, training books and Bible studies. Additionally, I duplicated cassettes for the Timothy Project parcels.

What was known as the "Timothy Project" was a leadership development training package consisting of Bible study materials, training books, and cassette tapes for ministers and church leaders. It was a non-denominationally oriented Bible-centered leadership training package.

My role in that project was the printing of study guides, duplication of tapes, and packaging the items together for transportation by our teams to church leaders in the East Block.

I also worked on other special projects. One of them was printing, collation and packaging of the first Literature Information Service (LIS) catalog for distribution to other organizations. The project consisted of information sharing with other likeminded allied organizations. The catalog contained organization names, types of literature being smuggled in with titles and regions of distribution throughout all of Eastern Europe and the Soviet Union. There was a risk-trust factor for some organizations who chose to participate. But many groups saw the value and did submit their information.

Getting the over four dozen Non-Government Organizations, each operating with their own security concerns about sharing information with other groups was an accomplishment for Hank. It required some negotiation, bridge-building and cooperative efforts with the many other groups who met in Switzerland and on telephone conferences. Protocols where put in place for the loosely allied sister agencies to share information as to the countries where they operated and the types and titles of books they provided to Eastern European Believers. The information was then compiled at our base. I printed it, sorted, and coded the information into the book of Cees' and Hank's design. Then a copy of the catalog was redistributed among the various participating organizations.

That effort helped each group reduce the overlap and redundancy of work conducted by others. Thus, every organization had the opportunity to become more efficient. This increased overall effectiveness of total efforts into Eastern Europe and the USSR.

In addition to the LIS program, the mission was also involved with other allied mission organizations in a program called the Sensitive Information Service (SIS) program. This program was designed for mission agencies to share information and learn from one another when one of their teams was detained and/or arrested. Information was gathered about each search event, including interrogation information, questions asked, items confiscated, and measures taken by the communist guards. Did the guards look for specific things, did they appear to be tipped off by going directly to the area where books were hidden, was the vehicle torn apart prior to discovery of the books, or did guards seem to stumble onto the books, etc.? The SIS program contained elements which could be considered to be an intelligence -gathering type of activity. Mike, the former Marine, was very involved with this program. Even within our small organization there were "need-to-know" levels. So Mike and I did not discuss his activities, but it was an important function within the mission. The LIS and SIS programs combined helped participating missions with stewardship of resources and mission planning, likewise enhancing safety issues for teams and the Christians in the East as well. Some groups had not taken as many security precautions as others. This of course could have some detrimental effects for those poorly prepared.

When the LIS catalog project was complete and catalogs mailed to participating organizations, Cees at the request of Tim Post, tasked me for work on The Christmas Card Project. Tim, one of our Dutch leaders in the Stichting Antwoordt (The Answer Foundation) section of the mission, spearheaded that project. The Project consisted of mailing pre-typed letters and Christmas card packages to Dutch Christians, who then mailed the cards to Russian Christian prisoners. The enclosed letters with Christmas cards printed in Dutch and Russian were mailed from Dutch people all over the Netherlands to Christian prisoners inside the Soviet Union and Eastern Europe. This resulted not only in encouraging the Christian prisoners but also let the communists know that people in the West knew about the prisoner. One prisoner receiving hundreds of cards usually had the fallout effect of better treatment for the prisoners.

When not traveling, after daily work routines team members might hang out together by breaking up into a couple of volley ball teams and play a few good games. Other times we would up break up into various smaller groups and go on bicycle rides, or play board or card games. Sometimes two or three of us would have excellent discussions on theology and various Biblical topics. More often than not, as the days grew longer during spring and summer many of us would ride bicycles to a Dutch village several miles away for ice cream or a bag of French fries, "mit mayonoaas."

Sometimes two or three of us would gather around to listen to my shortwave radio in the evenings. Most of our major news was obtained by listening to the BBC, Voice of America, Armed Forces Radio out of Germany and Radio Free Europe. Sometimes for entertainment we listened to English language versions of Radio Moscow propaganda broadcasts, which provided a combination of laughs and at times disgust.

Listening to Radio Moscow reminded me at times of the stories I had read about Tokyo Rose, the Japanese propagandist in World War II, and heard about Hanoi Hannah from Vietnam vets. We would listen to the English version of the communist propaganda regarding the Soviet war in Afghanistan at the time. The radio programs would boast of victories over the resistance or capture of CIA operators. Radio Moscow also had cultural awareness broadcasts about the greatness of the communist state, where life under the equal conditions of socialism was superior to life in the West. We knew better. We could only listen to it for a short time before laughing or getting irritated; then we would change frequencies back to the BBC, VOA or Armed Forces Radio.

I enjoyed listening to the Armed Forces Radio, old *Fiber Magee and Molly* radio reruns from the 1940s. They were a kick. The World Service News from the BBC had good stuff too. Sometimes I was able to tune in information about the situation in Poland and events about the Solidarity Movement and the imposition of Martial Law in Poland. The communist leadership of Poland under pressure from the Russians had declared prohibitions on travel and communications due to strikes and work shut downs by Solidarity. In December of 1981 the Polish government declared a State of Martial Law.

On January 31st I picked up a program on the *Voice of America* shortwave broadcast called *Let Poland be Poland*. President Reagan and several US celebrities spoke about the need of the Polish government to allow greater freedom for the Polish people. The program reinforced my view about the worth of the projects we were involved in for the betterment of the people living in Eastern Europe. The LIS Project, the Christmas Card Project and the Timothy Parcels (cassette and syllabus leadership training packages) I had been involved with for the past few months were definitely worth the efforts.

In late May, I found out that I would be traveling on a three-man team traveling with literature into Czechoslovakia. We would be traveling with Ed from California and Bruce, a Canadian guy.

The Typewriter

In the first part of June our three-man team headed for Czechoslovakia. Team members consisted of Ed, our team leader who was well experienced in the east, Bruce the Canadian, who would be making his first trip, and me with two missions under my belt plus some knowledge of circumstances beyond the wall. We had done all of our pre-trip training, planning, and preparation and responsibilities had been assigned. Contact addresses, personal information, routes to contacts were memorized, and certain routes were preplanned. We were good to go on June 12th and left The Farm early in the morning.

We left the base and drove several miles heading south toward the Belgian border, pulled over into a deserted parking lot in the wee hours, and switched our car plates, near the mission safe house apartment. We dropped off the other license plates for the Lada at the apartment as per instructions from trip planners. After switching and dropping off the plates, we traveled on into Belgium toward Antwerp, then swung east toward Germany. We spent most of the day on German autobahns, which was an interesting experience in its own right. I would have liked to be driving a hot car like a Porsche, a Camaro with a 396 under the hood, or a Vette myself! We were passed by many Porsches, BMW "Beamers" and Mercedes, who were doing 90 MPH or more in sections of the Autobahn. But we were in our Lada (Russian Fiat) moving along at about 50 to 55 MPH towing a specially prepared camping trailer. We had to treat those babies kindly, as the trailer was running heavy with the hundreds of Bibles, books, and typing equipment we were hauling. That night after dark we found a camp at a place called Hirscham in Germany and set up our rig.

Next morning, we broke camp had a short time of prayer, scripture reading, and a team meeting. As team leader, Ed lead planning sessions. After the team meeting we headed southeast for Cheb, Czechoslovakia. Once again, ten kilometers prior to reaching the border we stopped for another time of prayer, final vehicle check, and also checked our religious type of conversations at the door—no more discussions about theology, God, the Bible etc. It was time to change our conversation habits and talk about nothing but sports, fishing, camping, famous cities, interesting places, cars, girls, etc., for the time being. Nothing about anything religious would be part of a conversation for a couple of hours.

The crossing though the West German check point out of the country was smooth with no special occurrences. Once again, we left the freedom of the west, drove through no man's land to shortly be in a communist controlled regime. As we headed into no man's land, we started seeing the barbed wire, tank traps, obstacles, and guard towers looming in the distance. The guard towers, manned by armed guards with search lights, machine guns and listening devices for monitoring conversations grew larger as we drew near. Near the Czech barrier gate, the road curved as we drove between tank traps; we had to wait in line behind several vehicles. It was finally our turn, and the gate bar lifted for us. We weaved our way through a couple of barriers, then pulled up to a building where the road widened and opened up into multiple split lanes. We were ordered forward; a guard with an AK47 asked for our papers. We handed over our passports and visas. Other guards ordered us forward for a vehicle search. After stopping, they began searching our car. They wanted to see inside the trailer too. We had to set it up for them. I was at peace about it all, thinking it was going to be interesting to see what would happen and how it would work out that time. I was not feeling cocky or arrogant about it, just calmly confident that our welfare was in the hands of the Lord. It was nice to just sit down on the curb, eat a Snickers bar which I had in my jacket pocket, and watch the guards search our ride. I knew God was in control. The guards didn't use mirrors that time to look under the camping rig like they did on occasion with other vehicles. They were satisfied after their search. The Bibles and books made it through, and the guards hadn't dismembered any portion of the car as we had seen happen to a few other vehicles. They did not drill holes in the sides of the trailer either. Once again, the Bibles and books we were transporting made it through the search and check point OK... thank the Lord!

We left Checkpoint Pomezi after about forty-five minutes from our arrival. It had been a quick and smooth crossing overall. The Lord had answered our prayers. I did notice there were a lot more soldiers with AKs than I'd seen at previous border crossings. Guard dogs were being utilized as well. But we crossed on through unhindered. The Lord was covering us! Then we headed toward Cheb, and after driving past the 10 kilometer point in country, we stopped our rig, got out, and checked the vehicle and trailer for tracking devices, ever aware of the potential for being tracked or followed. It was a normal protocol for us. While in Czechoslovakia, our conversations would need to be guarded. We needed to be watchful about what we said when in public environs, even when just traveling through cities. It was an interesting challenge for us who naturally talked about God or theological topics as a matter of course, especially since those were common denominators among us. When we spoke of the mission itself, we referred to it as "The Company" or "The Farm." When talking about God or mission leadership in public, we referred to them as "The Boss," not being sacrilegious because we knew full well whom we served and answered to. These were certainly interesting changes. We were not being disrespectful, but just needed to make sure we were taking precautions and not putting the people we were coming to help at risk.

There was a fork in the road at Cheb which we took and headed to Karlovy Vary; then we headed onto Reonico, then Slany, and east to Melnic. We by passed Prague, and at Mlana Boleslav we headed northeast, toward Turnov. Outside of Turnov we started looking for a place to set up camp and register with the authorities. It was getting later in the day. We wanted to meet with our first Czech contact that night. We found a campground at a place called Zdar outside of Turnov. We set up camp, dropped the trailer, then continued north in the Lada on to Jablonec, close to the Polish border. During the entire drive, we were mindful that Poland not far north of us was in a state of Martial Law. The Warsaw Pact Nations under the direction and led from the Soviet Union were threatening an invasion of Poland. Our team leader and Bruce made contact with Brother Georg that evening. They had a time of fellowship with him and set up a drop time and location for the following night. Next morning, we played tourists in Turnov. In the afternoon, we returned to camp Zadar. We opened the system and removed Bibles and the Czech literature while in camp. We had some trouble with the system. The system jammed due to malfunctioning doors and lift system, making access a challenge; but eventually we got it fixed. Ed and Bruce took off to Jablonec to hook up with Bro. Georg. My job for that night was to hold down the camp, stick with the trailer, stay behind, and pray for the other guys. I read some in the little New Testament with Psalms, and said prayers for team safety. I waited and prayed, waited and prayed, prayed and waited some more. It was a long wait.

They finally got back late that night, around midnight, from a successful drop; but the round trip distance was further than they had expected. I was beginning to get concerned. They almost ran out of gas, and stations were closed; but they prayed that the Lord would stretch their fuel as it was running low. (The only gas stations, by the way, were all State-run.) They couldn't find a place to fill up with Benzine (gasoline). The vehicle guage had read empty for a long time, yet they were able to drive on several miles making it back to camp. They came in on fumes. The Lord certainly seemed to help out in that pinch. They firmly believed He stretched the mileage of the vehicle.

The next day, the first goal was to get gas. We had a small gas can with fuel at the trailer so we added it to the tank. Fortunately, we found a Benzine station not far away. We headed out to Jicin, then onto Hradec Karalove, Svitny, Olomuc, Hranice, Novy Jicin, and Pribor. We were headed for a place called Frydek-Mistik about fifteen kilometers southeast of the city of Ostrava. It was near here that we located a campground and set up camp. Ed and I had a contact in a rural area several kilometers northeast near the Polish border in a rural area. The Solidarity movement was going strong just north of us in Poland; and Poland was still under Martial Law, previously having restricted foreign travelers from entering the country. Travel restrictions were in place throughout the country at that time. The Soviets were pressuring the Poles with threatened invasion, including the use of not only Soviet troops and tanks but troops from East Germany and Czechoslovakia as well. The international situation was tense. The Czechs were massed on the Czech, Polish border. There were a lot of troop movements operating in the area where we were, and we had seen a lot of them. We dropped the trailer; Ed and I left Bruce in camp and headed out and told the gate attendant, "Weir gahen zum die stat fur essen und trinken." (We are going to the city for eating and drinking.) That city would have been Ostrava. Instead, we headed north for a remote area eighty degrees away from that city into the countryside east of a little place called Cesky Tesin up on the Polish border. We were to set up arrangements for a typewriter and printing supplies to be delivered near the Polish border. We would not have been surprised to learn that it was going to be used to make bulletins and posters inside Poland for use in the hands of Solidarity people.

The good thing about traveling with the Lada was that the vehicle did not stand out. It's a Soviet Russian made car. We could drive around in the Czech countryside and blend in a lot better than the vans I had traveled in on previous trips. Ed could pass for a Russian. He was a bear of a man, barreled-chested, with a rounded red-faced complexion and a full beard. I could have passed for a Czech or East German. So we fit in far better than Bill and I had in Romania with the dark-haired, dark-eyed Romanians.

We were several kilometers from at camp. The countryside terrain was rolling hills, high grass, and mixed types of trees. We made it into a remote area northeast of Cesky Tesin. Ed had me drive up a narrow deserted looking, single lane, worn old oil sand road full of pot holes. There were pine trees on each side of the road. It seemed like we were within a few hundred yards of the Polish border. We drove up a bit of a grade; then the road curved close to ninety degrees to the left, turning west. He had me stop and drop him off at the curve, and he took off on foot through a pasture headed north. Our prearranged rendezvous point for us was to be back down the road behind us a few hundred yards, in just over one and a half to two hours. I drove on up the road a short way continuing northwest after I had dropped him off; then I flipped a U-turn and drove back down the road to our rendezvous point. I parked off the side of the road next to a tree line of conifers, slid low in the seat, adjusted the rear view mirrors so I could watch what came up behind me, including Ed, and waited. It was getting past dark. I waited, and waited, and waited some more. After well over two hours, I was getting concerned; but I had no option at that time except to continue to wait. After two and a half hours, I was still waiting, starting to worry. Only one vehicle drove up the road toward me during that time. Thankfully, it was not a military patrol or the VB; I was relieved about that. Finally, just after dark I saw Ed coming down the road in the rearview mirror. He was in a quick step especially for a man his size. He was close to breaking into a run. He came up to the driver side door breathing heavy and with urgency in his voice said, "Move over, let me drive, we've gotta get out of here! I'm being followed!" I quickly slid right lifting myself over the gear shift into the passenger's seat. He slid in and started the engine, popped the clutch, took off with a lurch, and we were out of there like a bat out of a cave. He explained hurriedly as he was driving that as he was hiking in country not far from the contact's rural home, he saw a man with a gun several dozen yards from where he was on the trail. He recognized it was not our contact, as he had met him before. Ed had to leave the trail and go overland, carrying a suitcase, then circle back to the vehicle using another route taking evasive action. He told me the guy with the gun followed him, so he took evasive maneuvers to come back to the car. I asked him if it looked like the guy was military. He said that he couldn't tell. I asked him if the guy was carrying an AK or if he could tell what type of gun the guy had. He said that he couldn't tell for sure, but didn't think it was an AK; it was too dark. He thought it was a shotgun or a long gun. That puzzled me. It was not easy to see because it was near dark when he first spotted and the guy. Ed could not tell if the guy was military or just a hunter out late. According to Ed, he didn't have on a helmet.

Questions filled my mind:

> *Only one guy, was he part of a patrol? He had a long gun, was it a rifle or shotgun? Not an AK, did he have a radio? Hmm, maybe just a hunter, but were guns in common use among civilians there? Why was he out so late and following Ed? Hunters don't usually hang out much after dark, and follow people. Maybe a sniper scout or a point man from a patrol? Maybe he was a lone hunter, or maybe part of a two-man military team and Ed may not have seen the other trooper who was maintaining an interval?*

Since we were so close to the Polish border with so many Czechoslovakian troops massed in the area poised for invasion of Poland, he could have been military. I hoped that he was not part of a team with a radio. I thought he was most likely someone connected with the military or border security. But I had more questions than answers.

It was a puzzle that we didn't stick around to get answers. Ed couldn't tell what type of long gun it was, but he said the guy was definitely following him, which drew me to the conclusion that he was mostly not just a hunter out too late. Ed was worried and in a big hurry to clear the area, as we were close to within a kilometer from the border. He was driving fast and we were moving! We made it back to the main smooth asphalt road, but it was still curvy and winding. We took some sharp curves going pretty fast, the car slid and the wheels screamed out as we slid around the sharp bends in the road. On one particular curve we fishtailed. I was worried that the speed we were driving would get us spotted and pulled over by the VB. I asked Ed to slow down a little. Speeding down the road would definitely draw attention and make us a target. We had made it out of the immediate area. There was minimal traffic and our headlights in the night made us stick out all the more. It was nearing 11 p.m.; the risk was high either way. We made it back to our camping spot sometime around midnight with no one following us or getting pulled over. Bruce had been worried and was relieved to see us when we rolled into camp. The hookup with the contact was not successful. We would need to use the alternate contact and Plan B the following night to deliver the typewriter.

The next day we traveled to Ostrava. We played tourists during the morning. Then that afternoon, we went back into Cesky Tesin. Ed and I met with an alternate contact at the edge of town not far from the river on the north side of town, in a little place up near the Polish border. It was a heavily patrolled area with a lot of military activity. Czech troops in transport trucks were all over the place. Our drop was just two or three blocks from where troops were staged near the border. We were just across the river from Poland. That night we met at the contact's apartment, passed on some Bibles, the typewriter, and supplies. Remember, possession of a typewriter without a government permit was illegal. We had smuggled it in with the books; it was supposed to be for the contact the night before, but it ended up with the alternate contact. That typewriter was contraband, not any different than an illegal gun. That is a hard concept for we Americans to wrap our minds around, yet that was the reality for the Czech people during the Communist Era. Freedom of expression was monitored. We needed to use caution even when delivering something as simple as a typewriter. I carried it to the contact's home in a suitcase. The Poles in the Solidarity movement just to the north were in need of typewriters, too. They were being used not only by the Underground Church but by the Solidarity movement as well. Typewriters were used to make Solidarity leaflets for distribution to the Polish populace, among other things. Once again, I was reminded about the facade of freedom in the East Block as even typewriters were considered taboo. Again, I was reminded that a permit was needed from the government to possess one. I wondered where it would end up. Would that typewriter make it into the hands of some Polish folks involved with Solidarity?

The Solidarity movement going on across the river was an area of high tension and conflict. The city of Katowice, just a few kilometers north of where we were, had seen demonstrations and clashes with Polish ZOMO shock troops. The ZOMOs were oftentimes hardened criminals given early release from prison to serve in paramilitary units against the citizens. The previous December, six months earlier, ZOMO troops had killed nine Polish miners in Katowice during demonstrations against the communist government. It was the closest large city north of our location, from where we had contacts in Czechoslovakia. That Polish city was roughly about thirty-five miles north of us, "as the crow flies," so to speak.

On June 17th, we left the Frydek-Mistek area and headed back toward the west, with two contacts yet remaining prior to returning to West Germany. We traveled to Olomouc, then through Svitavy; we continued northwest toward Hradec-Kralovethen and cut off to Paradubice, and from there down to Podebrady. So far, things were good—no vehicle difficulties, no problems from authorities, made it out of the militarized zones close to the Polish border, and the three of us were still in a state of good health. We had been careful not to drink the local water sources, unless boiled first, and had a few gallons of water from Holland. We utilized our own food, which we cooked in camp, and didn't eat out. Team unity was still intact, although slightly strained at times, we played mental trivia games and quizzed one another on Bible knowledge, as well as small talk and sharing stories as we drove. Ed had come out of a tougher home life with some challenges; Bruce was a mellow guy who grew up in a stable home environment. We had theological discussions about scriptural topics while on the road, and enjoyed the journey, too.

Team spirit and morale was helped by relaxing and playing card games in the evenings or reading books we had brought along. Another thing which helped keep up our morale was the morning team devotions and prayer time. We prayed for our contacts, for their safety, and for the other teams which were traveling, operating in Romania and East Germany. I really appreciated having the little pocket New Testament along, too. I especially liked reading the Psalms.

Up to this point our trip had been successful, contacts made, literature left with network contacts and we had no major problems. As we drove along, Bruce read aloud from some of the travel guides we had on the history and information about cities we passed through. We took photos of the countryside and sights as we traveled. We drove on toward Melnik, and had to cover a lot of miles because our next contact was in Prague. We made it to a place not far from Prague called Veltrusy that evening.

We found camping sites there, setup camp, made some dinner. Then after chow Ed and Bruce headed for town. I stayed behind again with the camp trailer. I read, waited, watched and prayed. I was drawn to reading the Psalms, in the little New Testament left with me. I read chapters 27 and 31. Psalms 31:19-21 states:

> "How great is Thy goodness which thou hast stored up for those who fear Thee. Which Thou hast wrought for those who take refuge in Thee. Before the sons of men! Thou dost hide them in the secret place of Thy presence from the conspiracies of man. Thou dost keep them secretly in a shelter from the strife of tongues. Blessed be the Lord for He has made marvelous His loving kindness to me in a besieged city."

That scripture had special meaning for me that night. Another verse which spoke to my soul during that time was Psalms 27:5-6a:

> "For in the day of trouble He will conceal me in His tabernacle; in the secret place of His tent He will hide me; He will lift me up on a rock. And now my head will be lifted up above my enemies around me."

I prayed that those scriptures would be true for our team. Up to that point God had certainly been doing that. He had been providing concealment throughout our trip. It was good to know He was with us as we had felt His peace on more than one occasion.

Ed and Bruce returned later that night. They were successful and had been able to make contact with "Stephen." They arranged for a literature drop the next night. So, we were a go with contact number three. Would not need to use the alternate. We racked out. Next day we were up, did devotions, prayed for the literature drop, ate, etc. Bruce our Canadian teammate and I got into the system, with Ed acting as the lookout outside. We had to beware of making too much noise and not alerting neighboring campers, who might be walking by too close when we had the system open. Ed signaled Bruce and me with warning taps on the trailer to stop a couple of times. We heard voices as people walked near the trailer; we froze. After they passed by, we resumed placing the Bibles, Czech New Testaments, Children's Bibles with picture, and other books into bags. Then we put the bags of Bibles in the suitcases from which we had removed our clothes. We covered the suitcases in the trunk of the Lada with jackets; then as an entire team we headed for Prague in the Lada. A successful drop was made with the contact at the rendezvous point that Eric and Bruce had set up. No problems…all went as planned for them. Literature drop three was a success—so far, so good. One more contact to go, but we were not back in West Germany yet. Next, we headed into old downtown Prague and played tourist. Although it was not the first visit for me and Ed had been there multiple times, it was a new experience for Bruce. The team headed toward the Saint Charles Bridge, the Prague Astronomical Clock, Old Town Square, and Wenceslas Square to play tourist.

The Charles Bridge which crosses the Vitava River is over five hundred yards long and ten yards wide. It was under construction from 1357 until 1402 and has three towers, including thirty gothic era type statues along its length, fifteen on each side. The statues are statues of the twelve Apostles and some of the Saints of Moravian historical culture. It has been the site of several historical events. It was just a short walk from the bridge to the Prague Astronomical Clock and the Old Town Square. The clock was built in the 15th century and still works. It was damaged significantly in 1945 by German Artillery toward the end of World War II, but it had been repaired and restored.

The Prague Astronomical Clock is one of the three oldest in the world, and it is the only one which still functions. It is an amazing work in itself. There are small statues of four figures on the sides of the clock, which represent Vanity, Usury, Death, and the Old Turk. There are twelve moving figurines representing the Apostles which appear every hour. It is located on the south facing wall of the Old Town City Hall, just west of the Prague Old Town Square.

After hanging out in old town Prague for a while, we drove over to Wenceslas Square and checked out a couple of shops along the street. I bought some pictorial books about Czechoslovakia from a couple of the shops. It was interesting that the city's history, in the form of its architecture, testified to the Christian heritage of the region; yet it was ruled by atheistic communists. We headed back to our camp in the afternoon after a few hours of checking out the sites. It was a few hours of a somewhat relaxing time, although we still had to be on our guard and maintain situational awareness. Soon it was back to the reason we were there and the business at hand.

On June 19th we departed from Veltrusy camp after breakfast. Bruce and Ed were good cooks; I could get by. Our meals were typically Dutch fare but prepared by some North Americans who liked to add our own seasonings. We didn't hurt on the nutritional end, and the food supply was good. We still had food. We headed northwest to Chomutov and a drop for our fourth and last contact, a local pastor in that town. It was only ninety-five to one hundred kilometers away so it was not a long drive .It was just over an hour away, God willing, depending on road and traffic conditions.

We arrived at Chomutov midday. We found a camping ground and set up camp. Ed and I again left Bruce in camp while we left to link up with Alexis, our contact. He was at home. We visited with him and his daughter. We gathered information about their circumstances and needs for the next team. We had left the trailer in camp, where we had obtained the last of the books and Bibles to be distributed in the Chomutov network. We delivered the rest of the Bibles and Christian books to Bro Alexis. While visiting with his daughter, my heart was touched as I listened to her story. She told us about pressure from the police and being under surveillance. She shared that their movements and activities were being monitored routinely by police. She became emotional and her eyes filled with tears as she told me about a couple of searches conducted by the police in their home as they looked for Bibles and religious literature. She told us of being taken to the local police headquarters for interrogation about her religious activity of going to church. She was open about her fears and concerns; it was clear she was holding back her emotions too. She seemed to be on the verge of breaking down, as she shared with us of the pressures put on them by the authorities because of being a Believer and follower of Christ. As she regained her composure, she became resolute in her determination to continue following Jesus. She commented about how grateful they were for the support from western Christians. As I listened to her share their stories, it was easy to discern the longing she had to be free from police pressures. But when she spoke about her appreciation of receiving help from Christians in the U.S., it was another reinforcement in my mind the need to continue doing what we were doing, and to share about what Eastern European Christians had to deal with. She asked us to continue, but to use caution. I determined in my heart not to let down in my own vigilance of support for Eastern Europeans. Ed and I would share their story when we returned to the West. When we left those Believers' home, we were alert for anyone whom we perceived could be watching or following us. We tried to be vigilant about our own situational awareness to detect any abnormal human behavior which would reveal a secret police agent as we headed back to our vehicle. We checked for tails as we headed back to the camp.

The next day we broke camp at Chomotov. After our usual breakfast, prayer and team meeting routine we headed toward Karlovy Vary, then onto Cheb. Then we headed to the border crossing for our exit at Checkpoint Pomezi. Once again, we guarded our speech and did not talk about God or things of a religious nature within several Kilometers of the border. We got to the border crossing and saw the guard towers and guards with AK 47s which was always a sober time, not a time for cavalier behavior. But I could feel the hope swelling up inside me as we were getting closer to the West German border. We made it to the checkpoint and saw the guards, guns and security patrols. Having just been in a part of the world where drab, grey and red were the primary colors, I was definitely looking forward to Germany and Holland. The border crossing went fairly quick, only about 45 to 50 minutes. They wanted to see our papers, wanted to know where we traveled while in the country, and checked our visas for the registration stamps from our camp grounds. They checked our passports and visa travel papers, which indicated where we had stayed and camped every night while in the country. After a search of the Lada and trailer which we had set up again, the border guards found nothing out of the ordinary. So, once again, we were allowed to leave and pass back to the West through no man's land. We were glad to be leaving, looking at the guards armed with AKs who allowed us to pass, then drive through the mine fields on either side of the road and look at the barbed wire fencing presented its own intimidating experience.

We held back our excitement for a few kilometers after entering West Germany, again because we did not want our vehicle to become marked for future teams. But after driving ten kilometers two Americans and a Canadian broke out into a spontaneous chorus of "God Bless America! Land that I love, stand beside her and guide her through the night with the Light from Above." We sang the song several times. I was thankful to be back in the West! We sang choruses and patriotic songs for miles. Then we offered up prayers of thanksgiving and for the well-being of those we had left behind. I thanked God for what we had seen and heard and for His provision and protection while we traveled in the Czechoslovak Police State. A place where people were oppressed by a repressive communist political machine. I believed that I would forever remember those we left who had to live behind The Wall. I hoped to return to them again.

We had covered over one thousand five hundred kilometers while on that mission, made four successful contacts, delivered close to a thousand Bibles and Christian books for the Czechs and Slovaks, as well as a typewriter and supplies for Slovaks or Solidarity. The Bibles we delivered were to people who had no Christian bookstores and could not purchase study aids or Christian books like we could in Canada, the U.S. and Western Europe.

The Christians who practiced their faith behind The Wall were harassed and sometimes arrested or thrown in prison for Christian activities. The political situation in Poland was continuing to grow tense, which affected Czechoslovakia too. But, the Underground Church in the East was doing well, in spite of political pressures.

We drove northwest to Koblenz, West Germany, before we stopped at a campground for the night. We made it to a good place along the Rhine River. It was a good way to finish up the day, camping along the Rhine in West Germany.

June 21st was spent driving to and hanging out in Bad Honningen, Bad Honneff, and Koningswinter. We drove by the remaining Bridge Towers which were all that was left of the Remagan Bridge where U.S.

army forces had crossed the Rhine into the heart of Germany in 1945. We picked up a couple of souvenirs as we made our way along the road toward home. We hit the autobahn, put the pedal to the medal, as much as you safely and legally could drive a Lada pulling a trailer.

We made it back to The Company Farm at about 5:20 p.m. Praise the Lord! It was good to be home! Staff at the Farm warmly greeted us again with joyful hugs and smiles; it was great to see familiar faces of friends who were like family. We had made it home, back to our refuge. God had been faithful! He continued to pour out His love and mercy. I was reminded of the scripture, "Be strong, and let your heart take courage, all you who hope in the Lord" (Psalms 31:24), which I had read while in Eastern Europe. The Word of God does sustain us, as it brought encouragement to me.

Next day was spent cleaning the Lada and trailer, then having team oral debriefings to trip planners; next, we started written reports which we wouldn't complete for another day or two.

During July, I led several early morning team devotions. So I oversaw meal preparation for courier teams and base staff, greeted new folks, and helped with orientation and housing placement of newer couriers. I helped Cees and John prepare vehicles for teams headed out and worked on Timothy Project cassette duplication. Additionally, I had some special printing projects, including development of a filing system for storage and cataloging those projects.

Additional positive news which encouraged our spirits at the base came as we learned about the recent success of the Open Doors, "Project Pearl" mission which included the beachhead landing of a million Chinese Bibles to the Christian people of China. That project resulted in the delivery of over seven hundred fifty thousand Bibles into the hands of tens of thousands of Chinese Christians. (The 2008 book, *The Night of a Million Miracles* by Paul Estabrooks, details the account of that event.)*

While Ed, Bruce and I had been delivering nearly a thousand Bibles and Christian books into Czechoslovakia, an Open Doors team from the U.S. and Australia landed a million Bibles onto a secluded beach in China. seven hundred fifty thousand Bibles made it inland transported by a network of Chinese Believers, before the beachhead landing was raided by a Chinese Army patrol. The remaining two hundred fifty thousand Bibles were confiscated. The Chinese Army tried to burn them. But they couldn't get them to burn well so the soldiers threw them into the ocean. There they surfaced and floated. The day after the Chinese military had left, many villagers in the area harvested the soaked Bibles from the ocean and dried them on their roofs. In addition to the three quarters of a million Bibles transported inland, most of the Bibles thrown into the sea made it into Chinese people's hands as well. So most of the million Bibles made it to the Chinese people.

A few of the Chinese Christians involved with the landing onshore failed to escape the Army raid. Some were put in prison. They had counted the cost, wanted to serve, and suffered. Out of their sacrifice along with many others' sacrifices, great things were to come for China from the endeavor. A revival began to ensue throughout regions of China. Some attribute the revival that began in China during the mid-80s that continued on into the 90s as having sprung from that event. Hearing the news of the success of the Open Doors "Project Pearl" team at our Dutch base in Holland was a huge spark of encouragement for all of us as well. What a daring mission that was! God would accomplish His purposes on the earth with a few willing souls.

*(Information about the book, *The Night of a Million Miracles* by Paul Estabrooks may be obtained from Open Doors. Contact information is listed in Appendix I.)

Sometime in the later half of the month Hank asked me to consider being a team leader for an upcoming trip into Czechoslovakia and Poland. I didn't have to think long about the decision. I would be returning to Czechoslovakia. We would be taking Bibles and books including some Timothy leadership training parcels for Czech Christian leaders. The trip would also include an excursion into Poland as soon as Martial law restrictions were lifted for foreign travelers. We would be providing books and supplies for a youth camp in the mountains of south central Poland.

Poland had been in a state of Martial Law since December of '81 and tensions were high in the country. Anti-government protests and riots put down by ZOMO troops had occurred in several cities. As a result, Russia was threatening invasion with armored divisions which would also include troops from the East German and Czechoslovak armies.

VBs, the STB and ZOMOs

The first part of August found our new team preparing for the mission into Czechoslovakia and Poland. The excursion into Poland would prove interesting. The situation there was politically unstable as the country remained under a general order of Martial Law. But travel restrictions were lifted somewhat as foreign tourists were once again allowed to travel into the country. Curfews in certain areas and travel restrictions remained in place for nationals. Emotions of the people were raw and on edge. Our team would be taking in supplies for the Underground Church in Czechoslovakia and a student youth camp meeting in Poland. The youth camp was to be held in the mountains of south central Poland. Part of the mission would include a rendezvous with one of our mission team members traveling in by train through East Germany, who would come in from the west. We would be linking up with Roda at a Polish contact's home after coming up from the south out of Czechoslovakia. She was to be a music leader at the mountain retreat. We were there as part of her support team. We would meet with her at a prearranged location in a smaller town not far from Krakow, in the southern part of Poland. Then we would transport her and materials that we would bring in through Czechoslovakia part way across Poland, to a hidden mountain location. Roda was a talented Texas girl with a master's degree in music from Texas Christian University. She played several instruments and had a beautiful voice. Her presence at the youth camp would be an effort to boost morale of a few Polish people by bringing hope and encouragement to a group of Polish students.

Our team would be providing some assistance to the Polish Christians with logistical support in this effort. We would be helping them transport supplies, including Bibles, books, music equipment, and food. We would be traveling in a van which had recently been prepared by Cees and John for these kinds of trips. Cees and John had put in a lot of man hours installing specialized compartments for book smuggling. On this trip, we would also be transporting several hundred Czech and Slovak Bibles and Christian books for contacts in Czechoslovakia. It would be a busy trip.

I would have staff coworker and friend, John "AJ" Murphy from Iowa, on the team. He was an honest man of integrity whom I valued as a close friend. We had spent a lot of time working together at the base on special vehicle and printing projects for Cees and just hanging out after work days in Holland. He was athletic and worked out with weights, which was helpful for carrying heavy book-laden suitcases. We had developed a good friendship over the past year, and I was glad he was part of the team. He's the kind of man in which I placed a lot of confidence and trust as a friend and teammate. I knew he would watch my back, and I'd watch his. He was dependable, not self-absorbed, but concerned about the welfare of others. He was a man of good character and a trusted friend.

The other team member, Lane, was new on board and from upstate New York. He had received a bachelor's degree from the University of New York at Syracuse, had a good sense of humor, was courageous and had some chutzpah. He liked to play soccer and was an intelligent guy who spoke a fair degree of German (better than mine) and had a good handle on the history and politics of Eastern European. The three of us would make a good team.

John had been working with Cees on the special preparation of the vehicle we were to use which had a new smuggling system that we would break in. It was its maiden trip so Cees was a little nervous about the function of the system on its first long trip out. John would be our team mechanic and vehicle specialist. Lane was our money guy and team treasurer, the go-to guy for the dinero. John and Lane would each be responsible for memorizing information on a couple of contacts as well. This time out, as team leader, I would have a couple of other items to be concerned about other than just my contact information: the welfare of the group, knowledge on the details of all contacts, work with the team to plan logistics and route, keeping with our planned itinerary, plus decision-making to keep us focused on the execution of our plan. Our maps would remain unmarked as usual. I would have the job of keeping us on our game, sticking with the mission plan. But we were a cohesive team, and I did not believe in an autocratic leadership style. We would work together and just have different jobs.

August 17th, up at 4:45 a.m.: time for us to head out. We had been preparing, doing our homework and quizzing one another about trip information, contacts etc. We had our drivers training review and brief interrogation training, plus rehearsal of our itinerary and aspects of the trip for three days. As on other trips, everything was committed to memory and no maps were marked. The day before, we had loaded up the vehicle with all the Bibles, books and supplies we would be transporting to Believers beyond the Wall. The night of the 16th the three of us got together and did a team check of each other's personal stuff, wallets, luggage, clothes, etc. That included checking clothing for any university I.D.s, Christian logos, sports shirts with identifying logos, missed papers in books, pieces of paper with notes, etc. We were leaving as little as possible to chance, no "tells" or give away of our history or purpose.

Earlier the previous day, after we had loaded up the vehicle, there was a base team meeting with all staff present. We all gathered together in a huddle. The base team placed us in the center of the huddle surrounding us. Then prayed for us and the success of the trip, team cohesion, travel mercies, safety, protection, etc. We had confidence that they would be praying for us every day, too, because we ourselves had done it for other teams.

We got the last of our personal gear loaded up and were pulling off the mission base at 5:30 in the morning. We had a full day of driving ahead of us before we would be close to Czechoslovakia. We headed south into Belgium, toward Antwerp. At Antwerp, we headed southeast toward Liege, then east in the direction of Aachen, West Germany. The Dutch-German border crossings in that area were a little more intense than the Belgian-German crossings for some reason. So we dropped south to avoid those crossings and then went up into Germany southwest of Aachen and crossed at a Belgian border. There was definitely no need to take extra risks, even in the west, as they were looking for drug smugglers. After Aachen, it was on to Koln (Cologne), then Frankfurt, down to Wurzburg, Nurnberg and Regensburg. We reached Regensberg after dark and then headed north toward a place called Cham. We found a camp ground between Cham and Furth im Wald. We were thirteen kilometers (7.8 miles) from Czechoslovakia. We had had a full good day of driving, sang some, told jokes, laughed, talked about sports, girls, politics, the Lord, and the beauty of Germany as we enjoyed its countryside while we drove along. Our team spirit was high and cohesion was good. We were not glib and unaware of the risks, but were praying and had given the outcome of our trip over to God. We had done what we needed to do to this point. We were in the process of putting feet to our prayers. At the end of the day I thanked the Lord that our first day out as a team had gone well, and team cohesion was good as we started to gel as a team.

We were up about five the next morning. But by the time we made breakfast, got our tent packed up and gear loaded, had team devotions, did a last check of papers, said some prayers, had our team planning session and rehearsed counter interrogation answers, it was getting on in the morning. We headed toward the border singing the chorus "King of Kings and Lord of Lords, Glory, Hallelujah…Jesus, Prince of Peace, Glory…Hallelujah!" The words penetrated our souls and the atmosphere as we sang. While we sang the chorus, a scene from the movie *Raid on Entebbe* flashed through my mind. It was a 1977 movie about an Israeli Army unit raid into Uganda, as a hostage rescue mission which was carried out on July 4, 1976. The mission was conducted to save dozens of Israeli citizens whose plane had been hijacked by terrorists. In the scene, Israeli army commandos while in flight toward the Entebbe Airport broke into singing "Hine Ma Tov," an Israeli national festival and Shabbat song. It was a stirring scene.

As we drove toward the border singing our own song, I was reminded of them. Thinking of that scene as we sang was encouraging, and it was good to have a little of that encouragement. We were not singing with false bravado, but with confidence that we knew whatever the outcome of this mission, the Lord would be in control. It was also an act of faith for all three of us. We had been blessed with team unity and were doing well. Our trust was in the Lord. We arrived at the West German exit check point that morning in good spirits.

Once again I was part of a team leaving West Germany headed east into an Eastern European no man's land, a strip of ground which was a few hundred yards wide with coiled barbed wire and fencing along the route and a mine field on both sides of the road. As we approached Checkpoint Flomava, the road curved then began a zigzag through barriers and vehicle obstacles which were part of the entry. A guard tower and armed guards overlooked the entry gate which had what seemed to be a ten-inch diameter black and white striped barrier pipe across the road. Vehicles were backed up behind it; a few at a time were allowed entry. We pulled forward slowly following other vehicles. As we moved closer to the guard tower we were seeing more troops on foot patrol with AK-47 assault rifles, some accompanied by leashed German Shepherd patrol dogs. We were not singing any longer, just engaging in small talk.

We were motioned forward and submitted our passports and visas when they were requested by the guard. Next some questioning began:

"How many days will you be staying in Czechoslovakia? Where will you be traveling? Why are you visiting Czechoslovakia? Do you know anyone in Czechoslovakia? Do you have anything to declare? Do you have weapons or religious literature?"

There was that question again. Then our vehicle was inspected after we answered everything to their satisfaction, completed the necessary forms, and paid the authorities the required per diem, the sum of money charged for each of us to pay for each day to be spent in the country. The vehicle search was not too extensive, and we made it through without a hitch. All things considered, the crossing was very smooth. It was one of the best I had been through yet. The Lord was with us; we felt His presence in a strong way. Thank the Lord for His mercy! Hurdle number one—we were in country!

Our first contact was to be made in the eastern sector of the country in the Slovakia northeast of Bratislava. We would be in for a lot of driving that day. We took a route driving along what would be considered secondary rural type roads in the U.S. Most all driving in that country was along rural routes. We drove through a lot of villages, some larger communities, and a few cities. Our route took us northeast up to Plzen; then at Plzen we veered right and headed east toward Brno, several hours away, considering our slower vehicle speed limit. We hit a lot of varied road conditions, everything from cobblestone to brick and concrete to asphalt. Some stretches of road had a lot of potholes which seem to be about six to eight inches deep. These seemed to crop up as cobblestone roads just on the outskirts of a village or as we entered into small towns. Occasionally we saw a farmer plowing a field with a horse and an occasional cart pulled by a cow. We saw a lot of Skoda's, the Czech national car; at least they were in several different colors. We even got to drive on a short stretch of Autobahn (freeway) between Brno and Bratislava. It was the best stretch of road that I've ever been on in Eastern Europe. John was driving. As we neared closer to Bratislav,a a Czech VB (State Police) on the side of the road with binoculars was scoping traffic a hundred or so yards before we got to him. He nailed us, pulling us over because John did not have on his shoulder harness seat belt. The VB cop waved us over, and then fined us. He charged us right there on the spot—judge, jury, and fee collector all in one. We coughed up some Ceskoslovenskych Korun which we had exchanged for Deutsch Marks when at the border, in order to pay the fine. Lane asked the guy for a receipt for our money. The VB guy seemed bothered by that request, and his continence fell. We speculated that perhaps he was going to pocket the money. After we finished up with the VB, John headed us on to Bratislava. We drove northeast from there into Slovakia.

We headed up toward Trencin, a larger city to the north of us. There we were to locate our contact in a village called Stara Tura southwest of Trencin. We hoped that our link-up with Bro Paval could be pulled off successfully that night. South of Trencin about fifteen kilometers was a place called Novy Mesto. There were camping facilities there, and Stara Tura was about fifteen Kilometers to the west from Novy Mesto, our chosen camp location. It was about dusk when we arrived at Novy Mesto. We checked in at the gate, found out the charges, and told them we would be staying the night. But we wanted to go into the city, "Fur essen und trinken" (eating and drinking). They were good with that and told us not to worry about paying yet. They told us we could pay in the morning and that we did not need to leave our visas and passports. We drove around the campground and found a camp site which we planned to use later that night. Then we headed out just as it was getting dark. We drove about six to seven kilometers down the road, John was at the wheel again. Then we spotted a VB State Police road block up in front of us. We were waved over and stopped. They lit us up with search lights from two vehicles (not good). There were two Czech VB vehicles and multiple officers. A couple stayed on the lights and two approached our vehicle. One spoke in Czech to John who was driving. We didn't understand. Lane spoke up in German and asked "Kampin, wo est eine kampin platz, bitte?" (Camping? Where is a camping place please?) I thought *good job*! But it didn't work. They were using their individual flashlights to shine down into the van; they didn't back off but kept pressing John. They were giving us a good look and visual inspection. The lead VB was not easily distracted, and he was not a friendly sort. He was a pretty stern dude. He did not respond to Lane when he spoke up but ignored him and abruptly took charge. He spoke sternly in Czech. He wanted to establish that he was in control and that he would be asking the questions. He then broke into limited German, wanting to know where we were going, "Wo gahen sie?" Ignoring Lane in the passenger seat, he addressed John behind the wheel. He wanted to see our papers; we coughed up our visas and passports which seemed to satisfy him some. I spoke up and said in a friendly tone, "Wir gahe zum die stad fur essen und trinken, den Kampin? "Wo ist eine Kamping platz, bitte?" He was lighting up our vehicle with his search light and wanted to see inside. He could easily see through the windows with his bright light. He pointed at some items. He wanted a book of matches which we had brought from Holland with Dutch logos and phrases written on them. *The guy is good*! I thought. *We could be in trouble.* Leaving those matches out in plain view may have been a mistake. We had better be sharper than that in the future. There we were sitting on top of a thousand Czech, Slovak Bibles, and some Polish Christian books, plus food supplies for the Polish. We were not in a good position. That simple slip-up could be incriminating enough to get us into some trouble. It could not only cost us, but some of the other Brothers and Sisters as well, just because of a road block in the middle of Czechoslovakia. This thing could "go south" easily and quickly. Our dependence was on the Lord for our cover, I knew. As we sat silently while the cops were checking us out, we were praying internally. We were placing our trust in the Lord. He was our strong and mighty deliverer. Just as in the Biblical stories of old.

 That Czech VB had three American males driving a French registered vehicle with food items from Holland in their possession. It was evident the cop was not stupid and would not be easily dissuaded. We were in a bit of a tenuous position. It could go sideways. But we needed to maintain our cool. After we handed over the matches, he and his partner started looking inside the van with their searchlights more intently and were shining them in our faces. The situation was not the best. Then, about that time they received incoming radio traffic. He gave us back our passports quickly, waved us forward and told us to go, as he headed back to his patrol vehicle. AJ slowly pulled out and took off down the road; all three of us let out a sigh of relief as we pulled away. "Thank you, Lord" was the prayer which quietly rolled off our lips. That incident drove home the idea that we needed to continue to be alert and as discreet as possible. The result of that stop may not have been over.

We headed on up the road. After the encounter, I was weighing whether or not to go forward that night to our contact or wait until the next day. The VB got into their cars flipped U-turns and headed out the other direction. We watched the VB patrol vehicles tail lights fade away in the mirrors. We left the site and pressed on. We found the route to Stara Tura and made it into the city well after dark; it was starting to get late. AJ dropped Lane and I at an area on the edge of town, and we walked into the part of the small town where we thought our contact's house was located. The neighborhoods and street signs were not lining up with the map and information we had memorized. It was dark and we were having problems getting oriented to the village. Lane and I walked around searching for the contact's apartment complex for quite some time. There were a lot of younger people out late on the dimly lit streets; of course they were watching us. Perhaps we were being a little paranoid, but it seemed like we were really being checked out. We needed to be discreet not speak and just keep on walking. It was not getting any earlier, and we were starting to become too noticeable. I wasn't comfortable about our circumstances…time to leave the area. We walked to the edge of town back toward the rendezvous point where we were to meet John. Finally, we saw our vehicle up ahead on a bit of a knoll, sitting in a dark shadow. We headed toward it watching for tails as we walked up the street to link up with him. It was time for us to "get out of Dodge." We were not successful in our first attempt to locate Brother Pavel's apartment. We headed out of town and somehow ended up on the long way around back to the campground and followed some road signs which pointed us to the right place. We just took the long way to get there. We ended up on a narrow winding country road in what appeared to be the middle of nowhere, with a lot of trees and heavy foliage on each side of the road which narrowed to just over one lane wide. Roads signs did not match up with the maps. We were in rolling hills and woodlands. AJ was doing a good job driving on that narrow curvy country road. We were all getting tired by that time and strongly feeling the need to be back at the camp getting some sleep. AJ kept hanging tough, doing a great job driving considering everything. It was after midnight, and it had been a long day with a lot of ground covered not to mention some stress. AJ picked up the pace in his driving. We finally came to a sign and a landmark which was on our map. We headed that way. AJ was pressing on at a good speed driving on a narrow poorly marked road and persevering well; even though he was so tired, he wouldn't cave into it. We christened him with the nick name "Mad Dog" that night, due to his dogged determination to get us back to the campground.

Finally, we made it back to the camping facility about 1:00 a.m., ready to play up the "Essen und trinken" role at the gate house. No one was there. Thankfully, the gate was not locked and no barrier bars were down. We drove in and found a camping site not more than fifty yards from a restroom and shower facility. We still had to settle in and all of us needed to use the restroom; we rotated turns at the sink, too. I headed back to the van after my turn. Lane saw me coming; he headed toward the showers. AJ was already in the restroom shaving. As I got back near the van, a security guard with a pump action shot gun stepped out of the shadows and approached me. He was not friendly! He wanted to see my papers. He got belligerent with me. He started telling me in German that we couldn't camp there. He told me we had to leave, and he was not friendly about it.

Knowing we needed to have our visas stamped every day for our border crossing exit to avoid a hassle and decrease the potential of a vehicle search, we needed to stay at that camp. The next campground was miles away; it was 1:00 a.m., and we were tired and did not have a lot of options. The likelihood of getting into some other location was slim to none. I told him in German that we would pay in the morning. The guard got more aggressive with me and stated we could not stay there. Once again "Gehe Sie!" (You go!), he said sternly. He insisted that we leave. My two teammates were still in the restroom and shower while that encounter was going on. I guess I started feeling a little irritable, but I stood my ground and replied, "Nien, wir slaffen hier!" He then raised and pointed the shotgun at my chest and said sharply in German, "Go, get out of here!" I replied, "Nien, Wir slaffen hier!" (No, we are sleeping here!) "Wir im der morgen bezahlen!" (We pay in the morning!). I held my ground, gambling that he wouldn't shoot me over a camping spot, a little tired and irritable myself. He told me again to leave. Using the business end of the shot gun as he pointed it at me, he jerked the gun to the left in an out of there motion. I respond with "Nein! Wir slaffen hier!" We were in a standoff, more precisely a Slovakian standoff. He didn't become more aggressive nor try to get physical. The shot gun was enough. I certainly didn't get aggressive; I just held my ground. He finally figured out that I did not plan on budging and I don't think he wanted any more of a silly argument at 1:00 a.m. He grunted, let out a huff, and stomped off, walking away grumbling in Slovak. I wondered if he would be coming back shortly with re-enforcements to make us leave. If so, I figured I'd deal with that when it happened; right then I was tired and just wanted to get some sleep. My teammates showed up a little later, and I told them what they had just missed. We said some prayers and then racked out. It had been a full day for sure, and what a way to end it.! Again, as I fell asleep, I asked the Lord for wisdom and for protection for our team and for the Bibles and cargo being transported to the people we would be visiting.

August 19th we were up around 6:30 a.m. It was a short night. We didn't complain… just happy that things were OK and that we didn't have any more trouble with the VB last night. After breakfast, devotions, prayer, and team meeting, we then reviewed contact info and plans for the day. We headed out of camp, paid our camping fees, and got our visas stamped. Then we drove out of camp, N. Meso. We headed for Stara Tura once again to attempt contact with Brother Paval. We made it there before midmorning. After checking maps again and reconnoitering the area, we located the street Paval lived on or was supposed to live on our map. We headed out of town and established a pick-up point to meet up with AJ later. He dropped Lane and me off about a mile from Paval's neighborhood. We walked into where the contact's apartment was supposed to be from another direction. We made it to his street, noticing that we were not being followed and that no one seemed to pay any attention to us. There were few people out on the streets that time of day at midweek; but as we walked toward the apartment complex address, we discovered that the local Communist Party Headquarters was on the same block as Paval's apartment complex just across the street. It was less than one hundred yards from his apartment. "Great!" We ended up walking directly across the street from the local party headquarters to get to his location.

We stayed on the opposite side of the road; fortunately, the Communists had not opened their office yet. We walked past that spot and came to the apartment complex address we had memorized less than a hundred yards from the local Communist Party office. We entered from the back side of the apartment to a doorway where the mail boxes were located, which had names on them. His name was not on the number we had been given nor was it on any of the mail boxes! It was a completely different name. *What's goin' on? We were given the wrong address. Lane had memorized the contact info so had we*! We had a little discussion, bewildered about what to do next. We had diligently studied the addresses and diagrams we had been given. *Great, what now?* We couldn't knock on someone's door and ask, "Do you know where Paval lives or moved to?" Lane and I had a brief discussion about it, keeping our voices low. He said, I'm sure this is the right address. This is where he should be. I know this is it, I know I memorized the right address." "Yeah, I know," I replied. It was what I memorized, too, "You're right, this should be it. We are at the right place, but we don't have the right name on the box." It was the right street number and street name. We checked all the other boxes at the apartment complex, but his name was nowhere to be found. We were definitely at the address we had been given and studied. We confirmed it. We had a conundrum which puzzled us, and I was wondering what to do next. He was scheduled as our first contact with the largest literature drop. Once again, we had to adapt and adjust to the conditions we were in. We had to fall back and consider our options. I quickly asked God, complaining a little too, as I asked Him for guidance and wisdom. I imagine Lane was praying as well. *Ok Lord, we have a lot of books, have traveled three days, over a thousand miles, taken risks crossing borders, had close encounters with police, just to get here and find out that he does not live here...just great! What now??*

We certainly couldn't start asking the neighbors! Lane was asking me, "What do we do now?" I was thinking praying, the same thing, *What now Lord?* As I was praying inwardly, I looked up the street about a block and saw a second line of apartments parallel to and on the opposite side of the street. I had a flash back to a planning session at the Farm. I had remembered seeing those apartments on a hand drawn map back at The Company; for some reason those apartments had a mark on the sketch map back in the file at the base. Maybe there was a reason for the mark on that map—something special about that apartment block. I felt an instinctive nudge, most likely from the Holy Spirit; that we should check it out. I started to walk up the street and cross it at a diagonal, cognizant of the Communist Party office just down the street from us. There was still no one stirring there, I noted mentally, as I quickly glanced over my shoulder. I had not yet said anything to Lane about what was going on in my head. We had to be discreet and keep our English conversation in a whisper and at a minimum. I said, "Come on." He caught up with me and asked with a bit of urgency in his voice, "What are we doing? Where are we going?" I replied in a low voice, "Just follow me." I didn't have time to explain that I was following a spiritual hunch. He quickly fell in step alongside me. We walked up the block after we had crossed the street at a diagonal. Then we went around to the back of the apartment complex. We found several mail boxes on the rear side of the housing unit near a door way with names on them. There it was, Paval's name on one of the mail boxes! Bingo! "Thank you Lord," rolled quietly off my lips. Things were looking up. Maybe we wouldn't need to use the alternate contact after all. It would certainly help us stay on track with our itinerary.

Lane and I entered the complex exercising caution, hoping not to bump into anyone headed out late to work or women leaving to go shopping. We heard no voices. Good, we kept going up. Walked up two flights of stairs. Then we quietly tapped on the door of the apartment number which coincided with the name on the mail box. Finally, someone answered the door after what seemed like 3 or 4 minutes; which seemed like a lot more but in reality was probably less than two. Actually, when standing out in a hallway at a public housing unit in a communist country, without permission from the communists to be there and not wanting to be seen, seconds can seem like a long time. A blond girl in her late teens cracked open the door a little. She didn't completely fit our contact information we had studied. But we did know he had kids so I took the risk. I said quietly, "We bring greetings from the West." She looked a little puzzled which made me think, "Oh no, wrong place." "One minute please," came the reply. I added, "Is Brother Paval home? We bring Greetings from Brother Hank." She opened the door wider, a little more quickly saying, "Come in, come in." She ushered us into the house and took us through a living room area; then she shuffled us off into something like a sitting room. She asked us to wait, then left and went through a sliding door, closing the door behind her. The two of us sat, and sat, and waited some more. It seemed like twenty minutes, but was probably closer to eight or ten. We started to hear muffled voices on the other side of the door. About that time, I was again beginning to have doubts about our security. My mind started racing; a little paranoia began to enter my thoughts. Maybe this could be a trap; maybe the girl was an informer and contacted the police. It could end up being not so good. Maybe the VB or StB (State Security Secret Police) would walk in, in a minute. More muffled voices were outside the door. I was not feeling comfortable about our position and neither was Lane. I could tell just by looking at him. Pretty soon a guy which did not fit the description of our contact came into the room, closed the door behind him, and spoke to us in English. Our briefings had informed us that our contact only spoke Slovak and German, not English. He didn't fit the contact physical description either. This did not make me feel any better. Lane and I were thinking what's up here? After talking to us a little bit, and asking us questions, with us asking him some as well, he began to lighten up some. Then left the room again, he came back in with another guy who fit the description of our contact, Paval. Relief began move through me. It seemed all was well. They were just checking us out, too. They had been nervous about us, wondering if we were a Secret Police set up.

It turned out that the guy who spoke English was a member of Paval's church and had just happened to come by for a visit that morning. They thought that we may have been secret police who had followed him. He was one of the few English speakers in the church. Our concerns turned out to be providential timing with the Lord having provided an interpreter. We also learned that the night before, when we were walking around searching for Pavel's apartment, unable to find the right area, that he was not at home. They had been at a mid-week prayer meeting. It turned out to be good that we didn't find the right neighborhood the night before. That way we did not bring double jeopardy into play by showing up at his house two times in a row. A local informant may have seen us. After rapport was established and we were becoming comfortable with each other, we began discussing our purposes there and then set up plans for a literature exchange.

While we were setting up details with Brother Paval for the drop and visiting, we learned one of our network contacts, a Brother Lubos with whom Paval did literature work, had recently been arrested and sentenced to sixteen months in prison for his Christian anti-State activities. So they were rightfully nervous. The communists had trumped up false charges against him. That also explained to us a little more about Pavel's caution regarding us.

That was just another example of why we needed to exercise care when working in Eastern Europe to support the dissident community. We worked out a plan with Paval for the hand-off of Bibles and literature in a remote wooded mountain area for that afternoon at 3:00 p.m. Paval and Matus drew us a sketch map with directions with Matus acting as interpreter to explain them. After Lane and I studied and memorized the map and directions, they were destroyed. We pin pointed the location on a map they had and then reviewed it with John when we returned to the van.

This drop had an interesting twist. After we gave them literature intended for the Slovaks, we would leave our suitcases full of the Czech literature for our other contacts with Paval and Matus. So we would enter Poland with only Polish literature. That way if we were caught or stopped at the Czech -Polish Border, the Czech literature would remain in Czechoslovakia. After the work in Poland we would head back into Czechoslovakia for a second rendezvous with Paval and Matus and retrieve the literature left with them.

Then we would head out for our Czech contacts unknown to our Slovak friends. We had been instructed by trip planners to leave all our Czech materials with the Slovaks. After our time in Poland we would return and reconnect with Paval and Matus. The extra cargo space and weight differential would also be helpful for transportation of supplies inside Poland.

After some time at Pavel's, Lane and I returned to meet with AJ. He was faithfully waiting for us when we made it back to our prearranged meeting point. We jumped into the van and left the area. We found a good spot to lay low for a few hours, ate lunch, then headed to the mountain drop point. We arrived in the area about thirty minutes prior to the drop. We scoped out the area and parked off to the side of the road. It was a good remote location, a good place for us to access the van's specialized storage compartments. There was still no guarantee that it would be safe. Two of us closed the van curtains and accessed the system; the third was our look out, outside the van. Any knock on the side of the van would result in an immediate stop of work and closure of the system. We would then cover what we had out with our opened sleeping bags.

We removed several hundred Bibles and books, placing the literature for the Slovakians in plastic bags and the other Czech materials in four suitcases to be left for safe keeping with Paval. We would reverse that exchange with him in four days hence.

They arrived at 3:00 p.m. as scheduled. We followed them a short distance to an exchange point which was more secluded. Our team handed off the Bibles and literature for them in bags and left the four suitcases of Czech materials in their safekeeping. We set up another meeting at the central train station at the nearby Slovak city of Nowy Meso. The next meeting with them was scheduled for 3:00 p.m. at the train station in four days. Thankfully, that particular exchange had no unexpected interruptions. We left them and made tracks headed for southern Poland. Our team headed north toward more familiar territory for me, the militarized zone of the Czech-Polish checkpoint at Cesky Tesin.

Cesky Tesin was one of the areas where Ed and I had been just a little over a month before to drop off a typewriter. Our team had another destination, though, this time on the other side of the Polish border. We made it up to the border town and found a camping place on the Czech side. We would be crossing into Poland the next morning. The food for the Polish and clothing supplies were hidden away intermingled with our personal clothing, camping gear, and food supplies. We also had book materials in the system for our Polish friends.

On August 20th the team was up early; we were on the cusp of another border crossing. This time we would be entering into a country under martial law with travel restrictions consisting of country road block checkpoints. Foreign visitors were now allowed inside the country. However, curfews where still in place, and communications and travel between cities was being monitored. We would be among some of the first foreign visitors allowed into Poland since the establishment of martial law months earlier. We made sure to fuel up on the Czech side of the border in Cesky Tesin. We knew that there had been shortages in Poland with fuel being one of them. We wanted a full tank before entering.

Later that morning we crossed the border into Poland without mishap; the crossing was quick, only about forty-five minutes. Not too many people were traveling into Poland. It was a pretty good time, all things considered. We were on the road inside Poland fairly early. We needed to kill some time before our meeting at Katowice, so we headed toward Krakow and then onto Oswiecim (Auschwitz in German), the location of one of the most notorious Nazi concentration and death camps of World War II.

It has been estimated that one to two million people perished in that camp, with over ninety percent of those people being Jewish. It is hard to describe the experience. It was one of the most sobering experiences of my life. Words cannot express what we saw and felt there. One of the first things we saw as we walked through the entry gate were the words written in German on the entry iron archway, "Arbiet Mackt Frei" (Work Makes You Free). We began to detect slight odors which smelled of burning flesh or hair. Some of the buildings had been darkened from the smoke. The place still smelled of death, even then.

We walked around looking at the old wooden guard towers, the double rows of electrified barbed wire fences, and the lanes which were also kill zones. We saw the "Execution Wall" where hundreds and thousands where lined up and shot. We saw one of the smaller ovens where corpses were incinerated after the people had been gassed, shot, or worked to death. We toured old barracks where the cells housed the remains of prisoners' prosthetic devices. Some of the old cells were full of glasses or clothing, and others had suit cases with names and addresses written on them, as a testament to the fate of innocents. The barracks' walls were also lined with photos of prisoners who had entered the place of horror but never came out. One of the things we saw was the camp gallows. The last use was for the execution of Rudolph Huss, the former camp commandant who was hung there, on April 16, 1947, after his sentencing at the Nuremburg war crimes trials.

The three of us spent about two and a half hours there. We didn't talk much; to say it was shocking and disturbing does not even adequately describe the experience. Being there at a time when the country was under martial law where we were having to watch out for ZOMO patrols and police road blocks added to the impact. Our normal light-hearted and happy depositions were squelched. It is a place which definitely needs to be remembered with reverential and somber respect as a memorial for those who perished. It is a testament of man's capability to become worse than beasts, when we neglect or shun the goodness of God and His love for people. I pray that the world will never forget the hellishness of that place. The sad thing is some humans become barbaric, forgetting the lessons of history pretty quickly. It is deplorable that there are still the sadists who clamor after power bringing about such things. Just looking at the history of Cambodia, North Korea, Red China, and the Soviet Union does remind me of the need for the loving-kindness of the Lord. It would pay if we humans would learn to follow the ways of peace, forgiveness, and kindness taught by Jesus.

The visit at Auschwitz was a good personal history lesson for us on one of the most gruesome places ever constructed to the detriment of mankind. But we needed to get back on the road in order to make our evening contact. We had seen enough to stick with us for the rest of our lives. We didn't need to see much more to bear witness to the evidence of the atrocities committed by the Nazis. We needed to bypass visiting the rail head entrance of the concentration camp in order to keep on schedule. We knew those rail heads had brought displaced Jewish people from all over Europe to their destruction. What we had seen there already had made a huge indelible impression on the mind. We needed to get back to our purpose for being in Poland. But it was fitting that one of our stops in the country was at Auschwitz. Especially since the country was suffering under martial law with ZOMO military units roaming the land and the additional threat of Czechoslovak, East German, and Soviet troops poised to invade the country.

We left the Polish village of Oswiecim in midafternoon and headed onto Rybnik. Rybnik was about one hundred kilometers west and south of Krakow, with a population of roughly around one hundred thousand. In 1939 after the German invasion of Poland at the outbreak of WWII, Rybnik became a German border town as Germany claimed some of the territories in the area as its own. After WWII it ceased to be a German-Polish border town. Most of the German nationals who had lived there during the war left for West Germany. In the post-war period the city had become an important coal mining town for Poland.

We left Rybnik and headed onto the city of Glivice. Here we were to meet our Polish contacts, the Zwolennik family. We were also scheduled to hook up with Roda, who had traveled out of Holland via train. When nearing the city, we saw a lot of police, military vehicles, army troops, and paramilitary ZOMO shock troops. Military patrols on foot with AKs were everywhere, usually in teams of three, four or six. The ubiquitous military units could be seen in groups of eight troops at times. Most of the troops we saw seemed to be the ZOMO thugs in smaller teams of 3 to 6. After we found a suitable location near what appeared to be a tourist area where there were a lot of shops and a few other cars with foreign plates, we parked our van on a side street. AJ and I headed for the contact home. While walking down the street, we rounded a corner just in time to fall in behind three ZOMOs on street patrol. We slowed our pace and did not come any closer than roughly 8 to 10 feet behind them.

We walked behind them for about a block, then took the nearest left off the street. We continued walking a few more blocks making right, left, right turns until we were sure we were not followed on our way to the address we had memorized. We made sure there were no ZOMOs in the area as we approached the front of the house. After a knock on the door, we were warmly greeted by the matron of the home, Mrs Zwolennik. She had us sit down in the living room and served us some hot tea. She told us that Roda was already there as planned and that she was cleaning up and taking a shower. It was great to see Roda when she came out to greet us. It was good to know she was OK and had made it through all the check points without problems—just minor stuff, having her guitar case searched and close papers checks. Mrs. Zwolennik, Roda, AJ, and I had a good visit and time of fellowship. The mountain Underground Youth Camp was still on schedule for two days out.

Shortly after we arrived at the home while sitting in the living room, four ZOMO troops armed with AK47's patrolled slowly by the front of the house. We immediately quelled our voices. After the patrol passed, we resumed our visit, remembering we were illegally there. Shortly afterward, one of the two Zwolennik brothers about our age entered through the back door and said something. After a short time, at the insistence of Mrs. Zwolennik, John went back and retrieved Lane; and we shared a home cooked Polish meal with the family. Although in short supply and hard to obtain, they shared a special treat of Polish Sausage (the real deal) with us, I think it was the last they had. As we ate, the youth camp was the topic of discussion. We planned our logistical tactics, support role, and rendezvous for meeting up and transferring supplies to a Polish contact. Our role was transportation not only by moving additional food supplies, a sound system and music equipment, but also by supplying Bibles, song books, and Roda. The Poles provided music equipment and the sound system which we added to the stuff we had already brought. It all needed to be hauled to the camp. They had asked if we could transport more stuff in our van. They had only one van which could be used. Benzene (gasoline) was in short supply, being rationed and hard to come by. They valued it as gold.

We placed the extra packages and boxes, including food, sound amplifying equipment, speakers, and the couple of extra cases of Polish Bibles in the right places, evenly distributing the weight. Roda had to travel with us. The three of us guys would crowd into the front seat and

Roda would be right behind us in front of the supplies. For equal weight distribution, that would be where she would get to ride for the next several hours; she was a courageous girl agreeable to the plan.

We had to plan a spot to meet up with one of two Zwolennik brothers for the exchange of materials and for Roda to move into his van. One of the other considerations were police road blocks, or ZOMOs, and military check points which could be set up along our route. Road blocks and checkpoints for checking papers and people traveling from city to city would need to be avoided. We would have to be careful about the route we chose. The Poles helped us with planning the route. Even then the road blocks could be fluid and change. Timing was important, too. We would have the excess materials in our van partially covered with opened sleeping bags, blankets, and clothes; there were increased the risk factors. The van's rear and side curtains would remain closed. That was our only concealment for the supplies which we would be transporting; we prayed hard. If we got stopped and searched at a road block or pulled over, it could mean some bad news. That trip would be over.

The three of us left the Zwolennik home and made it back to the van with no problems and had plans to return before sunrise the next morning. Roda would stay the night; we would pick her up the next morning. We headed back to Rybnik where there was a camp ground adjoining a popular tourist motel restaurant and resort area. We drove to the camp ground, and after checking in, decided to check out a restaurant adjoining the campground for a snack. As we were walking along the footpath, the people we saw appeared hostile, angry and frustrated, with harsh facial expressions. The locals appeared more discontent than any place I had ever seen in Europe. The countenance of many displayed angry scowls, frowns and scorn. We saw many a wrinkled brow that night. We weren't comfortable even walking through the area, as we caught many glares and stares. There was a lot of drinking going on in the crowd. It seemed as though we were on top of a powder keg. We would be glad to be out of there the next day.

Logistics and time required for us to prepare that night before in order to be ready the next morning. It was already getting late. That night we got into the system, prepared and arranged our supplies, and checked our maps and directions for the rendezvous points and off-loading the next day.

We were up well before sunrise for the drive to Glivice and our pre-dawn meeting at the Zwolenniks to load supplies and to pick up Roda. Most ZOMO patrols did not start that early. We arrived at the house in the wee hours, well before daybreak. We backed into a garage-type shed in the early hours and loaded the rest of the food, Bibles, and equipment which could not be hauled in the other van. After loading up, we headed toward the southeast of Poland for the Gorce mountain region a few hours to the east. We were to meet our contact at 4 p.m. that afternoon at a roadside rest stop a few kilometers east of a place called Nowy Targ, Poland. We headed east and skirted around Krakow, avoiding the metropolitan areas although that was no guarantee we wouldn't encounter a road block along the way. Roda was in the van with us riding in a cramped position, but she was a good trooper. We made it to our arranged meeting place about an hour ahead of schedule. We had to wait even longer. Finally, sometime in the afternoon the youngest of the Zwolennik brothers arrived in his van. He pulled up and asked us to follow him. We tailed him several more kilometers east. Then we took a right turn onto a dirt road headed south into a wooded mountain area, kicking up dirt. We drove about half a mile and crossed a bridge over a beautiful mountain stream several feet wide. After we crossed the bridge, the Polish guy pulled off to the side of the road. It was a fairly wide spot on the right shoulder about sixty to seventy feet past the stream, on the uphill side. I turned in behind him at a right angle, where our van back doors lined up perpendicularly with the rear of his van. We jumped out making sure no one was coming. As far as we could see, everything was all clear. Then we off-loaded all the cargo into his van with five of us working quickly. All the supplies were transferred in short order, taking just a few minutes. We closed the back doors to both vans and had a brief visit with him asking us about life in the U.S. and what we did there. We could not spend much time socializing; wisdom and vibe said we needed to leave. "Thank you," and bear hugs from him., "God Bless you" all around, and we said our goodbye to Roda as she got into his van. We wished her God's blessings and protection. She left with the Polish guy, headed to the youth camp. Roda waved goodbye as they drove up the dirt road. We hated to see her go. As we walked back to get into our van, they had gone about seventy-five yards up the road and swung left unto another dirt road, stopping to make a three-point U-turn. We got into our van and closed the doors. I started the motor and started to back up. As I was looking over my right shoulder, I saw a

Polish military ZOMO patrol come over the bridge, heading right toward us. There were three guys with their Kalashnikovs and a driver in a rover-type patrol vehicle as they were driving toward our position. I said in a whisper to AJ and Lane, "Time to talk to the Boss." It didn't look good. But instead of stopping and questioning us with raised AK's, the ZOMO patrol motored by slowly, looking close and checked us out, giving us the "eagle eye," as some of my Texas relatives would say. Thankfully they just looked us over and kept driving slowly past us. They continued up the dirt road, then past the back of the Zwolennik's van driving between us. I turned and said to John and Lane, "You guys pray hard." The patrol continued up the road. They did not stop at the van Roda was in either. That could have been bad; an American girl riding with a Polish guy, miles from anywhere, would have certainly gotten her into some difficult circumstances. But the patrol kept on driving up the dirt road into the mountains, headed south toward the Czech border. If they had driven upon us two to three minutes earlier, we would have been dead meat.

But just to make things more interesting, as I was backing up and watching the ZOMO patrol drive just past the Polish brother's van trying to ease us out of there, a kid appearing to be in his early to mid-teens walked up out of the stream bed below the bridge with a fishing pole in hand. Unknown to us he had been fishing and apparently watching us. Lane had seen the kid across the road off to the left as I began pulling away from where we had been parked. Lane who was watching the kid out the back window saw him set down his pole and write down our license plate number on a piece of paper. Lane told me what was happening and commented that he thought the kid might have spotted us passing off the stuff we had for the Poles. I guess he had been watching us from seclusion, from that low-lying stream bed. All we needed was for the patrol to turn around or for the kid to begin yelling out to the patrol, causing the patrol to hear him, and turn around and bust us. As I began pulling away, I said to John and Lane lowly but with urgency, "You guys pray like you've never prayed before. We've gotta get!" I got squared away on the dirt road and headed out of there, drove hurriedly but not crazy back to the main road, and headed back west. I asked the guys to start checking the maps for a camping spot up in the mountains west of us, not far from Krakow. We wanted to put as many miles behind us as quickly as we could without speeding. Remembering the crazy drive with Ed a few weeks earlier, I kept the vehicle close to the speed limit, trying not to exceed it too much. As we talked with each other, we were hoping that the ZOMO patrol would keep going for miles before turning around, if at all.

I was also hoping that the kid's parents were pro-Solidarity and not communists, in case he rushed home to tell them. Maybe they would not pass to the police what the kid saw. Also, I hoped that he did not call the police directly. We made it a goal to be out of the country as early as we could; if he gave the info to anybody, hopefully we'd be gone before it passed through channels. We did need to get out of there, not recklessly speeding; but we didn't need to dilly dally around either.

I headed west toward Krakow posthaste. I asked the guys to keep checking the maps for a remote mountain camp ground. We needed to find a safe location to lay low and fairly close to Krakow, yet not far from the Polish Czech border so we could leave the country quickly. The vehicle was empty now and light, with no stress on the system, so we could drive at the speed limit without worrying about road conditions like bumps and pot holes quite as much. We planned on getting to a camp ground as soon as we could without stops. Lane and AJ checked maps for camping spots while I drove. We planned on a mountain camping place as far away from Nowy Targ as we could get by night fall. The guys found a site on the map which seemed to be somewhat isolated south of Krakow. We set course for that spot. It was getting dark as we cruised through the southern forest of the Polish countryside.

Late that night we rolled into the recluse mountain camp that the guys had found. Hopefully it would be a good place to remain low key. The next day we would have to spend the required amount of Polish zolities on some touristy type stuff for the border exit to meet our visa requirements. Then we would leave the country. It was nearing midnight; it had been a long day and we were tired.

We made our dinner and set up a small dome tent for Lane, about thirty feet away from the back of the van. AJ and I slept in the van. Sometime after midnight, not long after "hitting the rack," I heard voices quickly coming in our direction. It was someone calling out, excitedly and repeating, "British, Americans?" "British, Americans!" "British, Americans!" with some Polish words I didn't understand. A Polish guy went over to where Lane was bedded down inside trying to sleep. He was continuing in Polish with "British, Americans," sprinkled in. I looked out the van back door and the guy was bending over in front at the door of Lane's tent asking loudly, "British, Americans?"

I thought, "Oh, great! Here we are trying to lay low, get some sleep after a long day, and this guy is bugging one of my guys. He's gonna wake up the whole camp, and bring too much attention to us." I needed to intervene and draw him away from Lane's tent so I called over to him, "Hey, what do you want?" He turned to me and replied something in Polish with "British, American's?" as he started toward me. "We're American's," I responded. When he heard we were Americans, he began a quick step over to the van and tried to engage me in small talk, like I figured he might. It was my intent to draw him away from Lane, but now I needed to deal with him. *Oh great*, I thought to myself, *I'm so tired I can barely stay awake, and this guy wants to wake up the entire camp.*

He asked, "Where oou from?"

"America."

"Oh, me love Americans. What mus oou lic? Oou know Beatles? Jan Wennin?"

I answered, "No," thinking how do I get this guy to leave so we won't draw more attention to ourselves, then get some sleep.

He asked, "Haave u .. cigaarettes?"

"No."

"Wwhiskie?"

"No."

"Playboy?"

"No."

He continued wanting to engage each time I responded shortly, "No." He asked more questions about movie stars, rock stars, life in America, etc. *How do I get this guy outta our hair?* I was thinking. After humoring him a short while, I told him "We go sleep, you go sleep too, OK!" using hand signals, pointing away from camp, then putting my hands together, to the side of my tilted head, in what I hope would be sign language for sleep. He finally got it, apologized saying, "Me sorry," and left. Finally, I got him to leave! I went back to my sleeping bag and fell into a heavy sleep by the back doors of the van, leaving the doors ajar because of the humid hot August night. I was sleeping somewhat perpendicular to the van back doors, on my right side with my head near the back door. Leaving the back doors ajar turned out to be a mistake.

Unknown to us the Polish guy came back. It had been a rather warm muggy night, so I had left the van doors unlocked and slightly open for cooler night air to circulate through the van, it was not secured. I was asleep on my right side, when suddenly an intruder reached into the van and grabbed and pulled at my sleeping bag near my head. Startled awake I responded to those hands grabbing at my bag, with a spontaneous reflex action, which happened to be a left hook. I tagged the guy right in the face. I punched even as I was waking. As his head snapped back he was knocked off balance which caused him to stagger back a couple feet. As I was stirred from my heavy sleep, I realized it was the same guy; but now he was mad coming back at me starting to throw punches. After regaining his balance, he came back swinging. I woke up finding myself in the middle of a fight, up on my knees half way in a sleeping bag, blocking his attempted blows the guy threw at me. He wasn't landing any punches on my core or head; I blocked everyone. Somehow, I quickly was able to jump out of the sleeping bag and van. I was on my feet outside the van in boxer shorts; to this day, I don't remember how I got out of the bag and on my feet. I immediately went into a fight mode, fists doubled and primed. Blocking blows, I moved quickly to throw a blow escalating the altercation by throwing some punches of my own. I was primed to launch a hard right into the middle of his face, followed by a left jab, then throw another blow, squarely into the center of his head. He was slower and in my emotionally charged reflex I was getting ready to launch a series of blows on the guy and put him down. Suddenly, it was as though time went into slow motion. In a nano second just before I hit him, gigabytes of information flooded my brain. The thoughts came, *Don't you see what is happing here! This is spiritual. A fight will attract more attention than you need."* About then headlines flashed before my mind, *Bible Smuggler Arrested, After Fight with Local Polish Man.* I didn't have much time to argue with God or myself in the middle of a fight. As I had jumped out of the van and moved toward the Polish guy, he had stepped back a pace. Instead of throwing a punch, I threw a jam yet stopped short of his face. I pointed quickly, sharply, and precisely with my finger to the middle of his face having stopped short. Simultaneously I growled at the guy. "You... leave now!!" At the same time, I silently prayed a rebuke toward the spiritual enemy, commanding, *The Lord rebuke you*! It was as though someone had hit him in the solar plexus. He stopped, dropped his hands, his shoulders slumped slightly, he tucked his head as though in shame, then he began trying to apologize, saying, "Me sorry, me sorry." I responded by pointing the way out of our campground and said firmly, "Leave now!" He extended his hand for a handshake. I had not settled down and adjusted into a *Your OK, I'm OK* mind set. He had trespassed, invaded our space, and gotten violent when repulsed. I really didn't feel like giving him an *It's OK, all is forgiven* hand shake or *OK* hug right at the moment. I pointed the way out of camp and said "Leave." He left, as directed. I thought I was coming up short in my peaceful Christian walk.

What a way to end the day I thought, as I climbed back into the van and tried to go back to sleep; but couldn't because I was too pumped up to sleep. I thought about what had just happened. I felt bad about hitting the guy and even more so about wanting to pound him. We were trying to be low key, and I had ended up in an altercation which could have aroused others in our camp—not a good thing.

Just as I was beginning to settle down I heard voices outside the van. I looked outside and saw that the guy was back in camp again. But this time he had a friend. I got out of the van again, still in my boxers. I told them we were trying to sleep asked him to leave. He started getting a little testy again. I thought I was gonna have to fight him after all and maybe his friend, too. I figured he wouldn't be too difficult to fight, but two at the same time might be another story. I held my ground and asked him to leave again; after a bit of testiness from him they left. It was after 1 a.m. when I finally got back into the van.

It was finally the close of another interesting day with a crazy ending. I'm not sure, but I think Lane may have slept through the whole thing. I don't know. He didn't get out of his tent. Maybe he slept though the noise. AJ had woken up and was sitting up in his sleeping bag, getting out of it, as I got back into the van. He did not see what had happened, but the ruckus did wake him and he was headed out to help. Well, another unsought adventure! Just a couple of nights earlier, we had been stopped by a Czech VB police road block, and later I had a shotgun stuck in my face by a security guard. We were in a country under martial law with ZOMO patrols all around and had been spotted during a drop where our plate number was written down. Then there was this altercation with the Polish dude. "Ole' Slew Foot" must not have liked what we were doing. What a trip!

As I lay there trying to fall asleep, I prayed for that Polish guy. I prayed for peace in his life and for his country. I prayed for the Polish people and Poland. I prayed for those whom we had seen in many places with anger on their countenance, rightfully so with the yoke of the communists put on their country. The communist government was using ZOMO troops, which were literally beating down the Solidarity movement, with Soviet communist armies threatening an invasion. You certainly couldn't fault the Poles. I reminded myself about the circumstances in the country. That Polish guy was probably just excited about seeing Americans. We probably were a little ray of hope to him from the West which excited him. Yet in a sleepy reflex action I had hit him, ending up in a fight neither of us wanted. I mentally beat myself up for that. I was sure that the Apostle Paul would not have wanted to pound on the guy, as he had said in his letter to the Romans.

> "Never pay back evil for evil to anyone. Respect what is right in the sight of all men. If possible, so far as it depends on you, be at peace with all men. Never take your own revenge ...but leave room for the wrath of God." (Romans 12:17-19a)

Finally, I fell asleep praying sometime in the wee hours of the morning. If we would have been there under different circumstances, I would have looked for the guy the next day to talk with him and tried to set things straight and encourage him. But we had to stay focused on our mission, especially with the close call the afternoon before. We had no time to waste and could not risk any unnecessary exposure.

Sunday morning came quickly. We slept, waking up past daylight. After breakfast we broke camp and headed into Krakow to spend the required tourist dollars before leaving the country. We finished a short team meeting and decided to have our devotion on the road. We hit the road and Lane read a few verses of scriptures as we drove; then we started singing praise and worship songs. We were having church as we traveled along. It was a great time as we temporarily forgot the circumstances and focused on God in worship! We sang songs all the way into the suburbs of Krakow.

As we entered the outskirts of the city, we rounded a bend in the road; a police road block was set up ahead. We immediately quit singing and approached slowly; we couldn't around—we were stuck. It was a regular police unit without ZOMOs. A Polish cop stopped us at a check point and asked to see our papers. We showed him our passports, visas and international driver's licenses. After checking us over with a quick look into the van, he smiled and waved us through. He was friendly as he waved us on. It was a nice change from a few nights back with the Czech VB. After we got about a block away, we started singing and praising the Lord again with another reason to praise Him! We were singing and having church as we drove. We headed on into the city making our way to the old city square, played tourists, and spent the required amount of solotys (Polish currency) for our visa requirement. I bought a few little gifts for friends and family back home in the Netherlands and U.S.

We stopped for lunch at a little side walk café while at the town square. The food was good and certainly beat the camp food that we had been eating. But soon after eating lunch while still at the table, AJ and I both started feeling bad. We were somewhat light-headed and nauseous. Maybe we weren't used to the food, or maybe it was something else. We both started feeling slightly queasy. It was time to get out of town. As we left town we wondered what was going on with us. *Was the food just too rich or did we have a mild case of rapid onset food poisoning?* Both of us did not feel well for a while. A little later after we got a few miles outside of the city, we both began feeling better. It was probably just a light food borne toxin. Regardless of what it had been, after we got out of the city we pulled over to "check the oil." We searched through our ruck sacks that we had with us in town, too. We also searched around the vehicle checking for tracking devices once more. We checked for any cars which may have pulled over after we did, checking our six, looking for anyone who might have been following. Then we made a beeline, heading south toward a campsite north of Cesky Tesin, our Polish-Czech border crossing. We stayed on the Polish side, north of the border. We planned on an early exit from Poland into Czechoslovakia early next morning.

We wanted to be at the Polish Czech checkpoint first thing when it opened, hopefully leaving the country early. When we arrived at the checkpoint, a line of cars had already formed of people wanting to get out of Poland and into Czechoslovakia (guess we should have been a little earlier).

Thankfully, the border crossing went smooth, taking under an hour to get though the whole process. We headed south back toward Nowy Meso to hook up with Paval and Matus. We were to meet them at the central train station at 3:00 p.m. We had a few hours of driving ahead of us.

We made it to Nowy Meso a little ahead of schedule. We reconnoitered the area around the station and figured out our approach and where we would park. We decided to park in the train station parking lot. Where we parked turned out to be an error in judgment on my part; hind sight is 20/20 as they say. We should've parked several blocks away and walked in again. But I was concerned about AJ and I having to lug four heavy suitcases full of books back to the van. Moreover, we figured that it would look fairly normal for a couple of guys carrying suitcases out of a train depot into a parking lot.

John was driving; he took us to the edge of the train station parking lot at about 2:40. We parked under the shade of a big tree at the edge of the lot. Even shade can provide a degree of concealment. AJ and I left Lance with the vehicle. We walked to the station about seventy-five yards away. I figured that wouldn't be too far to carry the four heavily loaded suitcases. When we entered the station, we noticed the layout to be similar to a square axe head with the waiting area and benches straight ahead and off to our left. The waiting area was about several dozen feet with an aisle way to the right running along a rail fence that separated the passengers from the ground level train-boarding area. There weren't any loading docks. We were on ground level with the train. A train schedule with arrival and departure times was mounted on the wall to our right. We noticed a guy sitting in the far-left corner facing the waiting area, who appeared to be reading a newspaper with a view of the waiting area and the long rectangular aisle way to our right, his left. He had a good tactical observation position. He was holding the newspaper unfolded as if reading it, but frequently glancing over the top. It seemed to me that the guy in the corner was most likely StB secret police. John and I casually walked over and looked at the train schedule and pointed at a few places as if we were planning on going somewhere. We spoke only in low whispers with our backs to the public area, hoping that our mouth movements and actions would not betray us.

A train idling out on the tracks was making a low rumbling noise. We could only stay in that position for a while before it would be obvious that we had been staring at the schedule too long. We moved over to a wall behind us and to the left, running parallel to the tracks far out in front of it. We leaned against an open space we found on the wall and faced each other, with one guy watching over the shoulder of the other without being obvious. Occasionally, we spoke to each other in low whispers. People were milling around somewhat, and some were sitting on the waiting area benches. A train left and another arrived. We waited and waited. Paval and Matus had not shown at 4:00 p.m. Although patient, we were both starting to feel concerned and uneasy; they were over an hour late. It was becoming a long wait, especially since the guy in the left corner had not moved nor left the station either. It appeared he was monitoring the area. Meanwhile, we walked over individually and checked the train schedule again for the sake of appearance. The guy in the corner kept peering over the top of his newspaper occasionally. His location and behaviors certainly fit those of a StB agent. Things might not be so good; I was concerned, as was John.

Finally, after 4:00 Matus and Paval came through the double doors on our right. They were both carrying camera cases slung over their shoulders. One of them was wearing plaid shorts, a short sleeve striped polo, and a really clean white cap. He was looking like a tourist. They both looked somewhat like they were headed on a day trip. They headed left in our direction, walked right by us intentionally, not even acknowledging us. They passed about six feet in front of us, but didn't stop. They walked on by with the ever-slightest glance and nod in our direction, faintly detectable. They did not have the suitcases. I was thinking that this was not part of the prearranged plan. Something wasn't good. I wondered what was up. But I was glad that they didn't stop at our location, since the guy over in the corner appeared to be conducting surveillance. What I learned in a few minutes really made me glad that they didn't have those suitcases and confirmed my suspicions. They walked about the inside perimeter of the waiting area, as though looking for a place to sit, all the while checking the place out themselves. Most of the benches were full. They headed down the hallway running parallel to the tracks and at a forty-five degree angle to our right.

Well what now? I thought. If they came back over to us, having walked right by us, it would really look suspicious to the guy in the left corner, if indeed he was a secret police agent like he appeared to be. After about thirty seconds I decided to take a walk over to my right, down the hallway where they had gone out of sight around the corner, following them. I knew that the guy in the back over in the left corner was strategically positioned and able to see the entire waiting room and hallway. I rounded the corner and saw Matus coming back my direction, out in front of Paval. That was a break, as he was the English speaker. With my back to the guy in the corner, I was wondering how to play this out. I walked up to Matus, as a stranger might, and asked. "Excuse me sir, do you have the time?" Initially Matus looked puzzled. I asked a second time, "Excuse me do you have the time?" He caught on quickly. He lifted his arm with the watch and gave me the time. We then stepped over to the fence railing, positioning ourselves between some people waiting for their train along the rail and the guy in the corner. We leaned on the fence railing looking out toward the idling noisy train. The first words Matus whispered, with some urgency, were, "We cannot give you the luggage now there are too many secret police in the area! Your vehicle has been spotted and your license number written down. A brother saw a man walk up behind your vehicle, drop a match book, bend over to pick it up, then write your license number on it! Your team has been spotted!" After hearing that, my heart rate sped up. AJ had walked over and joined us at the rail. About that time a Czech VB police officer started walking across the train tracks headed straight toward us. As he was nearing us getting to within a couple of dozen of feet away, a little paranoia hit me. I started thinking, *Oh, man this is starting to look bad, looks like we could get busted.* Then an absurd thought hit me. *This is like a scene out of a movie, or an old episode of Hawaii Five O, where Dano would be in the process of busting someone. Then the captain walks up and says, "Cuff 'em Dano!"* Except we could be the ones about to get cuffed! My imagination was beginning to get a little active. The absurdity of those thoughts hit me while the cop was approaching. It seemed as though the CZ 9 mm pistol on his hip was getting pretty doggone big as he drew nearer. I had focused on it, watching for hand movement to the gun, assuming the gun could come out of the holster at any second. When the cop was only about fifteen to twenty feet away, the absurdity of the moment hit me, a little humor floated through my mind, and peace came over me as I glanced up. and caught his eye. I saw the look on his face and smiled. Interestingly, the little bit of joy didn't leave. I remained still and nodded my head as an acknowledgement, continuing to smile as a greeting. He smiled back and walked past us down the fence line. Matus of course had quit talking when he saw the cop coming our way. The 9 mm CZ pistol I had focused on started fading away as the cop walked past. A relief rolled over me, but I can't say I relaxed a lot though. Whew, another close one!

As soon as the uniformed officer got further away. I quietly asked Matus, "What's the plan?" He started whispering instructions to us, quietly but quietly. I asked AJ to listen in closely as a backup for me, in case I missed something. Matus instructed us to drive straight down the road in front of where we were parked, turn to our right at the first stop light, then turn left after coming to a second stop light and crossing some railroad tracks. "After the next light, drive several blocks to a stop sign; turn left. Then follow the road to the west until you come to a fork in the road," Matus further instructed, "At the fork you are to continue on the main road exactly one kilometer. There will be a green Skoda pulled over with the hood up." He gave us the plate number. "When you get to the Skoda, pull over and ask them if they are having car trouble. If they say *yes* and there is no traffic, the suitcases will be transferred. If they say *no*, it is not safe. You must keep going. Drive below the speed limit. They will follow you at a distance. When it is safe, they will catch up to you and signal for you to pull over, so a switch can be made." It was the plan, and the train station was not the place to ask questions.

We broke off from him headed back to the van, discreetly checking that we were not being followed by the guy in the corner. When we got back to the van, I saw that the shade had moved. This because of the long wait in the train station for the two Slovaks. Our vehicle was highly visible from the nearby road, making Lane's position more vulnerable to prying eyes. Poor guy waited in that spot. I wish he would have moved the van a little. No wonder someone wrote down our license number. It made me frustrated with myself for having asked John to park the van in that spot; it was way to visible with the movement of the shade. I approached the van from the rear on the driver's side. Lane had seen us coming and was faithfully sitting in the driver's seat. I asked him to move over so I could drive. It was easier than trying to re-explain the directions. John and I jumped in, I fired up the Fiat, and we took off, making sure to obey speed laws. Lane asked where the suitcases were; we explained what had just happened as I drove.

We followed the directions to a tee. I asked AJ a few questions about our route, and he verified our course. We got to the fork in the road with no mishaps. No police on our tail, no cars following us. We were leaving town and getting out into the country side with no tails, so far. I was beginning to feel some relief. The road was straight with only two lanes, and it was smooth. We could see a good distance behind us and down the road. We drove the one kilometer, past the Y intersection, with no vehicles behind us. But there was no green Skoda alongside the road where it was supposed to be. We drove for two kilometers then for five kilometers, but there was no Skoda. No green Skoda caught up with us either. We decided to turn around and head back to the fork in the road and retrace our path because we did not want to just sit at the one kilometer mark. Who knows? A VB could pull up to us to check us out. We ended up back at the fork in the road again. On route we met other Skodas including a green one, but it had the wrong license plate number. After we flipped a U back at the fork in the road, we headed back toward the one kilometer rendezvous point. There was no Skoda, but no VB police either so that was good. We were questioning what had happened to the other guys and wondered about the deviation from the plan. Maybe they got busted.

After we had turned around again heading west and driving slower, a green Skoda caught up to us and passed. It had the right plate number; it was our guys. They got to the one kilometer mark past the fork in the road and pulled over, with us not far behind. They jumped out and popped the hood open. Ok, at least we were in business. We pulled over and got out. Lane posted to the rear of the van as lookout. John and I walked up to the Slovaks and asked if they were having car problems. They replied that everything was OK, then popped their trunk and opened the rear passenger door, handing us our four suitcases full of Czech Bibles, Children's Bibles and Bible studies for our remaining contacts. The handoff took seconds with cars and no VB's driving by. We took off and the guys in the Skoda followed, lagging far behind us for miles. After a long distance, they passed us. They drove in front of us for a few more miles. We passed by a small sign on the side of the road. Then we came to a small country store and wide spot in the road. The Slovaks pulled over and waved us over. We got out, and they told us we were now in the Czech Republic. Then Paval explained to us that the VB were not quite as hard on Christians there as in Slovakia; so they wanted to visit for a short while. I was not feeling comfortable with it, but obliged them.

Slovakia is closer to the USSR than the Czech part of the country, and the authorities out of Prague were not as dogmatically oppressive. While they were strict, allegedly they were not as harsh as the Slovakian authorities. We sat down on a small concrete wall not far from the store; one of them went in and bought some soft drinks. There we sat sipping sodas with them talking about life. It was a short, but good visit. They asked us about the church in America. As we visited, Paval asked us to pray for them. He requested prayer that they would remain strong in faith and not pulled away from the Lord because of materialism. The pastor, through the interpreter, expressed concern about materialism in his church and country. I was thinking *What, he is worried about materialism in the church?* He was concerned about materialism; I was expecting something like protection form the secret police or relief from persecution. But his request amazed me, as I mentally compared life there to life in the U.S. After speaking with him on his circumstances, it was a prudent time to leave. We prayed together then said our farewell. Blessings were exchanged: "God be with you." "And with you." Bear hugs were exchanged; then we had to leave. Continuing west, the three of us quietly digested what we had just experienced. Our next contact was to be in the city of Brno. We arrived there that evening and camped just south of town.

Our ETA at Brother Franc's home in Brno was for about 10:00 a.m. the next day. We reconnoitered his neighborhood upon arrival. He lived in a block of apartments on the side of a sloping hill with a slow downward long curve in the street through the neighborhood. We parked in a parking lot about four blocks up the hill from his home. Lane tried to make contact that morning, but Franc was not home. We came back later. Since he was not home for Lance's attempt, we felt it would be best if John and I tried the second attempt. We didn't want Lane to be seen a second time within a few hours, just in case there were any nosy neighbors or informants in the area.

The second attempt was made, and again Franc was not home. As we were walking back up the long sloping urban sidewalk with our backs toward the van, I spotted a lone man who just didn't fit right, smoking a cigarette on a second level balcony at a small mall on a second level tier, when we had go, about a half a block away. He continued slowly taking drags off his cigarette, standing smoking at the rail. He then began a slow descent along some stairs at our ten o'clock position, which perpendicularly intersected with the sloped sidewalk we were walking up. Occasionally he stopped along the rail, taking a puff on the cigarette and gazing out toward our nine o'clock position. He was attempting to be as smooth as he could, but it appeared he was trying to time his descent to fall in behind us a few yards. I believed he was watching us. He would take a couple of draws off his "smoke," as he leaned over the banister, pause for a moment; then take three or four steps toward our direction. His time leaning on the stair step rail seemed too short, out of place, as did his draws on the cigarette. Most people just walk down stairs, smoking. This guy didn't. His movements stood out. He didn't fit. *Oh man not another secret police agent.* It appeared that he was. As we approached, the guy moved a few steps in our direction, timing his descent down the walkway and stairs to where he would be coming out on the sidewalk behind us. We passed by the stairs; the guy came in behind us about sixty-five feet as we were walking back to the vehicle. He definitely was following us. It was not good at all; we had to go back to the van, and we were too close to it to walk on by; we were at a dead-end spot at the road too. Lane was waiting in the van. There was no corner to round, no other street to turn down, and no block to walk around. The only thing past the van was a vacant lot. If we walked by the parking lot, there was no other place, housing or businesses to head to in order to double back around. There was just an open field straight ahead. *Should we walk past the vehicle and not go to it?* It would really raise more suspicion, especially since our van had foreign plates and we could be identified as westerners by the discerning eye. If the guy behind us had seen us get out of the vehicle earlier, walking past it would be a dead giveaway too. We were at a choke point, very limited as to what our options were. The best thing would be to be direct and leave the area as quickly as we could. We had to play out our hand. Fortunately, the agent/informant had not seen which apartment complex from which we had come. We picked up our pace, quickening our step a little to put distance between us and the guy following without going not too fast. We to have a proper gait, trying not to be too obvious. We made it back to the van soon enough and got in quickly and quietly with the keys ready. Lane started to sit up from lying on the floor, where he had been waiting for us. I told him to stay down as we got in. I started the van and quickly backed out without looking back, but checking the mirror for the guy to see if he took down our license plate info. I didn't see him get it. We headed for downtown to play tourist, hoping the guy following did not get close enough or have time to get our plate number. We needed to clear the area immediately and completely, so we headed to the Centrum; perhaps we would return that night. Perhaps we would need to try the alternate contact in Prague. If the guy at the rail who followed us was secret police, they would most likely be monitoring the area for the next few days. We had stuff to think about for our next course of action.

We decided to head back to try the contact in Brno one more time with only one of us making the attempt. If unsuccessful, we would head for the alternate in Prague the next day. Franc was not home after the third attempt so we drove north of Brno to a little place called Stoky, and camped there. It made me think of Ray, the California guy, who was out with another team now. He would often say when thinking something was cool, "Hey cool, I'm stoked!" Thinking about Ray prompted me to pray for him. Before our team racked out we said some prayers. I included Ray and the success of his team in my prayers.

The next morning, we headed northwest toward Prague. We arrived there in the afternoon. We attempted contact with a Brother Jiri and his wife that evening, but struck out after a couple of attempts. Our success rate was not looking good about then. We had struck out with Franc and decided not to risk any more attempts with Jiri so we headed to the alternate. Brother Miklos who lived in another part of the city was our secondary. We would go there because we needed to stay on track with our time in country to abide by our visa restrictions.

Miklos's apartment was on the second floor of a complex near a business district. We took the usual precautions and parked about five or six blocks from his home. Lane was the faithful standby, staying with the vehicle. John and I set out on foot utilizing the usual zigzag approach method to the apartment, stopping a couple of times with one of us doing the shoe-tie maneuver, with the other facing toward him watching our back to see if we were being followed by the StB secret police. We performed street crossing maneuvers where one of us would casually step up the pace walking slightly in front of the other, then discreetly scan back over the shoulder of his partner. Stepping ahead of your partner a little, then looking back for anyone following was a useful maneuver. We could see no tails. But we could not use that maneuver too much as it could have become too obvious. We arrived at Miklos's home later in the evening. It was summer time, and it was dark as it was getting a little late. After a knock on the door, Miklos answered and ushered us inside. We spoke in low tones letting him know we were a link from the west. He was somewhat alarmed, but courteous. He put a finger to his lips and whispered, "Shh, please be quiet; I think I might be being watched." He gestured in a Czech accent as he pointed upward like there was a listening device nearby. Then he whispered, "Things are not good here. Please leave, go outside to the street, turn right, walk slowly, and I will catch up with you." We left.

AJ and I did as he had directed, heading downstairs out of the apartment complex. We turned right, walking slowly down the street and we came to a "Kino" (cinema) after about half a block. Stopping on the far side, we pretended to be looking at a wall-mounted poster advertising the next attraction. We only had to stare at the thing for a couple of minutes before Miklos caught up with us. I ask him to walk with me. AJ to fell back slightly behind us; he watched our back as tail gunner. I asked him to keep track of where we were to remember our route so that we would not get lost and could make it back to our van. I was focused on the conversation with Miklos.

We walked along at a quick pace. Miklos had urgency in his voice. "Please do not send people here, for a long time. It is not safe now!" he exclaimed, in his thick Czech accent. "One of the women from my church has been arrested and questioned. I think I am being watched." He then told us about a girl in his congregation who had been arrested for questioning. He also let us know that he had been questioned and believed he was under surveillance. That of course did not sound good. I made a mental note for our debriefing reports when we returned. I asked him if there was anything we could help with, any particular materials, books or aid that he believed would be good for his people and that he would like to receive when things became safer. When inquiring about that, I asked him if he could receive the materials that we had with us. He responded in the affirmative, although he was nervous and rightfully so. As we walked down the street discussing materials preferred for any future drops, he asked if we could get them copies of the book by Watchman Nee, *Sit, Walk, Stand*. I told him we would pass on his request along with the information about his circumstances.

There was a decent amount of foot traffic that night out on the sidewalk as we walked along. We had to keep our voices low, aware of people approaching when we spoke. We would walk a block and turn right, walk another block and turn left. This maneuver was performed more than a couple of times. We learned from Miklos during this hurried visit that there was a move of the Holy Spirit within the Catholic Church. More Christian literature was definitely needed he explained to us. But he encouraged us to exercise caution, especially in any return to his home. He would get word out via contacts. He was definitely nervous about our contact. We told him we were making attempts to be careful.

As we walked Miklos said he would arrange for a drop, but explained it was not good for us to return to his home. We understood and agreed.

We came to a telephone booth at a street corner. He slid into the booth to make arrangements for the literature drop. John and I remained nearby. We leaned against the wall of a brick building about twelve feet away from the phone booth, concealed somewhat by the shadows from the building and trees along the outer edge of the sidewalk. We had positioned ourselves on a side street with the least foot traffic. I was facing east toward the street that we had just crossed and AJ was facing west. We were both watching over the shoulder of the other. I picked up on a guy who was walking out of the shadows from where we had just come. He looked out of place; he was walking our direction in the middle of a cross walk at a pace that didn't fit with the rest of the crowd while smoking and taking draws off his cigarette. He was walking across that street like he was taking a stroll through a park, taking long purposeful drags from his cigarette. I thought, *This guy looks like he's takin' a stroll through a park. And he's in the middle of the street. What's up with him?* I didn't have a good feeling about him; he stood out.

He continued in our direct after crossing the street. As he was approaching, I whispered to John, "Shh, don't say anything. There's a guy comin' our direction. Keep an eye on him after he walks by." We were quiet as he strolled past us. After about twenty seconds I asked AJ in a whisper, "What's he doin?" He responded, "He just slid into the shadows about fifty feet past us, has put out his cigarette, and is watching us from the shadows." That was way not good; we were being followed. Miklos finished his call and stepped out of the booth. I casually stepped over to Miklos, placing my body between him and the guy in the shadows, interrupting the direct line of sight. I gently touched Miklos elbow and pushed it away in the other direction, indicating that we needed to head the other way. We headed back the direction we had come from, then stepped to the right around the corner of a building and broke into a quick step down the street. Luckily, there was a lot of foot traffic, yet just sparse enough for us to maneuver through and provide some cover. I quickly told Miklos in a low voice, that we were being watched and maybe followed. He hurriedly told us an address as the location for a delivery point first thing in the morning. He told us to be there no later than 8:30 sharp. "No later," he said with emphasis. Then he added, "Don't send any more people to my house now." I again made a mental note to place his circumstances in our debriefing report. We made it down the block to the street corner, making a quick turn to the right, around the corner of the brick building which provided cover. Miklos broke off to the left in a few feet heading across the street at a diagonal. That was the last time we saw him. We continued down the block, making another right turn behind the corner of the brick building. The street was dark. We quickened our pace and headed in a diagonal direction crossing the street to the left. We checked our six position behind us as we turned left again at the next corner, then headed back to the van fast.

John did a good job guiding us back to the Fiat. I was certainly glad he was with me. We didn't detect anyone following us after having taken an indirect route back to meeting Lane. When back in the van, we headed to our campsite being alert for lights which could be continuing to lag behind us. We were also alert for any new cars coming off side streets which may have stayed behind us, too. We left the area, seemingly not picking up any tails. We headed on to our campground several miles outside of the city. It was pretty late when we got back to camp.

By the time we got to our campsite and ate dinner it was around midnight. We still had to plan for the next morning, get into the system, and retrieve the literature for the early morning drop. Then we needed to plan a route to the address we were given. It was going to be a bit of a challenge, not being familiar with traffic patterns and potential congestion. It was after 1 a.m. when we hit the rack and we needed to get up between 4:30 and 5:00 a.m. in order to get squared away, have a quick bite to eat, then make it back into town and not get stuck in commuter traffic in the large metro area we were unfamiliar with. Compounding the fun, we were in a foreign country where we couldn't read the street signs and at times those street signs and our maps didn't match up. Next, we would have to find an inconspicuous location to park and from there carry four suitcases full of Bibles and literature several blocks and arrive at a strange apartment by 8:30 a.m. sharp. There was no MapQuest or GPS in those days, either. We would work to figure it out and get it done.

While we were accessing the system and planning, we had to be on the alert for activity in the campground and work quietly without making any noise which could arouse suspicion. We needed to remain inconspicuous and be noise free. Once again, we needed to "be wise as serpents and innocent as doves" (Matthew 10:16) The incident earlier in Brno where the guy followed us from his balcony position was still a concern for me as well as the fact that we had been watched as Miklos was in the phone booth. Indeed, we had experienced some incidents that

I was concerned about. Although we were back in our camp and had not detected any StB or VB (regular State Police), we knew we needed to keep our guard up. It was not a time to get lax at all, especially after all that had been happening on this trip.

We opened the system and Lane acted as lookout. AJ opened cabinets and accessed the books at the access point, working by dim flashlight under the cover of closed curtains with blankets thrown over us. We worked quietly, just whispering in low tones when necessary, realizing how one noise can travel long distances through cool night air. As usual, we placed the books and Bibles into trash bags, then into four suitcases. A route to the address Miklos had given us was planned. We finally made it to sack time around 1:30 in the morning. It would be a short night. But I had dealt with short nights before just to get up early go out fishing.

The next morning we were up at 5:00. We quickly dressed, and ate a fast, light breakfast, then headed into town. We prayed as we drove, following the route John and Lane plotted just a few hours earlier. The route to the literature drop might prove interesting. We found a park in the city of Prague as a marker for the area where we needed to be. We parked our vehicle near there. We figured it would look normal for a western vehicle to be at a park. We found an area where AJ and I could get out of the van discreetly, hopefully where no one around would see us exit the van with the suitcases. Lane acted as lookout. When the coast was clear, he signaled for us to get out with the suitcases. John was in good shape from working out and able to carry a heavy load some distance so he got out with two cases. I followed with two more, and we headed out with our four book-heavy pieces of luggage toward the memorized address.

We walked for under a block before setting down the heavy suitcases to readjust the grip and check behind us. We had to do that several times to make it to the apartment. We also included a couple of fake shoe-tying stops to check behind us as we approached the apartment complex. Those short rests also gave us a break from carrying the heavy suitcases. As we drew near to the complex, we had not detected anyone following us. We made it inside the apartment complex and ID'd the correct address and name on a mail box. We had made it to the right place and it was just past 8:30 a.m. Next, we headed up two flights of stairs and went down the hall looking for the apartment number we were given. It was 8:34 a.m. when we knocked on the door; we were 4 minutes late. I hoped that the girl we were told about would answer. We both stood there with suitcases hoping no one would step into the hallway from out of one of the other apartments. It was a tense moment. Soon a brunette with short, dark straight hair opened the door. She greeted us with a warm and friendly smile and spoke to us softly in German, quickly ushering us into the apartment; then she switched to accented English. After a quick greeting, she began to roll an upright piano away from a nearby wall. Moving the piano revealed a large hole in the wall behind it. She quickly motioned and told us to put the Bibles there. John and I quickly removed the bags full of literature from the suitcases and placed them behind the piano. We helped the girl roll the piano back into place. We wished her God's blessings, and she thanked us likewise with God's blessings. Then we left with four empty suitcases. We were there just a couple of minutes; total time at the apartment was probably under a minute. We quietly peeked into the hallway before exiting the apartment then slipped into the hall and down the stairs. Next, we needed to make it back to the van without bringing attention to ourselves. The same evasive techniques were utilized for our return, but we didn't need to stop because of the weight this time. The last of our Bibles and books had been delivered.

We made it back to the van where Lane had been waiting with no problems. The team headed toward the Charles Bridge, the Old Town Square, and the Prague Astronomical Clock to play tourist and spend some per diem money. That afternoon we left Prague and traveled west toward the German border. We drove to checkpoint Flomava, arrived around 4:30, and had a smooth exit through the checkpoint with only a few questions and a lite search of the van. Made it back into Germany around 5:30 that afternoon. It was good to be back in the West! A load was lifted and all three of us started to feel light-hearted as soon as we exited no man's land leaving the barbed wire, tank traps, machine gun towers, guards armed with AKs and patrol dogs behind us. All three of us wanted to sing, but held it back for a while. I felt like I wanted to shake the hand of the first American GI I saw and thank him for his service. I didn't see any...probably a good thing.

Was it ever good to be back on the west side of the Iron Curtain! After we drove ten kilometers, we broke into spontaneous singing. We sang patriotic songs and praise songs to God. We were grateful to the Lord for His faithfulness to us. We had experienced some close calls, yet God had been with us. We talked about some of the events which had happened and remembered the people we had met during our travels. We prayed for them as we drove. We headed on toward Nurnberg, stopped, and had dinner before getting there. By the time we finished dinner it was late, so we found a nice country road with a wide parking area off the side of the road and parked to sleep just outside of the city of Nurnberg. It was nice not to have to check in at a campground and register with communist authorities—a blessing of its own. That night as we settled, in we talked about Auschwitz where we had visited just a few days before. We talked about the Nazi War Crimes trials held in the city where we were that night. We had personally seen and been witnesses to the cruelty of totalitarian governments on multiple levels. It made us grateful for the U.S. and the freedoms we enjoyed. While not a perfect place, America was about one of the best places on the planet. What a journey we had just experienced!

The following day our team traveled west from Nurnberg to the Mannheim area on the autobahn. We then headed to the Rhine and drove north following the river from Mannheim to just south of Bonn. Being in Western Europe, it was almost as though you could taste the freedom in the air. It seemed as though the grass was greener and the skies were bluer. I believe I probably commented on that more than once on our trip back to The Farm in Holland. But to me it really did seem like the skies were bluer and the grass was greener in Western Europe than they had been Eastern Europe.

We drove down to a small village called Erpel near Linz on the east side of the Rhine, south of Konigswinter. We came to some towers which were all that was left of a large bridge that once crossed the Rhine. On the opposite west bank of the river was the town of Remagen.

There stood the bridge towers, which were all that remained of the Ludendorff Bridge, also known as the "Remagen Bridge." It was at this location on March 7th, 1945, where soldiers from the US Army 27th Infantry Battalion, as part of the U.S. 9th Armored Division captured the Bridge. It was at that place where a bridge head was established by the U.S. Army in WWII on the German-held side of the Rhine. Allied armored forces established a vital bridge head from where allied military forces were able to punch through and cross into the German heartland, shortening the war in Europe. They held their ground and constructed pontoon bridges up and downstream from the primary bridge. Units from the Army Corp of Engineers labored to increase the capability for armor and mechanized infantry to get across the river. The Bridgehead was a big psychological victory for the Allies in World War II. It was utilized as a route across the Rhine into the heart of Germany. The bridge stood for ten days before it crashed into the Rhine after it had suffered stresses from explosions and bombing attacks. The pontoon bridges continued to be used as transportation routes across the Rhine by U.S. and Allied Forces. It was from this point where the allied armies were able to press into the heart of Nazi-occupied Germany and destroy the forces of the regime controlled by Adolf Hitler. As I reflected on the history of that battle, I imagined that we had just finished with our own spiritual bridgehead of sorts into communist Eastern Europe.

As our team continued north along the Rhine near Konigswinter, we found a nice restaurant with outdoor seating overlooking the famous river. We enjoyed a good meal and a beautiful sunset with rays of sunshine turning the skies into hues of yellowish orange and pinks, making the sky look like a beautiful canvas work of art. The food was tasty and the view was great. The cool mild breezes off the Rhine were crisp and refreshing. We could almost taste the freedom in the air. What a special gift and blessing it is! Some of the Christians we had met told us how they prayed for us in the West. They prayed that the church in the U.S. would remain strong and free; I had heard that several times from Eastern European Believers. It was slightly disturbing for me to sit there in freedom thinking about the ones we had met and left on the east side of the Wall. I felt some remorse for having to leave them. We talked about what we had experienced over that dinner and about the decent Christian people we had met who had to continue living on the other side of the political Wall called the Iron Curtain. We would never forget our experiences in Czechoslovakia and Poland, and we would remember the persecuted ones the rest of our days.

It was to be our last night on the road together as a team. We had many blessings to be grateful for: a safe return to Western Europe, a good meal, a decent place to camp, and most especially the delivery of about a thousand Bibles and books to the other side of the Iron Curtain. It was special to be back where we did not have to register with police authorities where we stayed. Although happy to be back in the West, we could not help but think of what life was like for the Christians of Eastern Europe. We talked more about the people we had met and prayed for them after dinner that night. We held the memories of those we had only spent moments with close to our hearts, remembering them in conversation for days to come. I still think of some of them to this day. The next morning, we slept in a bit before getting up and heading back to Holland and our home base.

We were ready to get back to familiar territory and see our friends at "The Farm" who had become like family. We headed north to Cologne, Cologne to Acchen, Acchen to Leige. Then we went from Liege to Antwerp, from there north toward Breda, and from Breda we were on the home stretch. We arrived back at the Company Farm late that afternoon. We were glad to be rolling down the farm road toward the mission base. We sang praises to the Lord as we turned left down its dirt and gravel driveway road. We returned as a unified team with our spirit having remained intact and high. I would have traveled with either one of those guys again in a New York minute, so to speak, especially since one was from New York. But we were happy and relieved to be safely home with our support team and friends. We were greeted with warm hugs, and we could relax somewhat now. I was ready for a shower. It had been a successful trip. All our literature had been successfully delivered. Since it was a Saturday our debriefings would not begin until Monday. It was good to be reunited with our friends at base. John and I were looking forward to seeing Cees and Nel. Perhaps we would have some good Dutch home cooking that weekend, which of course would include some potatoes.

Mike and Sam, a newer member on staff, were planning on going to a movie in Rotterdam that night. Mike asked if I wanted to go along, but I had been on the road and was tired. After a refreshing shower, however, I tagged along to spend time with my buddy, Mike, and hang out with them. It was good to be back in Holland. I enjoyed a movie in English with Dutch subtitles. As I sat there watching that movie, I was still processing in my thoughts what our team had just experienced. Again, we had learned about the conditions Believers were living under in Czechoslovakia and Poland. After the movie with Mike and Sam, we went out for coffee and I shared some of our team experiences with them. Although I still needed to be careful with what I said, even in Western Europe. Discretion was still important. Since Mike was on the SIS team, I gave him part of an informal debriefing while sipping on some coffee at a sidewalk cafe. We went to church the next day. It was good to see my Dutch friends, the Bos family.

We began Monday by removing our gear from the van and cleaned it up. That afternoon we gave a verbal debrief to Hank. We started the written trip reports including vehicle issues and mileage, fuel used and costs, food, and other itemized expenses. Individually, we documented some of the various things we witnessed, including contact reports. God was moving on the other side of the Wall, but there were needs the Czechoslovakians and Poles had that we needed to report. Written narratives were continued the following day. We documented what we had learned about the arrests of Christians in our network in Slovakia and the pressure that others were under from the government. Yet, they kept pressing on and wanted more Bibles and literature. They continued to need and want support of various types in the form of food, clothes, money, printing equipment, and car parts. We also noted that things like letters and cards for Christian prisoners sent from the West with words of encouragement were helpful, which we were told.

    On August 31st shortly after John, Lane and I finished our debriefing reports, we learned that Solidarity demonstrations had broken out once again in several Polish cities across the country. Much later I learned that demonstrations were held in dozens of cities. A few people were killed with hundreds and thousands wounded having been beaten by the ZOMO riot squads. A little over four thousand people were arrested. The communist government squashed the anti-government Solidarity demonstrations at that time. Had the Polish communists not acted then, most likely Soviet tanks, Czechoslovakian military, and East German troops poised on the borders of Poland would have come in and done it for them.

    After our trip to Czechoslovakia and Poland, both John and I returned to duties around the base, and Lane returned back to the States. John continued helping Cees with vehicle maintenance, and I worked on printing and reproduction projects during the month of September. Both of us assisted with helping other teams prepare for trips into Eastern Europe.

    On September 29th, Mike and I left for Israel for a twelve-day trip. We visited with Brother Dave who was working on a Kibbutz in southern Israel. It was good to see him and spend time with him. We also visited with friends of Mike's in Jerusalem and Haifa who were teaching in Israel. We shared testimonies about what God was doing in Eastern Europe with two groups of Believers in Israel as a result of the contacts there. We were fortunate to be in Jerusalem during the Feast of Tabernacles and met Believers from countries all over the world; it was an interesting time. We visited the Dead Sea, the Sea of Galilee, the Wailing Wall, the Diaspora Museum, and the International Christian Embassy in Jerusalem while there. During the time in Israel, where we shared about conditions for some Christians in Eastern Europe with several people. We flew back to Holland where we went back to work at The Farm. After a few days I started to prepare for a return to the US.

Near the end of October, I had to leave my friends in Holland, which was tough. I had mixed emotions about leaving and returning to the U.S. I hated to leave close friends who had become like family, but was looking forward to seeing my loved ones at home. Mike Lee and John Murphy drove me to the Schiphol Airport outside Amsterdam. After giving them a bear hug at the boarding area I turned, walked through the security gate, and looked back at my two good friends. The expression on John's face looked as though someone had just died. I waved to them and stepped onto an escalator taking me down to another level proceeding to the boarding area. As I headed down that escalator tears welled up in my eyes and I nearly bit off my bottom lip to keep from crying. Leaving those two men who were like the brothers I had never had was a tough time for me. They were some of the best men I had ever worked with to this day.

After returning to the states and having a reunion with family, I shared testimonials in some churches and youth group meetings about our experiences in Eastern Europe. In those meetings, I shared about the circumstances of the Eastern European Christians. Then in early December I traveled to Mexico as part of a disaster relief team for a couple of weeks. During the day, our team worked to repair structures which had been damaged by hurricane gale-force winds. Our project was mostly removing what was left of damaged roofs and replacing them with new ones. After construction work during the day, in the evenings we would go out to villages in rural areas and show hygiene films and share testimonies. Then a local pastor would preach. I shared testimonies in a couple of villages about what was happening in Eastern Europe with Christians I had met and the importance of the Bible.

Upon returning from Mexico, I spoke to youth groups mostly and a couple of smaller churches. I plugged into a local church, ushered some, and participated in prayer groups. I did a little more speaking to some small student groups and in small churches. I spoke at a Biola College missions' conference sharing in a break-out session with Voice of the Martyrs' Sabrina Wurmbrand, the wife of the Romanian pastor Richard Wurmbrand referenced earlier.

After consideration of my options, I went back into the work force. I attended a couple of denominational churches, but then I began attending a non-denominational church and joined a missions' committee and prayer group. I participated in prayer ministries and attended regularly. It was a blessing to know we did not have to worry about informers and secret police being in the congregation. Concern about the plight of Believers behind the Iron Curtain and persecuted Christians remained in my mind. I continued to send financial support to EEBM and Open Doors for their efforts behind the Wall. Being in the U.S. was good but I missed my Dutch friends and the Americans I had worked with in Holland. My desire to return to help Eastern Europeans remained. I hoped for a return trip to Europe in the future as the timing and provisions worked out according to the Lord's plans and purposes. But it was not to be as soon as hoped.

More Important Than Gold, Silver and Precious Jewels

During the mid-80s, the situation for Believers in Eastern Europe continued to be on my heart. Our nation has truly been blessed by the Lord. But realizing the blessing of religious liberty we enjoy, I could not forget those behind the Wall who did not have it. I continued to contribute financially toward support efforts for the persecuted and the desire to return was ever with me. Until I could return, I sent money and prayed. Besides the church prayer team and missions' committee, I participated with different prayer groups. During the summers of '87 and '88 I was able to return to Eastern Europe.

Thankfully, the supervisor at my job saw the merit in my involvement helping the persecuted. He was sympathetic to the need for additional time away from work. So he approved leave of absence time off work to piggyback onto some vacation time. His action enabled me to return for short term service as a team leader. The following testimonies are stories from those missions.

During July of 1987, a team of four of us headed east from southern Holland for Czechoslovakia. We traveled to a village outside the city of Kosice on the far eastern side of the country, just a few kilometers from the Russian border. I had the privilege of seeing Brother Daniel once again, whom I had met a few years earlier when traveling with Bill Larson and Vance. We arrived outside the city at the village late on a Sunday evening around 9:00 p.m. The strategy we planned was for my teammate Jim and I to be dropped off at the edge of the village and for us to walk in. The other two team members, Mickey and Pricilla, would wait at a roadside pullout approximately a mile outside the village. We had previously reconnoitered the area and selected a road side pullout which would make for a good rendezvous location. After the meeting with the contact, Jim and I would make it back to the rendezvous point to hook up with the others. Our teammates dropped us off at the edge of the village about four blocks from our contact's hacienda style home and headed off.

We had prayed earlier asking the Lord for his protective covering for this meeting. As Jim and I approached to within two blocks of the house, we noticed it was very quiet; not one dog in the village had barked, possibly alerting someone with prying eyes. All was quiet, still, and peaceful. We hoped it would remain that way.

As we walked through the small village toward Brother Daniel's home, then into his courtyard, all had continued to remain quiet—no dogs barking, no human foot traffic, or vehicles. We were grateful as we sensed the Lord's presence with us. When we approached the front door of Daniels home, we could see that the door was mostly glass. We could see inside the house and saw an inner stairwell leading up to the second level. As we began knocking on the front door, we saw a middle-aged man come down the stairs. He flipped on the porch light, then immediately a huge smile crossed his face. He jerked open the door saying "Allelujah!" He grabbed us, giving us big bear hugs; we had not yet uttered a word nor opened our mouths to speak. Yet he had become animated, was hugging us, and proclaiming, "Alleluja! Alleluja!" Before we could even say a word, he started excitedly speaking in Slovakian to us. Neither Jim nor I understood a word. I inserted, "Bitte spreaken sie Deutch" so he switched to his limited German. He was still speaking very fast, and I couldn't keep up. So, I asked "Sprechen sie longsum, Bitte,Meine Deutch is knick zo gut." (Please speak slowly my German is not so good.) He slowed down and said, "Eine stunde, eine stunde," (one hour) and held up one finger. He began to slow down and explain, and we began to figure out that the hour before we arrived, they had been praying and asking God to send someone from the West with Bibles. As the story unfolded, we learned that they were leaving their village first thing early the next morning headed for Russia. Coincidentally, we just happened to have some Russian Bibles for them. He wanted to know if we could get the Bibles to them that night. We explained that we were going to need to walk back and find our team parked somewhere along the road, approximately two to three miles outside the village, then recover our Bibles, and return. Perhaps it could take two hours or more before our return. We would need to find our team, then get into our system (which we didn't tell him about), and bag up the Bibles. We had been planning on a drop the next day, so the Bibles were still in the system. He insisted that we come back that night. I explained again to him that it would be some time before we could make it back, and it was already late. He told us no problem and asked for us to return as soon as we could. He was insistent about it. After some discussion, we agreed to return later in the night, which could be after midnight. He stood up and said something akin to "We don't have much time." It was time to go so he escorted us to the door. He instructed us to drive our van right into the courtyard of his house, as it was late and there would not be police around that late on a Sunday night.

Jim and I left and headed back at a brisk pace toward the rendezvous point. We thought it would be over a mile down the road and figured that it could take us thirty minutes just to walk to the van. We turned left onto the upcoming street...still no dogs barking, no traffic, thankfully. We walked to the next block, then left again at the end of the street. All continued to remain quiet. We made it to the next block, turned right, and broke out onto the main road. Immediately we saw head lights coming slowly in our direction. The vehicle approaching us about was about a block away and driving too slow to be regular traffic. I thought that a vehicle driving that slow at that hour could only be the VB State Police patrolling the neighborhood. Jim and I locked arms over each other's shoulders, looking down at the ground. We slowed our walking pace and added a slight stager, like two close buddies who had been out drinking. The vehicle kept on coming slowly toward us. We were both concerned hoping it was not the VB. I don't know about Jim, but my heart rate was increasing and it wasn't from the brisk walk. As the vehicle got to within about twenty feet away, I glanced up and had a huge surprise! It was our vehicle and our teammates! Mickey was driving! Jim and I headed quickly to the van. I asked the driver to slide over, explaining what was going on. Jim jumped into the back. We were thankful and wondered what they were doing there. They explained to us they had been praying while waiting at the rendezvous point and felt the Lord leading them to drive back into the village very slowly.

Well, I knew they had heard from the Holy Spirit! Talk about timing!

I don't think it could have been planned and practiced with much better synchronization. We drove back into Brother Daniel's courtyard about five minutes after Jim and I had left. This time Daniel's wife came to the door. She wanted to know why we were back so soon, thinking we had returned because we forgot something, seeming slightly unraveled. She was not expecting us for a couple of hours. I explained that we had the Bibles! She seemed shocked showing an expression of disbelief. Still, not a dog had barked in the whole area. Everything continued to be quiet. Daniel showed up. I quickly backed the van close to a back door and we got into the system, with van curtains drawn. Then we pulled the Russian Bibles out of hiding, placed them in the thirty-gallon trash bags, and carried them into the home. Daniel acted as lookout. We quickly placed the Bibles in a storage room on the first floor. We unloaded over a hundred Russian Bibles and additional Christian books in record time. After giving them the Bibles as we stood around those bags, I noticed big tears rolling down his wife's cheeks. As we prepared to leave, Daniel asked that we pray together; we prayed thanking the Lord for His provision. After a short time of fellowship, we said our goodbyes wishing each other Godspeed.

As we were walking back to our van, a cat in a dark shed at a forty-five degree angle about forty to fifty feet to our right let out a loud blood curdling screech which sounded like someone or something had stepped on it, "Ye..weyow!"

That woke up what seemed to be every dog in the village. All of a sudden it sounded like about a dozen of them started barking simultaneously. Daniel quickly dispatched his son to check the outbuilding to find out what was going on. He rapidly turned to us and said, "Gehen Sie, Snell, Snell!" (You go quickly, quickly!) We broke into a quick step back to the van and jumped in. While the others were getting in, I started the engine, threw it into gear, and we were out of there! When driving away we heard dogs continuing to bark throughout the neighborhood as we rounded the corner headed out to the main road. We cleared the area and headed toward our camp for the night. It was a literature drop, made in record time. Normally, a drop was a one or two-day process. That exchange happened in just over an hour and a half of total elapsed time, an interesting event full of Providential timing. Amazingly, in just a few hours the several hundred Russian Bibles we had carried in would be inside the Soviet Union. All was by Divine appointment—God's timing at work.

One of our next contact meetings included Sister Anna of Czechoslovakia whose husband, a former pastor, we were not able to meet. They held youth camps for teens. He had been arrested and warned by the communists not to teach children under the age of 18 about Jesus. However, he continued to hold secret youth camps in the mountains. He was discovered again holding the youth camps and unapproved meetings. He was arrested and interrogated, which may have meant beatings. He was defrocked by the State. His approved state-approved Preaching License was revoked by the government. He was forced out of his state-approved pastoral position and placed in a job as a mail carrier.

We asked how they dealt with the fact that they had a call of God to youth and teens, when they had been prohibited by the communist government from doing just that. She replied, "Oh, we have four children," and with a twinkle in her eye and clever smile, she continued, "and they have many, many friends. We tell them all about Jesus."

In our visit with her, I asked what living in Czechoslovakia was like for them not having religious freedom. A puzzled look came to her and she replied. "I do not know what you mean. But, if it is what I think you mean, whether I live in a big mansion, this humble home, on the street, or in a prison cell...I have Jesus in my heart and no man can take that away from me. That is what makes me free." I did not know how to respond to what I had just heard. Mickey said something. And we thought we were there to help them! Their story brought the gracious convicting love of the Holy Spirit to my soul. I really didn't know what it was like to pay a price to serve the Lord. These people did. The honest humility we witnessed was convicting.

Later that afternoon after bringing her the Bibles which we had for them, she picked up one and clutched onto it, holding it tightly to her chest. Tears began to flow down her cheeks and she softly said as she wept, "These are more important to us than gold and silver, better than precious stones, jewels and diamonds. Thank you, thank you. God Bless you."

I was close to speechless, convicted about things taken for granted, like the multiple translations of Bibles I owned, the ease of attending church services, purchasing Christian books, and the comparative amount of religious liberty we had. We went there to help, encourage, and strengthen. But as I walked away from that home I felt humbled and challenged. Her testimony definitely had spoken to my heart. As we returned to our vehicle, being alert for the presence of secret police and informers, neither my teammate nor I said a word for quite some time for we walked along contemplating the things we had just heard and seen.

The Texas Medic and the Romanians

Upon returning to Holland the summer of '88, I was happy to be reunited with some of my Dutch friends. It was really great to see Cees and Nel, his wife, and kids once more. Also, being able to visit with Dutch friends from the church was special, I was able to visit with the Bos family again; it was good to see close friends. Seeing Hank and Mona was a blessing. Several of the old team members were no longer at the Company Farm, having moved on; but there were a few. After getting settled in, I met Hap and Iris. Hap was a confident Texan and former Korean War veteran. He had been a combat medic and Iris, his wife, was a retired army nurse involved in Texas politics. Since Dad was a Texan, and I had family in east Texas not far from their home, we began to hit it off, being familiar with some of the same places.

After a few days, I was given my assignment. I would be taking Hap and Iris into Romania as their team leader. It was their first trip to the other side of the Iron Curtain. Hap was a retired army colonel. This would be an interesting trip. My mission was to take them in where they would be meeting Romanian Christians and learn of the conditions for Christians wit in communist Romania. Hap and Iris would then be speaking at various Chapel services in Western Europe and the U.S. Upon returning to the States, they would share their experiences and the needs of the Christians in Eastern Europe. Hap, a decorated Korean War veteran and retired colonel, was able to gain access to several army post chaplains.

We would be taking in a few hundred Bibles and books of encouragement in the car's specialized compartment. The trunk of the small sedan we were driving was also packed full of extra food for our contacts. One interesting development for me was that we would be staying in motels. I had always camped before so this would be a little more luxurious, but possibly somewhat riskier. Oftentimes with luxury there is a price. The motels in Romania were often places where agents of the secret police apparatus frequented to monitor foreign visitors. The likelihood of picking up a tail increased for us significantly. Also, it was known that many of the rooms in the hotels were bugged and had hidden microphones, so we would need to be very cautious with our speech. Hap had a bit of a handicap, too. He walked with a limp when he tired, as the result of a flare-up from an old Korean War wound. He could not carry heavy loads long distances; thus I would not only be the team leader but the team "bag man." The political climate of Romania was getting more intense in the late 80s as Ceausescu tightened his grip on the nation. While some reforms were beginning to occur in other Eastern European countries Ceausescu did not want to lose control of his. There would be some challenges ahead for us.

The previous year on November 15th in the city of Brasov an estimated twenty thousand factory workers and some local citizens marched on the Communist Party Headquarters shouting slogans to overthrow the dictator. Specialized Securitate units and the military were brought in and the demonstration was put down by force. Fortunately, no one was killed. But approximately three hundred were arrested and the rest dispersed.

Romania had a force of approximately sixty thousand Secret Police which worked to maintain the power base of Ceausescu and the communist state keeping the people under control. This included religious and Christian activities. The despotic control of the communist regime was notorious for its harsh treatment of its German and Hungarian ethnic populations and Christians. Many Christians were considered to be enemies of the State. Some had property and homes confiscated, were placed in work camps and prisons, and were beaten and tortured in the Romanian Gulag. Some even died from the beatings.

During briefings and training sessions prior to leaving for Romania, we learned that the Romanian regime was destroying Bibles, even turning them into toilet paper. Later when meeting with a Christian brother during our trip, this was verified. A Christian we visited shared with two of us about a time when he had to visit a public toilet. After using the facility, he reached for the sanitary paper and noticed it had little dark flecks on it. Those turned out to be letters of the alphabet and parts of sentences. As he examined the paper more closely, he was able to decipher some lines which turned out to be scriptures. The printed lines on the toilet paper were verses from the Bible; of course he was deeply grieved. I can't imagine the depth of sorrow he felt, as he had shared how it grieved him. His own country was turning Bibles into use for dung. The thought of that caused indignation to rise in me and my blood to churn as well.

> (Note: In mid-1985 an article in the *Wall Street Journal* revealed that twenty thousand Bibles donated by the World Reformed Alliance for Hungarian Christians of the Reformed Church in Romania were intercepted by the Romanian government. It alleged that the regime confiscated the Bibles and turned them into toilet paper. Weeks later this was the topic of letters submitted to the journal. Congressman Mark Siljander asked for a cancellation of Romania's most favored national trading status. An ethnic Hungarian and Romania dissident, Laszlo Hamos, was quoted in the article in the journal. According to Ion Pacepa in his book *Red Horizons*, Ceausescu had previously been so angered by demonstrations organized by Hamos that Ceausescu had ordered him killed by professional criminals. Of course, this did not happen [6].

After arriving at one of our contact cities, Hap and Iris dropped me off for a walk down a Romanian street to set up a meeting with some Christians. My job was just to walk down the street and drop a message in the mail box of an intermediary contact so we could later meet with a Romanian Christian leader. It was a balmy August afternoon with overcast skies and an elevated humidity factor. The air was mostly hot, humid, and still. There were no air conditioners in Romania; most people were sitting outside on the steps or porches of their homes. I was fully aware of people watching me as I walked by, well over a mile from the mail box where I was to drop the message. It seemed as though every eye in that neighborhood was trained on me, watching my gate, the way I walked, sizing up my every move. Although somewhat experienced with traveling in Eastern Europe I was feeling rather vulnerable. Thoughts of informants and secret police kept flooding my mind. Attempting to be casual and trying not to appear out of place, I was not at all comfortable. I definitely did not feel like I was out for a nice evening stroll. I was trying not to feel nervous, let alone not feel out of place. A conversation I had with a European friend a few years earlier came to mind.

"Even if you dress like us we can tell you are from America."

"How is that?" I inquired.

"By the way you walk," was his response.

"By the way we walk?"

"Yes, you walk free. You smile, hold your head up, walk happy and proud."

That conversation flooded my mind while walking down that Romanian street. How do you walk as though you're not free went through my mind? I attempted to walk as though a little dejected with shoulders slumped and my head slightly bowed. I did not smile and tried not to look happy. My gaze was slightly directed toward the ground as I tried to maintain situational awareness. I didn't walk too fast, but I did not shuffle. I was not feeling particularly courageous, but exposed. So, I started to pray internally as I walked along. I couldn't think anything to pray; no spiritual Sunday morning prayers came to mind for sure. Only the simple request came, *"Lord, I don't know what to pray right now. You know what is going on, so I'm just gonna ask the same thing Brother Andrew (God's Smuggler) prayed. Lord, you made blind eyes to see, so I'm asking that somehow you make seeing eyes blind... that somehow these people do not see what they should not see and that you protect the Christians we are going to visit."* Interestingly, as I continued to walk toward that mailbox, the humidity must have hit its dew point for after a few short minutes it began to rain. The result was as you would imagine. Most of the people out on porches and steps went inside their homes. They could not report what they wouldn't be able to see. The Lord had provided protective cover once again and watched our back. Wow! Who says that there is no God which doesn't answer prayers on behalf of His people? Maybe there was some Romanian farmer out there praying for rain as well; all I know is that my prayer was answered too. I got a little wet, but it was well worth it.

As I neared the address where I was to drop the note in the intermediary contact's mail box, there was not a person on the street. I crossed the street to my right, glancing over my right shoulder as though checking for traffic. But more importantly, I was looking for anyone who appeared out of the ordinary behind me. The closer I came to the mail box checking the addresses, the more alert I was for out-of-place individuals who might be following me. I adjusted my gait somewhat as I neared the mail drop. I verified each address as I drew nearer to the drop box. There it was, the address which I had memorized, a mail box on a wall next to a side yard entry gate. Again, no front yards in this urban area existed. After checking my surroundings, I dropped the note with greetings and rendezvous time in the box. All the while this kid was hoping the contact had not moved, been arrested, or for some reason would no longer be living at that address. But as per the most recent information, I was at the right place. After my earlier experiences in Czechoslovakia and Poland I had concerns. I was hoping most especially that someone else other than the contact did not live there, who might tip off the police. I guess we would find out at 8:00 p.m. that night. It was a simple and brief note in English, "Greetings from the west, 8 p.m."

We returned at the designated time that night, with the continuing cover of rain which had gotten heavier. Hap dropped off Iris and I about a block away for the walk to the house coming in from the opposite direction from where I approached earlier. Not knowing whom we would meet, we remained alert for anyone who might be secret police lookouts or informants as we approached: Anyone on top of buildings, moving curtains in windows, someone peering out a window at us, or lurking in the shadows. Thankfully, it continued to rain. After a knock on the wall, a woman perhaps in her early to mid-thirties opened the door. She was tall, large, and big boned, but not rotund, with a bit of a peasant look. She was glad to see us and animated. We were relieved that our contact was there! She enthusiastically and warmly greeted us with big hugs. Then she told us that she and her daughter would lead us to her uncle. The four of us in two groups of two walked back toward the pre-designated meeting point with Hap. He pulled up simultaneously as we arrived at the corner. The rain was a great cover. There we piled into the little Opel. Five of us were crammed into the little car. Two were in the back seat with most of our luggage because the trunk was full of food. In the back seat there was actually only room for one, yet two squeezed into the narrow space in the back seat with three of us in the front two bucket seats. It was a full load. The contact's daughter, a fairly large woman, was on my lap, in the right front seat, as I sat in the shot gun position. She gave directions to Hap on where to go. Iris and the lady's daughter crammed into the small space in the back seat. Thankfully, it was dark and rainy which provided us a bit of concealment. Hap drove following the indirect route he was given by the woman. We headed toward the Romanian believer's home.

The man which we were about to meet had been a leading Christian musician and pastor in Romania. He had spent five years in prison. His crime was practicing his Christian faith. He walked with a significant limp, was handicapped, and could not stand for extended periods of time because of torture and beatings. While in prison, the guards broke his legs in order to keep him off of his knees in order to keep him from praying.

He was a talented musician; his gift helped him survive while in prison. He wrote several dozen songs while in prison, memorizing most; the songs and melodies were hidden in his heart. The music in his soul was something which helped him to endure. He made a handwritten song book including musical scores full of worship and praise songs he had sung while in prison. He put over three hundred fifty songs on paper after he got out of prison, writing them all by hand. While visiting with him in his home, we were blessed with being able to look at and hold that handwritten song book. He sang some of hymns out of it in a beautiful baritone voice just for us. There I sat holding a song book with three hundred fifty handwritten songs of beautiful music in a country where it could not be reproduced because of State repression. The music we heard was as sweet to the ear as honey would be to the palate. He played the piano with a crippled arm and hand, yet did not miss a note. The beauty of the music resonated in our souls. Praises to the Lord birthed out of prison. It was seasoned with peace, love, and humility. Even though we could not understand the words, the melodies were full of rich music of the soul full of love for God. His face radiated adoration for God. As I listened, I glanced up at the Colonel, he himself another kind of hero. The highly decorated Korean War veteran, who had received two Silver Stars and two Bronze Stars, had tears rolling down his cheeks. It was a special moment that words fail to describe.

As I sat there listening to the Romanian sing, I could not help but think about some of our experiences we had just getting there to visit with him in his own home. We did not have permission from the government to visit with him and his family, which the communist government required and most likely would have denied. It would have further placed him on the government radar screen and put him at further risk from the Ceausescu regime. We had to be covert in order to be there, just to visit with him and listen to his music.

I thought of the border crossing at checkpoint Vidin-Calafat between Yugoslavia and Romania. There while the border guard was searching our car, the female guard turned and asked me, first in Romanian and then seeing I didn't understand, in German:

"Do you have guns or Biblia?"

Not understanding the word for guns in German I asked her, "Wass?" (What?)

She said, "Haben sie, pistole?" (Do you have pistol, guns?) in a heavy accent with a sharp tone, while pointing her finger and saying, "Kennen sie"(know you).

"Bang, Bang,.. pistole," I replied, with a degree of forthrightness, "Oh, No!... No guns!

She said, "OK," not persisting with the question about the Bibles.

She stepped back to the rear of our little Opal and asked me to open the trunk. It held the LPG tank where the Romanian Bibles and books were stored. After opening the trunk, the guard asked me what we had in the trunk and began examining our food stores. We had extra food in the trunk destined for Romanian Christians. I was glad she was focused on the food and not the LPG tank, although she did ask about it. As the guard was going through the trunk search, I was remembering the instructions Cees had given me in Holland. He had told me, "If the border guards pay too much attention to the LPG tank and asks you to take it apart, say, 'No,' nicely. Do not agree to take it apart, let them do it. If they start to take these screws here out," as he pointed to some assembly bolts, "if they start to loosen these bolts you walk away! You walk away fast, no run, they will shoot you! If they loose this bolt, it go boom, LPG tank explode! You no run, walk away fast! You run, they shoot you! Remember this, very important!"

That was enough warning for me. As I was watching the guard fumbling around in our trunk, trying not to be focused on the LPG tank, those words kept circulating through my mind. After examining our food supplies; the guard turned around and told us we had too much food; instead of continuing an interrogation about weapon and Bibles she assessed a tax and charged us for the food. That did not make me happy. But considering all the alternatives, I was OK with paying the tax. I did not show it, but kept a straight face. I was just glad to get through the checkpoint and out of there having been cleared to pass into the country.

Continuing to sit in the Romanian musician's home listening to his music, my mind skipped back to days earlier when after getting into the country we needed to access the LPG tank and retrieve Bibles from the LPG system. We had to access the tank system to get Bibles and books for the very people we were visiting that night. We had been driving on a rough road and encountered road construction where traffic moved slowly. We were in a narrow mountain pass with hillsides to our left and a river to the right. The hillside was somewhat wooded, but ahead up to our left we could see a slopping grassy meadow through the tree line above us. It would be a good place to open the system and prepare for our stops. Up head we saw a dirt road that turned off up toward the meadow. We took the road and drove up the hillside into the meadow. Trees and bushes somewhat obscured the view from the road way. We drove the car up the hillside and turned a buttonhook U turn, facing the little Opel toward the flow of traffic. We were approximately one hundred fifty to two hundred feet up the hill from the road way. We had positioned ourselves in such a way that only someone in an airplane or on the peak of that hill above would be able to see into the trunk. We stopped, got out, and opened the trunk, pulled out a tarpaulin, spread it on the ground and began to prepare a diversionary picnic. Anyone below us on the road way would see three people preparing and enjoying a picnic lunch. While Hap kept watch, and as he handed food stuffs and picnic items to Iris, I removed the sleeve of fuel from the mostly hollow LPG tank, giving us access to the storage area which held the books and Bibles. Intermittently I handed the Colonel lunch stuff, a jar of jam, some peanut butter or bread. Then I returned to pulling out Bibles and books, placing them in bags, then rearranged luggage and supplies. Part of the activity included Hap and I taking our clothes out of the suitcases and placing them in bags. While doing that, one of us would hand Iris more picnic stuff, like more bread or one of the various condiments. Hap and I covered the Bibles with clothing and supplies.

Iris made some pretty good ham and cheese and PB & J sandwiches that day, as she took her time spreading the peanut butter and jelly or placing the extra cheese and lunch meats on slices of bread. This while either Hap or I would hand her utensils or food stuffs while the other worked rearranging our supplies, alternating the time in the trunk.

Shortly after we removed the Bibles and I replaced the rectangular fuel tank sleeve in the hollowed LPG tank, a lone man pulled to a stop just down the hill from us. He moved over to the side of the road. He was in a light tan sedan which looked something like a knock off of a 1962 Chevrolet Biscayne. Hap and I sat down with Iris on the drop cloth and we all enjoyed our lunch in view of the agent just below us in the tan sedan. Who knows perhaps he was assigned to us because of the extra food at the border. We would never know. But what we did know is that we were being followed and would need to be very cautious and discreet, exercising extreme caution when attempting to meet contacts. While we were having our picnic, rearranging supplies and placing Bibles in the suitcases, he sat below us acting like he was waiting for the construction work on the road. But several groups of cars passed though the detour while he sat there, appearing to read a newspaper, all the while glancing up at us occasionally. He was a plainclothes "Securitate" secret police watching us.

While having our leisurely picnic, we made causal conversation about our lunch and talked about the beautiful countryside. We managed to redistribute our supplies and hid the Bibles in our suitcases without seeming to appear out of the ordinary. We had removed our clothes from the suitcases and placed the books and Bibles in bags then put them in the suitcases, all the while appearing to have a nice leisurely picnic. We enjoyed some good sandwiches that afternoon, while handling the Bread of Life. Our position on the hillside had placed us on the high ground so anyone observing us from below could not see what we were doing in the trunk. In this case, that someone below us had all the behavioral characteristics of the Secret Police. We kept the Bibles below the level of the trunk opening while redistributing and repackaging them. A few trees and some bushes down the hill had partly shielded us from view as well. The secret police agent left after we finished our lunch, and began replacing our stuff and the tarp. Our high ground strategy had paid off. The agent could not see what we were doing in the trunk, and our actions made us appear like we had just stopped to take a break for lunch, a common occurrence along the roadways of Europe. Fortunately for us he did not drive on up the dirt road toward us. After we finished lunch, replaced our supplies, and drove away from that spot we kept our eyes open for that agent or anyone following us. The Lord had been with us as we sought to be "as wise as serpents and as innocent as doves."

Thinking about the border crossing and our diversionary picnic, then the evasive actions we had taken just to visit this notable Christian was an experience which had impact on us. This Believer had been tortured in prison or his faith. Hearing his testimony, translated for us by the young woman, and listening to him sing, blessed us like few others have been blessed. Few in the West have experienced such things. I wish I could somehow capture the moments, bottle them up, and pass them along to you. Having to operate clandestinely, meeting discreetly, exercising caution just to visit this Believer, worship, and pray with him in his own home is hard for us in this country to imagine. Why was the communist regime so afraid of Christianity and this humble man? His crime was believing in a religious philosophy of peace and forgiveness, different from their philosophy of global domination. He was one who believed in God, loved Him, and loved his neighbor. This was further evidence to me that the communists were not only intolerant of Christianity but simply God haters, although they claimed otherwise. How fortunate we have been in the U.S. to have the religious freedoms we enjoy.

While many do attempt to repress truth by fear, intimidation, coercion and abuse, truth will eventually prevail; many have suffered in the quest for it. The politics of fear, control, and power embraced by communists did not stifle what was in that man's soul. The love for God and the desire to worship Him was not taken from this man even after five years of prison, beatings, and torture.

The costs were many for this brother who had been tortured because of his faith, but he had not bowed to his sufferings. He continued with steadfast perseverance and hope in his dedication, devotion, and service to the Lord and God-fearing people.

We left his home headed back to our hotel, after spending well over an hour visiting with him and his family. The three of us were really touched as a result of the impact of that visit. We felt blessed and simultaneously convicted. Hap drove again as we took his daughter home, then found the way to our hotel. We were aware that the rooms most likely were bugged or a secret police agent may be lurking in the lobby. We could not talk then much about what we had just experienced until we found time when driving on the country roads. Hap and Iris would share of this experience in chapel services throughout West Germany and the U.S.

Hap, Iris and I had another contact in the northern part of the country which proved to be as interesting two days later. We were to meet up with the Budia family, where we would make arrangements to drop off a few books and Bibles and also gather information about the circumstances for Christians. We hoped to verify the truth about the reported destruction and razing of a few Romanian villages do to Ceausescu's State collective plan of Systemitization.

Our team plan was set to have Hap stay with the vehicle and drop Iris and I off for the long walk to the Budia home. Hap had suffered a war wound in Korea when a jeep he was driving was blown up by a landmine. Luckily for him he had lined the floor of the jeep with sand bags which he attributed to saving his life. Years later a combination of the wound and an arthritic condition had impacted his ability to walk long distances. He had a significant limp when tired; long walks exacerbated the condition.

Hap dropped Iris and I off after we reconnoitered part of the area and established a rendezvous point. We would meet up with him at a predetermined location along a river parkway in an hour to hour and a half. Our join-up location was down a frontage road on the far side of a river near the contact's home. On our approach to the house and on our return trip Iris and I would need to cross a bridge over the river which ran though the city. It was a bit of double jeopardy, but it seemed to be the best route in order to leave Hap at a decent standby location at a park along the river. The rendezvous location would appear to be normal to the casual observer. A man sitting in a car along a river parkway would not look out of place and hopefully not draw attention. I had a light backpack and emptied it, placed my stuff in the trunk of the car, then filled the ruck sack half full with Bibles. I filled the remaining space with canned foods for the family. Iris and I walked the three blocks to the Bridge. All seemed well; we had not detected anyone following us. There was little foot traffic on the bridge sidewalk. We crossed the river, then turned left onto the first street headed away from Hap toward the neighborhood where the Budia family lived. After a couple of right and left hand turns down a few blocks. we came to the address we had memorized. We hoped that it was still current information and the family still lived there. It was late morning when we arrived; no one was home. Other apartments were close and there was potential for informants in the neighborhood. We had to walk along a corridor with neighbors on the right side of their home to access their porch. It was not wise to sit and wait, and we did not want to increase the risk of exposure because of multiple visits. I elected for us to go back and meet up with Hap, then come back in late afternoon. We did not retrace our route back to the bridge but varied it slightly. But we would still need to cross back over that bridge on the return to hook up with Hap. On the way back to the vehicle, Iris and I emerged from behind the trailing side of a brick building located on the river front onto the sidewalk leading up to the bridge. As we turned right heading toward the bridge, we both simultaneously spotted a Romanian cop standing on our side of the sidewalk on the far side of the bridge. Iris broke step, backing behind the cover of the building on the street corner. She whispered with urgency "What do we do now?" As I was wondering the same thing, I uttered a quick prayer in my mind, *OK Lord, what now,* while quickly considering our options. I knew that to go the opposite direction would mean we would be headed away from Hap and into territory with which we were completely unfamiliar. We didn't have a map and knew the next bridge crossing over that river was a sizable distance away from us. The river was a natural barrier between us and Hap. We didn't know how far down stream we would have to go before finding another crossing over the river. It meant walking several kilometers through the city increasing the possibility of being spotted by other officers or informers as well. It would take a considerable hike for us to make it to another bridge across the river. That would significantly delay the rendezvous time with Hap, causing him worry. But more importantly, it would increase his exposure time as well and with it the risk of being spotted by an informant or the "Securitate." If he were noticed sitting in one place for too long, his risk factors went up significantly. While quickly assessing our circumstances, a scripture suddenly popped into my mind, "The wicked flee when no one is pursuing but the righteous are bold as a lion." (Proverbs 28:1) A sense of boldness hit me. I couldn't even remember where I had read that scripture, or where the text was located. But by the suddenness, timing, and content, I believed it was from the Holy Spirit. I quickly whispered back to Iris:

"Stay with me; we're gonna cross the bridge. Stay close to me, do not look at the cop, look at me, move your lips like we are having a conversation as we approach. But do not let any sounds come out, as we get near to him. When we get close to him, continue to look at me! Do not look at him and do not talk."

I stepped back around the corner of the building and headed to the bridge toward the cop on the far end, with Iris sticking right with me. We continued our causal walk straight for the far side of the bridge, where the officer was standing right on our path, although he was not looking in our direction. He was standing at the corner of an intersection, just on the other side of the bridge. He had only glanced toward our direction.

As we approached I mumbled a quiet prayer to the Lord and we prayed as we continued. Iris mouthed something of little importance about the weather or something to appear as though in conversation. When we got to within several feet from the communist drone, we quit any resemblance of speech. About that time two teen girls walked up to the cop from the far side of the road and began talking with him. He was focused on the two girls and didn't pay much attention to us. The two of us walked right past him with me carrying half a backpack of Bibles hidden under the remaining half of canned food goods. Although I had a twinge of tightness in my gut, I knew the Lord was with us. As we walked by the officer, he did not even seem to notice us. He kept talking with the two girls who had captivated his attention. When we reached the corner of the intersection still in view of the officer, we turned left. We walked up the road and disappeared down a bend in the road, then continued toward our link up with Hap. We spotted him sitting in the little Opel near the location we had agreed upon, a long row of trees near the water front not far off the river. There was no one near him; we did not see anyone loitering in the area or curtains move in the surrounding apartments as we approached. It appeared that the coast was clear, and we were good to go for a direct approach to the vehicle. We hooked up with him and were relieved at the reunion. We got in, and he drove us away from his nice cozy spot close to the river.

Later that afternoon we located another rendezvous spot for Hap to park not far from the previous one. Then Iris and I struck out on route to the Budia home once more. This time it was closer to the dinner hour. Upon our arrival at the family home we were warmly greeted. We gave them the Bibles and canned goods that we had with us in my rucksack. They asked us to share a meal with them. We accepted under the condition that we could not stay long. Iris and I had an exceptional visit with the family, which lasted about an hour. Over dinner with them we learned that the family's oldest son, a young man in his twenties, had fled Romania months before as a refugee fleeing the oppressive regime of Nicolae Ceausescu.

Mr Budia told us that his son had confided in him he was going to flee to the West, but did not tell him the specifics of his plan. The father and son had worked out an agreement. The communists often punished the families of defectors. Sometimes family members were arrested and placed into prison, where they endured torture and suffering for the deed of the family member who fled. They had agreed that after his son did not return home for two days, the father would go to the police and file a missing person report asking them for help in locating his son. The son fled, and after two days the father carried out the preconceived plan.

They later learned from a mutual family friend that their son had made it to the U.S., where he was living in southern California with an ethnic Romanian family. While having dinner, Brother Budia asked if we could relay a message to their son when we returned. He wanted us to tell their son that they were OK and did not suffer any harm from the communists after he had left the country. I heartily agreed to contact their son. Mrs Budia went into the back room and came out with a small piece of paper with an address written on it. She copied the address onto another piece of paper which I hid on my body for our return to the vehicle.

After hiding the address, the young man's little sister a girl perhaps the age of ten or eleven came up to me and sweetly thanked me in English for bringing them Bibles and food. She also asked us to tell her brother "hello" and that she loved him and missed him. As she came up to me and said thank you, it touched my heart that this family was separated because of political oppression. I told the family I would see their son and brother and take word to him of their welfare.*

* *A few weeks after returning to the U.S, I traveled to southern California and located the little girl's older brother. There I passed on greetings and well-wishes from his dad, mom and little sister. I was able to share with him, as his dad had requested, that his family was doing well, and hadn't suffered any repercussions from the communists after he left. That was a special meeting. It was then that I learned his side of the story. The younger Budia shared with me that a girlfriend had taken him by car into neighboring Hungary, also a communist country but relaxing in its attitudes toward the West. There they drove south*

to a remote location along the Danube River. She dropped him off, and after hugs and tears he swam across the river, evading military patrols. He made it into what was then Yugoslavia and was able to make it to a U.S. Consulate where he sought political asylum. After weeks in the Consulate, U.S. officials released him to a sponsoring Romanian family in California. I felt privileged with getting to be a small part of the story, by passing on to him the good news about the welfare of his family, of which he was unaware, due to mail censorship in Romania during era the of the communist regime. His family could not write to him nor he to them for fear of repercussions against them.

That evening Iris, Hap and I made it back to a hotel room and registered with the authorities. I was able to retrieve the Budia son's address from Iris, then copied it in code inside a Robert Ludlum novel I had brought along to read. As most travelers are aware, it helps to have reading material for the down times, like waiting at airport terminals and checkpoints.

The next contact, set for the following day, in another city, was to be for Hap and Iris. I would stay with the vehicle. This was an information gathering contact; primarily just a few books were given Christian couple they visited. I dropped them off close enough for Hap not to be stressed by a long walk, and would meet them at a park about three blocks away. They would not have to carry any additional weight, in the form of books or food on the return to the car. Hap and Iris would be interviewing a couple about the conditions in Romania for Christian families, so they could return to the U.S. and share their experiences and findings with church groups.

I dropped them off a block or two from the Romanian home and around the corner from a park about three blocks away from the contact's location. After dropping them off, I drove to our prearranged meeting spot at the far eastern edge of a park with a lot of trees. It was the afternoon and I was in the shade of some trees as the sun inched its way toward the western sunset.

As I sat in the car a vulnerable feeling worked on my nerves. It would be better to be walking. I sat in that little car ready to go the minute Hap and Iris returned. Perhaps I would have been better off relaxing in the park. There were only a few people there and just a few pedestrians walking down the sidewalks north of where I sat. I sat there reading part of the *Parsifal Mosaic*, by Ludlum, occasionally taking a break checking maps and travel guides.

After having been there for what seemed like an hour, I continued to feel uneasy; yet I tried to maintain a relaxed composure as I sat in that vulnerable position and read. Then, a slight, dark haired Romanian character wearing a disheveled dark shirt and pants began to walk toward the car. He was coming from across the street headed to the left front of the car. It was a hot day in August so I had the windows down of the little Opel. The guy approached and began to speak to me first in Romanian. Then seeing that I didn't understand, he switched to German and said in his thick Romanian accent:

"Woher kommen sie?" (Where do you come from?) He proceeded, "Kommon sie aus die Netherlands?"

"Nien,"

"Kommon sie aus Kanada?"

"Nien," "**Uu, S, Ah,**" I responded.

He leaned over closer to the window, lowering his voice asking, "Haben sie wissskkey?"

"Nien, I replied"

"Haben sie, ciggaarettes, playboy?"

"Nein," I reply again.

He then reached deep into his pocket pulling out a huge roll of cash of Romanian "Lei" dollars. He leaned in closer, lowering his voice more and asked,

"U wanna changa monnie?"

I responded, "No thanks."

In German, he persisted, "Give deal."

I asserted, "Don't you know it is against the law in your country to change money!"

He was trying to get me to do a black market currency exchange. That encounter had "Bad Deal" and "Set-up" written all over it. We had been warned and briefed back at The Farm about illegal currency exchange and stings by the police. With my response to him about exchanging money being against the law, it startled him and he walked off irritated. I kept my eye on him. He walked about half a block, going up to another guy who was coming toward him. The other guy was more nicely dressed. He was a polished looking guy with a cosmopolitan look, clean pants, a white shirt, unfastened at the top two buttons, having a lower neck line, revealing a gold chain around his neck. He was also wearing a nice high-dollar watch. He had a slight swagger in his gait and walked directly to the other guy in a confident manner. I sat there watching those two characters talk over the top of my book. The first guy headed back in the direction the slick dude had come from. The more polished looking guy walked confidently several yards straight up to my car window and repeated the same thing the first guy had asked. I was thinking about then, *Oh, so the trainee didn't score, so now the teacher is giving it a shot.*

"Woher kommen Sie, aus die Nederlands?"

"Nien!" I replied.

"Kommen Sie aus Kanada," he asked.

"Nein!" was my reply, short and direct.

The two guys had to be secret police trying to set me up. The second guy was using the same line of questioning as the previous guy, almost word for word. It was a canned speech. He came to the last part of his spiel; and exactly like the first guy, he leaned in close to the car window lowered his voice, then pulled out a big roll of cash; then as I expected, said, "Wanna changa money?" This guy didn't know that I had been briefed about this kind of set up. The Romanian Secret Police was known for setting up foreigners with black market money exchange deals. After the traveler took the bait, they would bust them, haul them off to jail, fine them, and take the belongings they wanted. After interrogation, they would either keep them in jail for a short time or kick them out of the country as "persona non grata." Knowing that, I looked the undercover agent squarely in the eyes and with a direct, matter of fact, non-antagonistic tone said, "Don't you know it is illegal and against the law to change money in this country?" I didn't need to continue any further. He immediately grumbled something under his breath with a tone of exasperation, turned, and walked off, back in the direction from where he had come. But that was not the end of it.

As I sat there watching the guy leave, the drama continued to unfold. The second polished looking agent walked back to the first guy who was walking toward him. I could see both of them easily, about a block out. I guess because they were so used to controlling people, they were sloppy and not even trying to be discreet. The slick looking dude spoke briefly and crisply to the first guy, appearing to lecture him having a sour, stern expression on his face. He walked off leaving the younger guy there. Soon the first younger guy just sat down on the curb. He was sitting there keeping an eye on me, what seemed like a sloppy surveillance to me.

It was obvious now they were secret police, and I was being watched by the less experienced guy. It was almost laughable. If I had been watching what just unfolded on a movie, I would have chuckled. But I was the one under surveillance, with the possibility of Hap and Iris coming back at any time, increasing the possibility that the Romanians might see them and jot down the car license plate, marking us and follow us. So, it was not funny. It never does pay to under estimate your opponent. I had no cell phone; those were not in common use yet and those few in use were big and bulky. I could not warn Iris to meet them somewhere else. So, I didn't have a lot of choices. I could have left the scene driving around in circles looking for them, but that would not have been smart. What if they came back another route and I missed them? I had to sit there and wait with that guy watching me. Hap and Iris were still gone and that location was set as our rendezvous point. I sat there and read for what seemed to be an eternity. It was probably just over an hour. But I was definitely not comfortable. Obviously it was not a good situation. Our rendezvous location was under surveillance. Hap and Iris could be walking up at any minute. I could not leave, and I certainly did not want him seeing Hap and Iris walk up. I prayed that the guy would leave. But he just kept sitting there on the curb. I was being watched and he wasn't sly about it. So I just kept reading. Occasionally I looked at a map of Romania, attempting to appear like I was taking a break from a trip. As I prayed quietly to myself, something like "Lord, make that guy leave," I remembered that sometimes nonverbal communication can influence the subconscious thoughts of others. Also, I was aware that Hap and Iris would be returning to the car out of the south or southwest. I knew that the guy watching the car would see them approach and get into the car. That would most likely really increase the surveillance on not only us but the neighboring area as well. That would not be good for the Christian family who lived a few blocks away. Perhaps it would enable the police to backtrack to the contact's home because of previously known Christian activities. It could even lead to interrogation. We were in a pickle.

Occasionally, I intentionally started to slightly exaggerate looking at my watch every few minutes, so that my movement would be noticed. Then I looked off into the distance through the park into the north or northeast away from the area from which Hap and Iris would be approaching. I would stare at nothing in particular, taking a long and hard look. I leaned forward and to the side somewhat, directing my gaze around the multitude of trees in the park. I acted like I was looking for someone in that direction. Finally, after about twenty minutes, the Romanian got up and walked off into the park, headed to the north. He disappeared out of sight. Shortly thereafter Hap and Iris arrived out of the south. As they were getting in, I started the car, made a quick one hundred eighty degree U-turn and we were out of there. While headed out of there, I quickly explained to them what had happened while they were gone, telling them that we needed to put some distance behind us. Being a former combat medic, Hap and his wife Iris, a former army nurse, remained curious, yet stalwart. As we left the city, we prayed for protection of the Believers and for our own covering from the Lord. In their meeting, they learned more about the two Romanian villages being razed and the inhabitants of the two towns being relocated into State housing projects. They would be sharing about it in public meetings in the West.

They were encouraged about their meeting with the Romanians, and said it went well. They said they had received a good testimony from the couple to share Stateside. They also added that they had not seen anyone following or watching them. We cleared the area not seeing anyone following us in tan vehicles or seeming to tail us, but remained cautious about the possibility. Hap and Iris had found out about the needs of the Romanian Christians for that area and brought back a newspaper article verification of villages being demolished. A few days later we crossed out of Romania into Hungary. The crossing went smoothly, although the Hungarian border guards did remove the back seat of the car and check under it; but that was a routine practice at times. We exited Romania not only having delivered Bibles and food, but with information verifying that Bibles were being turned into toilet paper and villages were being destroyed to make room for communist collective industrial sites. Hap and Iris had obtained a newspaper which had an article with photographs about the State relocation program and the razing of two villages for taking back to the mission. The names of the villages were mentioned in the article.

The border guard at the Hungarian checkpoint Bors about thirteen kilometers northeast of Oradea removed the back seat of our car during the search at the border. But the paper was hidden away in our system. We left the country, having cleared the Hungarian-Romanian border. We breathed a sigh of relief to be out of Ceausescu's Romania. But we knew full well we were not home yet. There was still our traverse through Hungary with peasant wagons and gypsy caravans on the roadways and then the exit at the Hungarian border crossing into Austria. The communists of Hungary were beginning to relax their grip on the nation so the crossing shouldn't be too intense. At that point, our biggest concern was for safe travel.

Later that evening we found ourselves in the "Paris of Eastern Europe." We enjoyed a relaxing ethnic meal at a restaurant in the beautiful city of Budapest. Our primary mission had been accomplished. As we enjoyed our dinner, we thought of those we had met and left behind. We still could not openly speak about the purpose of our trip or the people we met. We did lift them up in prayer later when back in the car. The meeting with the Budia family really stuck with me, as I thought about the little girl and her big brother she loved and missed.

In Budapest, Hap, Iris and I played tourists and purchased a few souvenirs for friends. We were unwinding and enjoying the beauty of Budapest. We were nearer the border of Austria and could almost smell the freedom being blown in on the jet stream from the west. We were grateful the Lord had gotten us into and out of Romania safely. Hap and Iris would have a lot to share about on their speaking tours.

The next day after the time in Budapest, we found ourselves at the German village of Erpel on the east side of the Rhine River; again I was at the remains of the ruins of the Remagen Bridge. It was a third visit to the site for me but being there with a WWII and Korean War Vet made it more memorable. For Hap, the veteran of WWII and Korea, standing at the location where Allied Armies crossed into the heart of Nazi German was a special occasion. As we walked around the location we took several pictures of the Rhine and what remained of the famous bridge. While taking in the scene, I took Hap's picture and he flashed the "V" for victory sign. A smile on his face and the twinkle in his eye reflected an expression of victory and thankfulness. The "V" for victory was common during the World War II era. It was a gesture by which one generation communicated a special sentiment to the next generation without a word exchanged. God had given us protection and we thanked Him that evening. Our next objective was to make it safely home to report what we had seen and heard. When driving northwest down the autobahn headed back to the mission base, Hap shared more of his Korean war stories. As a combat medic he had saved many lives. Perhaps inside his soul he felt like he had helped save some Romanian lives too. The Bibles we took in contained the Gospel message of eternal life, hope, and peace.

Upon our return to Holland, Hap, Iris and I were grateful to be back at the base. We rejoiced with the rest of the team for our successful trip. We thanked God for it. We prayed for those whom we had met as well and pledged to ourselves that we would always remember them. We completed briefings and trip reports. I returned home to the U.S. Hap and Iris stayed on in Europe traveling around Germany, speaking at chapel services. Shortly after my return to the States I traveled to southern California to visit with the Budia's son, taking word to him about the welfare of his family. After Hap, Iris, and I continued our separate ways, the work of EEBM continued, ministering support to the Underground Church and dissidents in Eastern Europe until the Wall of separation between East and West came down in 1989.

The Wall Comes Down

During the spring of 1989, I was again making plans for leave of absence time from work for another return trip to Eastern Europe. I had contacted the mission to make arrangements for a trip in late summer or early fall. Things were looking good for another trip. I was contacted by the mission and given a green light to return. Then the transmission went out in my truck, and the work load at the job went up. It looked like I would have to postpone the trip into Eastern Europe. I had to call the mission and cancel. It was certainly a disappointment. But I hoped to make an excursion into Eastern Europe the following year. That trip was not to be.

While monitoring CNN news during the summer and fall of 1989, I was seeing that things in Eastern Europe were changing. Cracks in the Berlin Wall were beginning to widen, and the Iron Curtain was developing significant fissures. I began to ask myself if these were the events which would bring the freedom spoken of by some Christians whom we had visited. A few had shared of prophecies heard in their church groups about the fall of communism coming to Eastern Europe.

A perfect storm for Eastern Europe had been developing. Several forces had merged in recent years to impact the reform movements on Eastern Europe and the Wall. The Catholic Church's Pope John Paul II, Karol Wojtyla, was a native of Poland and had experienced living under the oppression of the NAZIs in the 1940s during WWII. He had worked as a slave laborer in a quarry and had to study in an underground Seminary for the priesthood. Once again under the communists, he experienced the oppression dictated by one-party humanistic socialism while a priest. He rose to the position of Archbishop of Krakow while being active in human rights issues in that region. After being appointed the first Polish Pope, he continued his advocacy for religious freedom and human rights. A 1979 visit to Poland he spoke about the Cross of Christ and the hope of the Cross infusing the Polish people with renewed hope and vigor. The Christian message of Christ's blood shed on the cross for forgiveness of sin, with the hope of eternal life, not only aroused the people, but also provided fertile soil for the growth of the Solidarity movement throughout the country.

The Polish Workers' Solidarity Movement while operating somewhat underground initially became openly resistant in the early 1980s, resulting in the imposition of martial law by the communist government in December 1981. But even after hostile treatment by the communist authorities, the movement persisted underground in its activities toward more reforms and freedom for Polish workers and the people.

In the late 1980s Catholic priests, students, Protestant ministers and dissidents continued to quietly resist with underground congregations and movements throughout Poland and Eastern Europe. But they were also beginning to become more emboldened and speak out more openly against the communists.

President Ronald Reagan, a staunch anti-communist conservative, and Margret Thatcher from the British Parliament's Conservative Party and the leadership of West Germany had joined forces. Prime Minister Thatcher from the United Kingdom like Reagan was an outspoken anti-communist. The U.S. and British governments under Reagan and Thatcher continued to pressure the Soviets with military spending and placement of weapons in Western Europe.

In June 1987, Ronald Reagan standing at the Brandenburg Gate in Berlin proclaimed to the people of Germany for the leader of the Soviet Union to hear, "Mr. Gorbachev, tear down this Wall." The pressure was on the USSR and the communists to change. Just as importantly the cry for freedom in the hearts of their own people was impacting the Wall of separation. The ability to act independently, think outside the box, write without censorship, creatively develop and grow, explore and apply new ideas was screaming to be released. Those cries of the human heart would not be restrained. The Wall which the communist dictators of Central and Eastern Europe had worked to maintain for decades was beginning to crumble.

In East Germany, Hungary, Poland and Czechoslovakia churches became meeting places for intellectuals, students, dissidents, and freedom seekers. The churches became locations where social reform, religious freedom and the Solidarity movement were discussed. Throughout Poland, Czechoslovakia and East Germany people met in churches, coffee houses, in homes, and on campuses in discussion groups to talk about the new *Perestrokia* and *Glasnost* policies established by Mikhail Gorbachev. What did it mean for their future? When could they openly express their options which differed from the communist elites? When would they have free multiparty elections? When could they engage in business, free enterprise, and open free trade with the West?

However, in Romania Ceausescu continued to use the Securitate to crack down on the people and enforce his Stalinist styled regime. But the people were beginning to murmur louder and complain more openly about the government even in that harsh regime. I had heard some of it myself by Romanians on the street, just a few months earlier in 1988. Even a few brave pastors began to speak out against the tyranny of the Ceausescus in Romania. Men like Peter Dugalescu and Laszlo Tokes were boldly outspoken The stage was being set for change in all of Eastern Europe.

In February 1989, the Hungarian Communist Party had sanctioned independent political parties. Then in April 1989 pressure from the Solidarity movement resulted in free elections being announced for Poland. On May 2, 1989, Hungary tore down an electrified fence at the Austrian border. On June 4, 1989, the Communist Party of Poland was defeated in open elections as the leader of Solidarity Movement, Lech Walesa, obtained the majority of votes for President. In parliamentary elections Solidarity candidates won decisive victories.

In July hundreds of East Germans sought political asylum in the West German embassy in Hungary. Nine Hundred East Germans fled into Austria from Hungary in what was called the Great Escape, or the Great Picnic.

Early in August 1989, communists in Poland came into agreement for procedural change enabling Solidarity leaders to take control of the governments.

In August Hungary opened its borders into the West, including Checkpoint Sopron into Austria. It was at that very border I had made my first crossing into the communist Eastern Europe in late 1980, riding in a van carrying a thousand Russian and Romanian Bibles and some

Hungarian Bible studies. Then in 1989, the Iron Curtain was initially opened at that very border crossing location. East Germans began pouring south into Hungary, then northwest into West Germany.

On September 10, 1989, Hungary granted permission for the hundreds of East Germans at the West German Embassy in Budapest to flee to West Germany. A huge fissure in the Iron Curtain with the eventual fall of the Berlin Wall occurred, thanks to the Hungarians.

September 11th saw the founding conference of a prodemocracy group in East Germany. In September East Germany closed its borders, completely forbidding foreign travel to Hungary. This resulted in the beginning of demonstrations in the streets of East Germany. The East Germans had seen the events of Tiananmen Square in China play out on their TV screens just a few months before. Conditions were ripe for the people to stand up against the communist task masters.

On October 9, 1989, over seventy thousand people demonstrated in Leipzig, East Germany, and on October 16th another group of five hundred thousand people protested and demonstrated for reform in East Germany.

Open demonstrations occurred throughout East Germany during October 1989. Eric Honecker, the communist dictator ruling over East Germany, resigned on October18, citing health issues. But growing political unrest in East Germany was most likely the real reason.

Mid-November saw protests erupt in Prague at Wenceslas Square. Then in late November Czechoslovakia was paralyzed by a two-hour general strike across all sectors of its economy.

In November Czechoslovakia opened the border with West Germany which allowed thousands of East Germans to flee to the West. Likewise, another 500,000 demonstrated in East Berlin.

On November 9, 1989, demonstrations were held on top of the Berlin Wall, as Berliners clamored to scale it. The Berlin Wall between East and West Berlin was opened in November and began to be torn down. On the night of November 9, my telephone rang; as I picked up the receiver I recognized the Colonel's voice. After saying a quick "hello," he excitedly asked me if I had on my television, which I did. We both were watching Germans celebrate on the Berlin Wall from separate parts of the U.S. He exclaimed, "Can you believe what we are seeing? It's unbelievable!" It truly was an amazing and wonderful sight as we rejoiced over the phone together, watching Germans dance on the Berlin Wall. It was spectacular. Truly amazing and hard to imagine, but there it was on international TV before our very eyes. I didn't know about Hap, but I had tears in my eyes. The Berlin Wall had been a symbol of communist tyranny most of my life up until that time. As a First Lieutenant, Hap had tended to wounded soldiers fighting communists in Korea. The fact that we were both watching the Wall come down together, although in different parts of the country, united us in spirit just as we had been when we had evaded Secret Police together in that part of the world only months earlier. It was an indescribable feeling. We were watching history in the making happen before our eyes for people we had worked to help. To say it was fabulous would be an understatement. But as we watched things unfold, we discussed the question of the Romanians and Ceausescu's hardline stance. What would happen there? We could only speculate.

In November 1989 as the Berlin Wall, the symbol of communist totalitarianism, was being torn down freedom was coming for the East Germans, the Czechs, the Hungarians, and the Polish. But in Romania, the socio economic political programs of Systemitization continued. The question the Colonel and I both had in our minds was, "What about Romania?" Ceausescu had determined not to lose his position of authority, tightened his fist, increasing austerity measures. He had resolved not to relinquish his power to the Romanian people. In October through mid-December the Securitate even increased their iron-fisted rule over the people.

The monitored telephone conversations increased in frequency, as more phone lines were tapped; personal mail was also opened often and read by government censors. While communication within the country had its challenges, it was extremely difficult to have open communication with people in the West. Romanian law required that all conversations and contacts with foreigners had to be reported to authorities.

However, that strategy would backfire. The undoing and fall of the Ceausescu Regime would be more violent than any other in Eastern Europe. During the late fall of 1989, Christians across Romania fasted and prayed regarding circumstances gripping their country. The increased heavy-handed application of Ceausescu's Systemization caused a rise in social unrest. The Securitate continued to crack down, and Ceausescu resolved not to cave into pressure. However, many did not bow the knee to atheistic communism. Men like Lazlo Tokes spoke out, as well as many other obscure, unsung heroes who had not surrendered to the Communist Party elite but to the Lordship of Jesus Christ and His ways.

On December 15, 1989, units of the Romanian police appeared at the parsonage home of pastor Lazlo Tokes, a Romanian born ethnic Hungarian who shepherded a Hungarian Reformed congregation. Tokes had been preaching and courageously speaking out openly against the abuses of the Ceausescu dictatorship. He had got the attention of authorities, and they intended to silence him.

The Securitate and police authorities came to forcibly remove him from his home and arrest him. Some of his parishioners linked arm in arm, in front of the apartment and around the block preventing the police from removing him. Friends, neighbors, students, and supporters began to challenge the authorities. It started with arguments which broke into pushing and shoving; then fighting erupted. Shortly thereafter people from all over the city of Timisoara began to protest. Rioting broke out and battles began to engulf the city.

On December 16th negotiators were brought in, which gave the government more time to mass Securitate forces and troops. December 17th saw an aggressive crowd march on the Communist Party Headquarters in Timisoara. The crowds burned portraits of Ceausescu throughout the city. The army used tanks, tear gas, and water cannons against the crowds. Elena Ceausescu and the Executive Political Committee ordered Securitate and army forces to fire live ammunition into the crowds. Allegedly hundreds of people were killed and the army began throwing bodies into mass graves.

On December 19th resistance against the regime began springing up throughout western Romania. Members of the army began to defect toward the side of the people. The Securitate continued firing upon the people. Nicole Ceausescu returned home from a visit to Iran and proclaimed martial law, blaming the uprising on Hungarian Fascists.

Then on December 21st Ceausescu addressed a crowd in Bucharest which was nationally televised. It was an address created by the communists as a show of support for the regime, but it had the opposite effect. The crowd became indignant, "Booed" Ceausesc, then became violent. They threw stones and rushed the compound. Riots and fighting erupted in Bucharest.

As I watched CNN on December 22nd, I could not believe what I was seeing. The rioting and battles had shifted into Bucharest; the Army led in fighting against the Securitate forces which had their own armored units. Fire fights between the army and the secret police were televised around the world.

That night I received another call from the Colonel. We again watched CNN together hundreds of miles apart in amazement. Just the year before he and I had smuggled in Bibles, books, and food supplies to the Underground Church within that Stalinist styled dictatorship. We had also brought out confirmatory information about the razing of villages and relocation of people from their homes into State apartment complexes in other cities. We had also verified that Bibles were being turned into toilet paper for use in public restrooms. During our time in country we had been all too aware of the presence of Secret Police agents. That was because of the oppressive rule of Ceausescu's Stalinist styled Police State.

As we watched TV wondering what the fate of the Romanian people would be, we talked about those whom we had met. We spoke of what they had shared with us. We had high hopes that Ceausescu would be deposed and Romania would be delivered from the bondage of dictatorial communist oppression.

Then on December 23rd, Nicolae and Elena were captured by the Army. A speedy trial was held. The Ceausescu's' were allegedly executed on Christmas Day December 25, 1989, for genocide and crimes against the people of Romania. The communists faded away quickly and a Mr. Ion Illiescu emerged as a leader of the National Front which made demands on the government. A provisional government lead by the National Salvation Front assumed control of State affairs.

Later on December 25, 1989, the bodies of Nicolae and Elena Ceausescu were displayed on national television. After eleven days of revolution the Romanian people had broken off the shackles of the Ceausescu regime. It was determined that elections would be held in April of 1990. The elections were actually held in May of 1990, when the people of Romania began the greatest move of self-determination since before WWII.

The events of the previous six months saw Eastern Europe on the path toward democratization. The people of the region had become free from the yoke of Soviet domination. In December 1991 the communist-ruled Soviet Union collapsed.

"What then shall we say to these things? If God is for us, who can be against us? He who did not spare His own Son, but delivered Him up for us all, how shall He not with Him freely give us all things? Who shall bring a charge against God's elect? It is God who justifies. Who is he who condemns? It is Christ Jesus who died, and furthermore is also risen, who is even at the right hand of God, who also makes intercession for us. Who shall separate us from the love of Christ? Shall tribulation, or distress, or persecution, or famine, or nakedness, or peril, or sword?" (Romans 8:31-35, NASB)

"Yet in all these things we are more than conquerors through Him who loved us.For I am persuaded that neither death, nor life, nor angels, nor principalities, nor powers, nor things present, nor things to come, nor height nor depth, nor any other created thing, shall be able to separate us from the love of God which is in Christ Jesus our Lord." (Romans 8: 37-39, NASB)

Ethics of Taking Bibles into Closed and Restricted Countries

After returning to the U.S. having traveled behind the Iron Curtain to help the Believing dissidents, I shared testimonies of experiences with a few churches and student groups. At the end of speaking times I usually offered a time for questions and answers. Although responses varied, during some of those sessions there would occasionally be an individual who asked the question, "Wasn't smuggling Bibles against the law in those countries?" Some of my responses at times included in some part information listed below which I submit below for your consideration.

In no way do I encourage anyone to break the fundamental laws of moral decency, public safety, health regulations, speed laws, etc. An individual should make every effort to comply with the higher laws of God and the laws of their host country that do not come into direct conflict with the law of God, to love your neighbor as yourself. However, I submit for the purposes of this discussion that there are two basic general classifications of laws in any culture: the laws of God, being moral statutes, and the laws of man, being civil statutes. God's laws are moral laws established for the good of mankind and societies. They are written in His word as codes of moral behavior and written in the hearts of humans around the world. "Don't worship idols or false gods, commit adultery, don't murder, do no injustice in judgment, don't steal and don't covet." These spiritual laws and the principles which surround them have not changed over the millennia. The Bible is full of God's directives to humankind for its welfare in social groups. He loves us and desires that we have healthy, well-balanced lives.

Many of the laws in the U.S. were birthed out of Biblical Law, "The Ten Commandments." The laws of the land should always be obeyed to the best of our abilities as citizens until they come into direct conflict with God's higher law. We must always attempt follow the higher law of love which God has for all of us. As the Scripture directs, as far as it be possible with us let us pursue peace and things which build each other up.

We must ask the question, what do the Scriptures and history reveal to us? Then we must examine what the governing entity is commanding us to do? Is it commanding the worship of false Gods, the defrauding of others by usury or theft? Is the authority directing us to be disrespectful of our elders or holy things? Is it commanding by statute the disdain of people with acts of violence against them? History is full of such examples: the Inquisition, the Holocaust, Stalin's purges, and Pol Pot's Killing Fields. When we consider God's moral laws, we can receive answers about injustice verses justice. When injustices exist we should pursue legal remedies first. If an individual has misgivings about smuggling Bibles, food, or providing assistance to hurting people when obvious oppression is occurring, then they should not be involved with it. Obviously, they must find a path in something else. Let's move on with examples of stories taken from the Bible and historical writings. What follows are examples where people of God did violate the laws of man to serve Jehovah.

In Numbers 13:1 the Scripture says, "Then the Lord spoke to Moses saying, 'Send out for yourself men so that they may spy out the land of Canaan, which I am going to give to the sons of Israel.'" Could that directive have resulted in the breaking of Canaanite laws? I would think so. So could the Lord have commanded Moses to break Canaanite law? What do we do with that one?

Joshua 2:1 says, "Then Joshua the son of Nun sent two men as spies secretly from Shittim, saying 'Go view the land, especially Jericho.' So they went and came into the house of a harlot whose name was Rahab, and lodged there." The story goes on to say in verses four and five that Rahab not only hid the Israelite spies, but she lied to the King of Jericho's men when they came looking for the spies. Then she misdirected the army of Jericho, telling them to chase after the two Israelites another way. Wow...a minimum of two misdemeanors! She also aided and abetted foreign spies and lied to investigators. I think those were most likely felonies in Jericho. Here is the conundrum: in Hebrews 11, the great "faith chapter," the scriptures say in verse 31: "By faith Rahab the harlot did not perish along with those who were disobedient, after she had welcomed the spies in peace." She misled the bad guys and was saved for it—she and her family. Did Rahab break the laws of the King of Jericho? Absolutely, she did. So it would seem best to correctly choose whose side you are on. So, in the words of Abraham Lincoln, "Sir, my concern is not whether God is on our side; my greatest concern is to be on God's side."

Also, consider these things. Three young Jewish men, choice Hebrew servants to King Nebuchadnezzer were to be executed for breaking the king's decree or law (Daniel 3:1-29). The Biblical account tells us they were thrown into a furnace filled with fire.

Daniel broke the decree (law) of King Darius the Mede when he prayed to God (Daniel 6:1-28). He was to be executed for breaking the law by being thrown into the lions' den.

Elijah broke the decrees and rules of religious law of Ahab and Jezebel when he destroyed the altars revering Baal and Asherah. Jezebel tried to hunt him down to kill him for it. He hid in a cave to escape arrest and death. According to the Pharisees Jesus broke the law when He healed on the Sabbath. Peter broke the law on several occasions when he was instructed not to preach about Jesus in the book of Acts.

Saul, who became the Apostle Paul, was hunting down Christians to have them thrown into prison because they were breaking the law.

In Acts 12:1 Herod the King was having Believers in Jesus arrested and tortured "to mistreat them." because they were breaking his decrees (laws). In the same chapter, verse two, Herod had James the brother of John executed for breaking the law.

In Acts 16, the Philippian jailer and his family were converted by Paul who had broken the law and was beaten with rods and thrown in prison for it.

Christians who broke the Roman laws were fed to lions and wild beasts. Under Nero they were burned as torches to light the city of Rome because they did not follow the pagan rules and law. They sought for God's higher laws.

The Roman Emperor Diocletian issued a decree (law) in 303 AD to destroy churches and the sacred writings read by Christians. Those followers of Christ, many who held high positions in government, also persisted in their faith and did not obey the law of Diocletian. They lost their civil rights and were deprived of their liberty. Christians who remained true to Jesus had a choice to break the law of the emperor or honor Jesus.

In the book *The New, Foxe's Book of Martyrs*, by John Foxe, one may read of men like John Wycliffe, Jan Huss of Bohemia, Martin Luther in Germany, Ulric Zwingle of Switzerland, Hugh Latimer of England, John Bradford of England, John Bunyan and a host of others who broke decrees and laws of religious leaders and secular kings. These people paid the price for their commitment to Jesus and the written Scriptures. Sometimes it meant harsh cruel and unusual punishment, torture in prison, etc., and sometimes an outright cruel death by being cut to pieces or burned at the stake (from where the Eighth Amendment to the Constitution of the United States— prohibition of "cruel and unusual punishment"— owes part of its origin).

Consider that if there had not been individuals who broke the religious laws of the King of England, English speaking people may not have had a Bible in English or heard the Gospel in England for several years later than they did. William Tyndale, thought to be born in 1494, educated at Oxford and Cambridge, and devoted to God's Word, is reputed to be the first translator of the New Testament in English. As such, he broke the law by translating the Bible from the Latin and the original Greek into English, the common language of the people. His Bibles were printed at Worms, Germany in 1526. Then they were smuggled from the Netherlands by Dutch merchantmen into England inside rolls of cloth and textiles. An edict was issued prohibiting Tyndale's New Testament translation anywhere in England. He was a law- breaker, considered a criminal for violating the King's statute.

In October of 1536 Tyndale was executed by strangulation and fire, being burned at the stake... this for breaking religious laws of man. By his work England received the Bible in the common language of the people. During martyrdom his last words were, "Lord open the King of England's eyes." Two years later King Henry commissioned a translation of the Bible. It became known as the Great Bible. In 1611 the fifty-four scholars who translated the Authorized King James Version drew on Tyndale's work. It is estimated that approximately eighty-three percent of the King James Bible New Testament is from the work of Tyndale, and approximately seventy-four percent of the Old Testament found in the

King James Bible is a result of Tyndale's translation work. We could safely say that we received our first Bibles in the English language because a bold scholar full of faith and love for God and people broke the laws and decrees of man.

The Scottish reformation which saw many come to personal faith in Christ occurred because men like George Wishart, martyred in 1546, broke the decrees and laws of kings and men as well. As Revelation 1:11 says, "not loving their own lives unto death," they chose to follow Jesus.

In Acts 5:29 after being given "strict orders" (legal directive) not to in the name of Jesus by the religious council known as the Sanhedrin, Peter and some Apostles replied "We must obey God rather than men." Those heroes of the faith chose to obey God. They were flogged for it and ordered again not to speak about the name of Jesus. They rejoiced after that and considered themselves blessed that they were worthy to suffer for Jesus. Then they kept on teaching and preaching Jesus as the Christ. You can read about it in Acts 5:12-42.

When I read the details of the ways many have suffered because they broke the decrees of kings and laws of men for the Gospel and think of those who've been beaten, tortured, and martyred, even now, because of their love for God, His word, and His people, I am humbled and convicted.

One could say that the United States of America was born because fifty-seven brave men joined together as representatives from their colonies, and signed the Declaration of Independence. It was an offense for which they could have been hung because they broke decrees (laws) of King George even though he had committed many abuses against them. It can also be said that the First Amendment to the U.S. Constitution was created because of our forefathers' knowledge of religious persecution in Europe in times past.

In the United States we have been blessed with a Constitution which includes a Bill of Rights. Many understand that in the U.S., it is the First Amendment which guarantees the freedom of religion and speech. It states the following, "Congress shall make no law respecting an establishment of religion or prohibiting the free exercise thereof; or abridging the freedom of speech, or of the press; or the right of the people peaceably to assemble and to petition the government for a redress of grievance." When living in a society where the freedom of religion is a guaranteed right protected by the rule of law and a bunch of men and women on the front lines of law enforcement and the military, it is easy to make short judgements. I encourage caution with such things. Remember also our federal, state and local governments utilize law enforcement methods and intelligence agencies to protect our security and freedom by conducting undercover operations.

In summary, a few Biblical and non-Biblical examples have been cited about following God or following the edicts of kings and men for your consideration. It is important that a person come to God in prayer about the matter. It is likewise important to become educated about the realities of life for Believers who are being persecuted and having their human rights violated. Then one can formulate an educated opinion.

As for me, I'm certainly grateful that Jesus allegedly broke laws created by religious leaders and that Paul, Peter, James and John, and thousands of others broke government and religious laws to spread the Gospel. They spread the Good News as acts of love for us so that we could learn about the love of God for us, salvation and eternal life. What are the higher laws?

Reliability of the Bible

According to the Eastern European historian Karel Bartosek, churches and people of faith were the biggest blocking force against the eradication of the mechanisms of civil society for the communists in Eastern Europe. In order to lessen the churches societal influence, the communists sought to bring them under the control of the State, then turn them into tools for developing and enforcing communist policy. The communists used the tactics of repression, attempts at corruption and infiltration to weaken churches.

Obviously, the Bible, as the foundational document and anchor of Christianity, was anathema to a majority of communists, but it became even more important to the clergy and laity within the various sects, regardless of creeds and denominational dogmas. It is a book of eternal inspiration containing messages of hope. The following can be considered when contemplating the relevance and importance of the Bible.

The Bible is one of the most unique books in all of human history, if not the most unique of all documents ever produced. It is a book of history, full of civil law and moral codes. It contains biographies, poetry, romance, prose, songs, correspondence, memoirs, history, prophecy, and parables. Billions of copies have been produced. Other written works have been produced in the millions, even a very few in the tens of millions. But the Bible, having been produced in the billions, is unique in the volume of its production, not only in its content. It has spoken to human hearts the world over, spanning centuries. The richness of its content and message is incomparable. It has proven to be a source of encouragement over the centuries to large populations in the world.

It is one document composed of sisty-six books, written by over forty different authors spanning a period of over one thousand four hundred years. Its authors consisted of kings, farmers, herdsmen, government leaders, fishermen, prophets, and warriors writing under inspiration from the Spirit of God, just to list a few. It was written on three continents and in three different languages (Aramaic, Greek and Hebrew). Its words were first inscribed on papyrus, then on parchments, on calf skins known as vellum, and eventually on paper. Meticulous methods were applied in ancient times to preserve its accuracy. Rabbis and Priests diligently copied its contents word for word s by hand. Copies were reviewed by other scribes Rabbis and Priests, if one mistake was made, the entire copy was destroyed.

The Bible is full of stories of inspiration, hope and courage, drama and sorrow. When read it can lift the soul as no other book can. It speaks of life and death. It tells of overcomers and those who were overcome. It is a literary work like no other. Many have made efforts to refute it, only to embrace it. It has stood the tests of time and history. It has been validated time and time again. Its overall message consists of moral codes, poetry, life lessons, and stories of deliverance, hope, eternal life, and salvation.

The Bible continues to be validated by its own internal content, fulfilled prophecies spoken of by ancient prophets, continued archaeological finds, and historical documents outside of Biblical testimonies.

Scholars debate such things as the authorship of the eyewitness accounts of the Gospels. However, the eyewitness accounts and testimonies of the Gospels continue to stand up under scrutiny.

Fourteen of the twenty-seven documents listed in the New Testament have been attributed to the Apostle Paul. His accounts validate the Gospel accounts being difficult to refute by those who choose otherwise. It has been established that Luke the physician was a personal friend of the Apostle Paul and documented the early events surrounding the life of Christ. Unbelievers and humanistic global socialists have continued with attempts to discredit the Bible and the Gospels. However, what is not up for grabs is the very existence of a religious sect of people known as Christians. This group exploded on the world scene of history and came into prominence during the first century AD. What was the beginning and ignition source of Christianity's historical development?

It is logically concluded that it was Jesus whom they espoused and proclaimed as Lord and Savior.

The book of Acts of the Apostle, and the Gospel recorded by Luke the physician record the story of the beginnings of the Christian faith. According to the archeologist and scholar Dr John McRay, in the Lee Srobel book *The Case for Christ*,* McRay states: "The general consensus of both liberal and conservative scholars is that Luke is very accurate as a historian" [7].

In the introduction to the Gospel of Mark in the New King James Version Study Bible, scholars claim the early church fathers Papias, Irenaeus, Clement of Alexandria and Origen all testified that Mark wrote the Gospel given his name.

Likewise, scholars writing in the Open Bible Study Edition of the New King James Version indicate that Irenaeus, a disciple of Polycarp and a follower of John, "bore witness" to the authorship of John. Irenaeus, in his work *Against Heresies* testifies that the Apostle John wrote the Gospel bearing his name. Clement of Alexandria, Theophilus of Antioch and Origen, and all early Christians also give credit to John for writing the Gospel of John.

Scholars associated with the New King James version of the Bible, also claim that the early church credited Matthew, the tax collector and the son of Alphaeus, with authorship of the Gospel credited to him. The early church father Eusebius quoted Papias as saying that Matthew wrote sayings of Jesus in Aramaic, as well. Early church traditions attribute this Gospel to the tax collector.

Irenaeus, a second century Christian, apologist and theologian who was a follower of Polycarp, a disciple of John the Apostle, wrote the following in approximately 180 AD in his work *Against Heresies*:

> Matthew published his own Gospel among the Hebrews in their own tongue, when Peter and Paul were preaching the Gospel in Rome and founding the church there. After their departure, Mark, the disciple and interpreter of Peter, himself handed down to us in writing the substance of Peter's preaching. Luke, the follower of Paul, set down in a book the Gospel preached by his teacher. Then John, the disciple of the Lord, who

also leaned on his breast, himself produced his Gospel while he was living at Ephesus in Asia [8].

Therefore, it can be said that historical testimonies, as well as writings of first and second generation Christians attest to events in the life of Jesus. This verification of the Bible by eyewitness accounts is also strengthened by the fulfillment of prophecies found within its pages. Many Old Testament prophecies of the Messiah-Deliverer have been documented as being written centuries prior to the recorded events fulfilled in the New Testament. Several ancient prophets foretold of a coming Deliverer, Savior, and Messiah. There were specific things spoken of about this coming Savior. Many scholars estimate there are well over one hundred prophecies about the coming Messiah found in the Old Testament. Those prophecies were fulfilled in the life of one man. The historically documented Jesus of Nazareth has been shown to be the one of whom all the prophets spoke. This is revealed by the historical eyewitness testimonies and the prophecies fulfilled in the life of one man. The miraculous events surrounding His life and historical testimonies all validate His Messianic role spoken of in the Bible.

Author Josh McDowell in his book, *The New Evidence That Demands a Verdict*,* cites Peter Stoner's book, *Science Speaks* when he states that the probability of just eight prophecies being fulfilled in the life of one man is one in ten to the seventeenth power, or ten with seventeen zeros behind it. That is estimated to be equivalent to piling silver dollars over the entire State of Texas two feet deep, marking one, mixing them and having a blindfolded man pick out the marked silver dollar! According to McDowell and Stoner, that is the probability for just eight prophecies being fulfilled in the life of one man. Specific examples of these prophecies may be found in McDowell's book. There are definitely many more than eight prophecies related to a coming Savior-Messiah which were fulfilled in the life of the one man, Jesus from Nazareth. A few examples of prophetic fulfillment follow.

In approximately 480-470 BC in the book of the Prophet Zechariah, it is written:

> "Rejoice greatly, O daughter of Zion! Shout, O daughter of Jerusalem! Behold your King is coming to you; He is just and having Salvation, Lowly and riding on a <u>donkey</u>, a <u>colt</u>, the <u>foal of a donkey</u>." (Zechariah 9:9)

Luke, in approximately AD 60 to AD 70 recorded the following:

> "And they brought him to Jesus, And they threw their own clothes on the colt, and they set Jesus on him. And as He went, many spread their clothes on the road." (Luke 19:35-36)

Some may allege that this could have been manipulated by Jesus. However, the place of his birth, manner of his birth and the details of his death could not have been manipulated. No person can plan how they were born, obviously. Additionally, people can-not easily predict when or how they will die, unless by suicide. The following prophetic passages and their fulfillment tell of the birth and death events surrounding Jesus of Nazareth.

It is recorded in the writings of the prophet Micah written sometime between 735 BC to 710 BC:

> "But you Bethlehem Ephrathah, though you are little among the thousands of Judah, Yet out of you shall come forth to Me, The One ruler in Israel. Whose goings forth have been from of old, from everlasting." (Micah 5:2)

Matthew, recorded the following written in approximately 40-140 AD, as historical documentation:

> "Now after Jesus was born in Bethlehem of Judea in the days of Herod the king, behold wise men from the east came to Jerusalem, saying, 'Where is He who has been born King of the Jews?'" (Matt 2:1-2a)

In Isaiah 7:14 the prophet said, "Therefore the Lord Himself will give you a sign: Behold, the virgin shall conceive and bear a Son, and shall call His name Immanuel."

It was recorded by Luke the physician and friend of Paul that the following occurred in about 6 or 7 BC:

> "Now in the sixth month the angel Gabriel was sent by God to a city of Galilee named Nazareth, to a virgin

betrothed to a man whose name was Joseph, of the house of David. The virgins name was Mary, and having come in said to her, Rejoice, highly favored one, the Lord is with you; blessed are you among women!" ... Then the angel said to her, Do not be afraid, Mary, for you have found favor with God. And behold you will conceive in your womb and bring forth a son, and you shall call His name Jesus. He will be great and will be called the Son of the highest; and the Lord God will give Him the throne of His father David." (Luke 1:26-28, 30-31).

During sometime around 740 to 686 BC, the prophet Isaiah said in Chapter 53, verse 5, "But He was wounded for our transgressions, He was bruised for our iniquities; the chastisement for our peace was upon Him, and by his stripes we are healed." The apostle Matthew states in 27:26: "Then he released Barabas to them; and when he had scourged Jesus, he delivered Him to be crucified." The fulfillment of Isaiah's prophetic words came to pass in Matthew's account over six hundred years after they were spoken.

Then in verse seven of the same chapter of Isaiah, he said, "He was oppressed and He was afflicted, yet He opened not his mouth; He was led as a lamb to slaughter, and as a sheep before its shearers is silent, so he opened not his mouth" (Isaiah 53:7). Again Matthew records over six hundred years later, "And while he was being accused by the chief priests and elders, he answered nothing."

Thus, with those words Isaiah's prophecy was demonstrated as having been fulfilled.

Again sometime between 740 and 686 BC it was recorded in Isaiah 50:6: "I gave my back to those who struck me, and my cheeks to those who plucked out the beard; I did not hide my face from shame and spitting."

Its fulfillment happened with this event just prior to the crucifixion of Jesus. It was recorded by Matthew: "Then they spat in his face and beat him; and others struck him with the palms of their hands." (Matthew 26:67)

In Zechariah 12:10, the prophet Zechariah spoke the following, "They will look on me whom they pierced." It is estimated that these words were written in about 480-470 BC. Its fulfillment occurred at the crucifixion of Jesus in AD 33 and is recorded in the Gospel of John, where the apostle says, "But one of the soldiers pierced His side with a spear." (John 19:34 AD 33)

Found in Isaiah 53:9 is the prophecy, "And They made His grave with the wicked but with the rich at His death." It was fulfilled in AD 33 with the burial of Jesus where Matthew 27:57-60 states, "There came a rich man from Arimathea, named Joseph...and asked for the body of Jesus... When Joseph had taken the body, he wrapped it in a clean linen cloth, and laid it in his new tomb."

In the previous few paragraphs eight prophecies and their fulfillment have been provided. Again, as a reminder, according to Peter Stoner the probability of these events occurring in the life of one man is equal to one in ten to the seventeenth power or a 1 in 100,000,000,000,000,000 (one in one hundred quadrillion) chance—a huge probability for just eight events spoken hundreds of years before they came to pass in the life of one man! [9]. There are dozens of other prophecies which can be added to those eight.

In addition to these prophetic scriptures, archeology also contributes its own reinforcement of the Bible. The discoveries of hundreds of artifacts by archeologists continue to strengthen the Biblical record, not contradict its content. While a few minor translation errors may exist within the Bible, due to the complexities of the transliteration of languages, Biblical content of the original scriptures remains consistent. The information found in the original Aramaic, Hebrew, and Greek texts continues to be reinforced by archeological discoveries.

The discovery of such artifacts as the Elba Creation Tablets, the Black Obelisk of Shalmaneser, the Cyrus Cylinder, the Assyrian Tablets found in the Palace of Ashurbanipal, and the Dead Sea Scrolls have yielded much information for scientists and scholars. These discoveries continue to reinforce what was transcribed by scribes, rabbis and priests being brought forward into our modern texts.

The discovery of the Elba Tablets in northern Syria in 1968 by Professors from the University of Rome reinforce the Creation account found in the book of Genesis. These tablets predate the Mosaic Genesis account by one thousand years. A section of these tablets record the following, "Lord of Heaven and earth; the earth was not, you created it, the morning light you had not [yet] made exist." (Elba Archive 259) [10]

This account speaks in the singular of a Creator. It testifies of a belief in Creation prior to the writings of Moses and establishes that a group of people practiced a belief in a monotheistic God, before the Jewish race existed. The Elba Tablets also reference the cities of Sodom, Gomorrah. Adam, Zeboiim, and Zoar as listed in Genesis. They also present judicial proceedings which are similar to the Mosaic Law Code found in Deuteronomy.

The Black Obelisk of Shalmaneser, a discovery in 1846 by British archeologist Austin Henry Layard, is a record of Assyrian Kings. It depicts an Israelite and speaks of Persia. The Shalamaneser Obelisk is considered the most complete Assyrian Oblelisk to date and speaks of the Israelite King Jehu referenced in II Kings 17:3, II Kings 18:9 and II Kings 9:13. Replicas of the artifact are located at the Oriental Institute in Chicago, Harvard's Semitic Museum in Massachusetts, The Catholic University of America, Washington D.C., and in the Netherlands at the Theological University of the Reformed Churches.

The Cyrus Cylinder, also called the "Stele of Cyrus" and found in the British museum in London, is so named after the Medio-Persian ruler Cyrus the Great who conquered Babylon in 539 BC. It was discovered in 1879 in archeological digs outside of Babylon in what is now southern Iraq, not far from Baghdad. This artifact mentions the repatriation of the Jewish people from Babylonian captivity back to Israel, listed in the Biblical book of Ezra. Information which can be found on the Stele is also mentioned in the books of Daniel and Isaiah in the Bible.

Tablets from the Palace of Ashurbanipal also testify of Assyrian Kings and Kings of Israel mentioned in the Bible.

The content of the Bible itself along with fulfilled prophecies and archeology all provide pieces of evidence which validate the Biblical record. Additionally, extra Biblical writings from historians and historical figures from the first century add to the trustworthiness of the New Testament portion of the Bible and accounts regarding Jesus of Nazareth.

The ancient Jewish historian Josephus wrote of Jesus in Book 18, Chapter 3, in his work *Antiquities of the Jews*, estimated to have been written between 70 AD and 93 AD. Scholars have debated that some of the quotes attributed to him as having been added later. Those portions of the quotation are not included here. The quote, excluding the debated portions, reads as follows:

> Now, there was about this time Jesus, a wise man ...for he was a doer of wonderful works - a teacher of such men as receive the truth with pleasure. He drew over to him both many of the Jews, and many of the Gentiles, ... and when Pilate, at the suggestion of the principal men amongst us, had him condemned to the cross, those that loved him from the first did not forsake him; ...and the tribe of Christians, so named from him, are not extinct at this day. [11]

Josephus documents the historical Jesus in this account. This observation is another source which reinforces that Jesus was not just a mythological figure created by religious zealots. Along with other documentation it demonstrates that Jesus was a real person who lived on the planet in ancient times.

The Roman historian Tactius wrote in AD 115 of Nero and the fire of Rome in AD 64 that Nero tried to place the blame of the fire on the Christians. The extra Biblical testimony recorded below also speaks about Jesus and establishes the pre-existence of the Christian faith prior to 64 AD. Tacitus wrote the following:

> Nero fastened the guilt and inflicted the most exquisite torture on a class hated for their abominations, called Christians by the populace. Christus, from whose name had its origin, suffered the extreme penalty during the reign of Tiberius at the hands of one of our procurators, Pontius Pilate, and a most mischievous superstition, thus checked for the moment, again broke out not only in Judaea, the first source of the evil, but even in Rome... Accordingly, an arrest was made of all who pleaded guilty: Then, upon their information, an immense multitude was convicted, not so much of the crime of firing the city, as of hatred against mankind. [12].

Pliny the Younger, a Roman governor, wrote of the Christians in approximately 111 AD:

> I have asked them if they were Christians, and if they admit it, I repeat the question a second and third time, with a warning of the punishment awaiting them. If they persist, I order them to be led away for execution; for whatever the nature of their admission, I am convinced that their stubbornness and unshakable obstinacy ought not go unpunished. [13]

In 221 AD Julius Africanus quoted the historian Thallus, who wrote history of the eastern Mediterranean region in approximately 52 AD. Thallus spoke in his *Third Book of the Histories* of a day the earth went dark in the whole region [7,11]. That darkening appears to correspond with the event listed in the New Testament during the Crucifixion, in the accounts of Matthew 27:45, Mark 15:22 and Luke 23: 44. Luke records the event as, "And it was about the sixth hour and there was darkness over the earth until the ninth hour." Interestingly, Amos the prophet wrote under inspiration in approximately 767 BC to 739 BC the following, " 'And it shall come to pass in that day.' says the Lord God, 'That I will make the sun go down at noon, and I will darken the earth in broad daylight.'" (Amos 8:9)

Further extra Biblical attestation of this event is documented by Paul Mair, author of the book *Pontius Pilot*. He notes in his book:

> Phelegon, a Greek author from Caria writing a chronology soon after 137 A.D., reported that in the fourth year of the 202nd Olympiad (i.e., 33AD) there was "the greatest eclipse of the sun" and that it became night in the sixth hour of the day [i.e. noon] so that stars even appeared in the heavens. There was a great earthquake in Bithynia, and many things were overturned in Nicaea. [14]

The Roman historian, Suetonius, wrote in his work, *Life of Claudius*, the following comments: "As the Jews were making constant disturbances at the instigation of Chrestus (Christus), he (Claudius) expelled them from Rome." [15]

In the Acts of the Apostles, the physician Luke recorded the following: "And he (Paul) found a certain Jew named Aquila, born in Pontus, who had recently come from Italy with his wife Priscilla (because Claudius had commanded all the Jews to depart from Rome); and he (Paul) came to them" (Acts 18:2). Once again the scriptural account does not differ from other historical records.

The Bible has been validated by written eye witness testimonies, fulfilled prophecies and historical documentation. It continues to be reinforced by archeology and historical documentation.

Volumes have been written about the internal content, historical, and archeological evidences supporting the reliability of its scriptures. This brief account has not begun to touch on what has been placed in volumes of books about the validity of the Bible. It cannot be covered in just a few paragraphs. Entire manuscripts have been dedicated to that end. But hopefully enough has been included to demonstrate that the Bible is well-supported by various sources of evidence which attest to its historical reliability. Hopefully this stirs you to further investigate the truths found in the scriptures. The reasons to trust in the contents of the Bible are many, much more than has been briefly discussed here. The Bible in its totality has demonstrated time and again to be more accurate than the sayings, teachings, works or writings of any other single guru, one religious figure, sage, or seer. It testifies of the spiritual truths about God and the One we call Lord Jesus Christ, Jesus the Nazarene, or Jesus the Messiah. The Bible testifies of His work to bring salvation and deliverance for our spirit. It is not only a reliable historical text but also contains prophecies which continue to be fulfilled. It is a book like no other which within its pages, hope may be found.

The Bible is a book which over time, has drawn many to the knowledge of God and encouraged millions of believers in their Christian lives. But more than that, it tells us of the history and love God has for mankind and His creation. A book of encouragement, hope and healing, it documents God's love for us.

I make no claim to be a scholar, just one who carried a suitcase for Jesus. But information from scholars has helped to strengthen my faith and encourage me. I do not consider myself a particularly brave soul and was not on a quest for excitement. I am far from a perfect man and was not seeking to be justified before God by performing religious good deeds. I just saw a job which needed to be done, and had a passion in my heart to pursue it.

Knowledge of the historicity of Jesus, knowing about the fulfillment of ancient prophecies in His life, aware of changed lives because of the

Word of God, and having experienced His work in my own life were all pieces which were part of a whole. Those things were part of my inspiration. I've touched on a few of the items which brought me to deeper faith, likewise giving me the desire to serve God and His people wherever that led. Taking Bibles into the communist world was a call of the Lord. A response to help those in need, just as the scripture says in Galatians 6:2, to "Bear one another's burdens and thus fulfill the law of Christ." This law of Christ, is nothing less than the Love of God for His Children which brought Christ's sacrifice on the cross. The knowledge of what was going on in communist regimes coupled with the outcry of Eastern European Christians was something from which I could not turn away.

[*Note: During the 1980s, I enjoyed theological discussions including Christian apologetics with my American coworkers and Dutch friends. I found the book by Josh MacDowell, *The Evidence Which Demands a Verdict*, to be a source of information and referenced it in discussions. I have more recently referenced the work of Lee Strobel, *The Case for Christ* in discussion. Due to its relevance to this topic, his references to McDowell's book *The Evidence Which Demands a Verdict*, and many of his citations being of historical nature, I chose to include his information as a reference. His book includes published works from the 1970s through the early 1990s. It is not my intent to claim this chapter as a memory from the 1980s; that would be a fallacious impossibility. However, much of the information in Strobel's book is historical and referenced from other works published prior to the 1980s. I did not read his book obviously until after the fall of the Wall. But his book and McDowell's work have been part of my life experience so they have been included in this chapter.]

Epilogue

In late 1989 and early 1990 the Berlin Wall came down, communism in Eastern Europe imploded, and Eastern Europeans became freed from the yoke of communist oppression. East Germans became reunited with their West German family. The German nation became whole once again after decades of separation. It was then the process of reconciliation and healing began. When I reflect on seeing West and East Germans standing on top of the Berlin Wall celebrating and watching people with sledge hammers break chunks off the wall, I consider myself blessed and fortunate that I was able to work with fine, good people like Bill Larson, Mike Lee, John Murphy, Cees Den Hollander, and Hank Paulson, along with many others to help bring the Word, hope and encouragement to Eastern European Christians during the Communist Era. I have a very small piece of The Berlin Wall in my home which reminds me of those times.

After the destruction of the Iron Curtain, Bill Larson and Nona, his wife, moved to Slovakia and served the people there for several years. They continue to return seasonally to assist the Roma gypsies and Slovak people in Slovakia every year. John Murphy married Michele, whom he met at The Farm in Holland, returned to the U.S., and attended Bible College. They became leaders in local churches in communities where they have lived. They have raised two children, a daughter who returned to Eastern Europe working with orphans in Romania and a son who attended seminary and is going forward in service. John and Mickey continue to be involved in a local church, send financial support to help persecuted Christians, and pray for their needs. Mike Lee returned to the U.S. and started his own construction business, building houses, got married, and has served on short term mission trips to Haiti and other locations.

Hap and Iris traveled to various U.S. military installations in West Germany speaking at chapel services on U.S. Army Posts. They encouraged the troops with the Gospel message in chapel services. They also shared about what life was like for Christians living in communist society, relating what they had experienced and learned on the other side of the Iron Curtain. Upon their return to the U.S. they passed on many testimonies in churches and military services.

In the early 1990s, not long after the fall of the Berlin Wall and the collapse of the Soviet Union, Hap and Iris traveled in Russia speaking to Russian youth in schools about the Good News of Jesus Christ. Hap actually was able to teach and proclaim the Gospel in Russian schools, as the USSR passed into the pages of the history books.

Hank Paulson and his wife Mona continue to work with youth and others in Eastern Europe in places like Moldova, Romania and Ukraine, having founded an organization known as 4D Ministries, out of Monument, Colorado. Cees passed on a few years back and went home to be with his Lord whom he dearly loved.

Individuals who served the people of Eastern Europe with Open Doors and Eastern European Bible Mission continue to follow the Lord in various forms of service. Groups like Christian Freedom International, International Christian Concern, Open Doors, Voice of the Martyrs, and others continue to serve oppressed and persecuted Christians in various places around the world. While there is no longer a need to smuggle Bibles, books, food or clothing into Eastern Europe, Christian humanitarian aid is still needed in sections of Eastern Europe in various forms.

The conversion from communist dictatorships to democracies in Eastern Europe was obviously a wonderful thing. Now most of the former communist nations have been reestablished as democracies which replaced the previous regimes. Several of those have become allies in the war on terrorism and increased trade with the U.S. and western nations.

Compared to the Communist Era, social conditions improved considerably, and economies in areas recovered and are doing much better. The political oppression of the past faded into a distant memory. Germany is no longer divided into East and West, finally were reunited as one people after World War II. Germany has flourished and become a major economic power in Europe. U.S. Military and NATO Bases have moved and are now located in Romania, Poland, and various other countries of the former communist bloc. More importantly, the people of Eastern Europe are in the healing process from political and economic injustices suffered from 1945 to 1989.

But even in a few areas local economies and social conditions do suffer. In places where poverty is present, poor living and health conditions are prominent. Poverty, alcoholism, and the crime of human trafficking still impact certain areas of Eastern Europe. The Romani or Roma gypsy minorities in the Czech Republic, Slovakia, and Romania as well as the orphans and some sectors of Moldova, areas of Ukraine are still in need of help as well.

Persecution in parts of the world is again rising in recent years and has come to national attention in the media. It plays out in parts of the globe where practicing faith can have dire consequences. Living in some countries as a Believer may cost fines, loss of job, economic discrimination, loss of home and belongings, harassment, imprisonment or torture and even the Christian's life. To learn more about the state of Christian persecution globally consider reading the book *Persecuted, the Global Assault on Christians,* by Marshal, Gilbert and Shea, published by Thomas Nelson Publishing. It is also recommended that you contact one or more of the organizations listed in Appendix I to obtain more current conditions and updates.

The work of providing Good News of hope and reconciliation of man to God in difficult areas is not over. There remain hundreds of thousands and millions throughout the world who would love to be able to read or have their own copy of a Bible, religious liberty, decent medical care, clothing, sanitary living conditions, food, and safe drinking water. Likewise, there are incidents of local and regional disasters throughout the world where involvement of kind Christian workers are needed to help in recovery efforts. Also, there are the handicapped and those with limitations who need to be accepted, loved, and helped. The task of spreading hope, love, peace, and salvation through Jesus Christ around the world is not over. It is for us to spread the Good News of His love to people, in neighborhoods and regions around the world.

Do the most you can, for as many as you can, while you can, starting by loving one at a time. But more, seek Jesus, love God and follow His call where He leads you. In that will be your fulfillment and path to your destiny.

In closing this account, I wish to use the words from the Lord Jesus. He said,

> "... even so must the Son of man be lifted up, that whoever believes in Him should not perish but have eternal life. For <u>God so loved</u> the world <u>that He gave</u> His only begotten Son, that whoever believes in Him should not perish but have everlasting life. For God did not send His Son into the world to condemn the world to but that the world through Him might be saved. He who believes in Him is not condemned, but he who does not believe is condemned already, because he has not believed in the name of the only begotten Son of God.
>
> And this is the condemnation, that the light has come into the world, and men loved darkness rather than light, because their deeds were evil. For everyone practicing evil hates the light and does not come to the light, lest his deeds should be exposed. But he who does the truth comes to the light, that his deeds may be clearly seen, that they may have been done in God." (John 3:14-21 NKJV)

> "Seek the Lord while He may be found; call upon Him while He is near." (Isaiah 55:6)

> "If anyone wishes to come after me, let him deny himself, and take up his cross, and follow Me. For whoever wishes to save his life shall lose it; but whoever loses his life for my sake shall find it. For what shall a man be profited, if he gains the whole world and forfeits his soul? Or what shall a man give in exchange for his soul?" (Matt. 16:24-26)

A Special Thanks

The Apostle Paul proclaimed in Romans 13:7a: "Render to all what is due them...respect to whom respect, honor unto whom honor." It is in that spirit that I extend appreciation to those who encouraged me to pursue this book. Likewise, to those who supported me during my season of service in Europe. The source of inspiration and motivation for this memoir have been my cousins, my mother, some close friends and those with whom I served.

    A special thanks is owed to my cousin, friend and brother in Christ, Bernie, for his support during that season of my life. I'm grateful for his many prayers then and now. A special thanks is owed to my friend, Randy, with whom I've spent many hours in prayer, and who encouraged me many times to share some of the experiences found here. Randy's continued encouragement is a huge reason this memoir was written. Special thanks to Brandi and Tamra for providing the motivation to write this memoir.

    Appreciation is also extended to Cory and Jon for their encouragement, having lit an ignition fire under me to begin this book. Additionally, I wish to extend thanks to John and the Saturday morning Bible study group who demonstrated interest in that part of my life, which motivated me to share this story with others.

    My friends Mike and Walt, thank you for your friendship, prayers, and brotherhood, as you have stood by me these past decades. Your faithful friendship over the years has meant much and continues to encourage me to press on.

    Mike, you were rightfully voted most inspirational on your football team in your younger years as you have stood by me and encouraged me as a friend through thick and thin, during the good times and the not so good for over thirty-eight years now. God bless you and be with you for your faithfulness, my friend and brother.

Walt, I'm glad we've been able to share memories of God's provisions about taking the Scriptures and the Good News into restricted countries and parts of the world, albeit at differing seasons I appreciate, love you and your fellowship, encouragement and words as a man of God. You are a sojourner and brother whom I continue to love, respect, and pray for.

Thank you to my close friends for the prayers and encouragements to go forward in service. All of you hold a special place in my heart.

Thank you, Joyce and Saundra, for your contributions to this book, and a special word of thanks to Sariah for the cover artwork.

Most importantly, I wish to thank the Lord for His faithfulness, the blessings He has extended to me and for the opportunity to live out these experiences and pass on this history to those who may be interested in it. As He has said, He would never leave me or forsake me; He has not. He has never left me, even when I have messed up and let Him down. He has not held my shortcomings against me, but extended forgiveness even when I've missed the mark. Thank you Lord for your past and present protection and provisions. Also to all my loved ones, uncles, aunts and cousins who prayed for me then and pray for me now I say, "Thanks and I love you." Dee, thank you for your kindnesses, all of the good things you've done for me and your love. Thank you for saving my life and helping me with all you did during one of the most difficult times of my life. I love you, Sweetie. Thanks is also owed to the publishing team for their help and assistance for production of this book. God bless and be with you all. This story belongs to God, and without Him this was not possible. I thank and praise Him. This writer is a cracked, clay pot who was used by the Almighty. May God receive the Glory!

Proceeds from this book will be donated toward aiding the oppressed and persecuted.

Appendix I
Organizational Contacts

Current and historical information about Christian persecution may be gained from contacting one or more of the organizations below.

Christian Freedom International
986 John Marshall Highway
Front Royal, VA 22630
1(800) 323-2273
www.christianfreedom.org

International Christian Concern
2020 Pennsylvania Ave.
NW #941 Washington D.C. 20006-1846
(800) 422-5441
http://www.persecution.org/

Open Doors USA
PO Box 27001
Santa Ana, CA 92799
(949) 752-6600
(888) 524-2535
www.opendoors.org

Voice of the Martyrs
PO Box 443
Bartlesville, OK 74005-0443
(877) 337-0302
(800) 747-0085
www.persecution.com

Appendix II
Excerpts from the Former Soviet Criminal Code Related to Religious Regulations

I. Soviet Laws Regarding Religion in the former USSR

The following former Soviet laws regarding religious activities were received from Keston College News Service, an organization which was located in the United Kingdom, which tracked and monitored religious human rights conditions in the communist countries of the USSR and Eastern Europe during the 1970's and 80's. The information provided below came from the booklet as printed, *"Soviet Christian Prison List, 1981,"* copyright 1981, by the *Society for the Study of Religion Under Communism,* formerly USA, PO Box 2310, Orange, CA, 92669; also known Keston College, Heathfield Road, Keston, Kent, BR2 6BA, England.

Index of Criminal Charges, Former Soviet Criminal Code

A. Religious Offenses - Organizing religious meetings for worship or study, teaching religion to children, printing religious literature.

Article 142 - Violation of laws on the separation of church and state and of school and church.
1- punishable by correctional tasks for a period not exceeding one year or by fine not exceeding 50 Roubles.
2- If previously sentenced, punishable by deprivation of freedom for a period not exceeding three years.

Article 227- Infringement of the person and rights of citizens under the guise of performing religious rituals.

1- Organizing or leading a group whose activity is connected with causing harm to citizens' health or other infringement of the person, or with inciting citizens to refuse to do social activity and likewise enticing minors into such a group, is punishable by deprivation of freedom for a period not exceeding five years or exile for the same period, with or without confiscation of property.
2- Active participation in the activity of such a group and systematic propaganda directed at the commission of the acts described is punishable by deprivation of freedom for a period not exceeding three years, or exile for the same period not exceeding three years, or correctional tasks not exceeding one year.

B. Military Offenses - conscientious objectors.

Article 80 - Evasion of a regular call to active military service is punishable by deprivation of freedom for a period of one to three years.

Article 249 Evasion of military service by maiming or any other method.
A- The evasion of military service by causing any kind of injury or by malingering, forgery of documents or any other deception, or a refusal to preform military duties is punishable by a deprivation of freedom for a period of 3 to 7 years.
B- The same committed in wartime or in a combat situation is punishable by deprivation of freedom for a period of 5 to 10 years.
(Under Article 249, a "refusal to swear the military oath" can be seen as a refusal to preform military duties.)

C. Political Offenses - protesters of human rights violations, including Freedom of Religion.

Article 64: Treason - offenses under this article include escaping from the country Maximum sentence is 15 years, plus 5 years exile or death.

Article 70: Anti-Soviet agitation and propaganda.
1- is punishable by depravation of freedom for a period of 6 months to 7 years, with or without additional exile for a period of 2-5 years.
2- If previously convicted of especially dangerous crimes against the State, punishable by deprivation of freedom for a period of 3 to 10 years, with or without additional exile for a period of 2 to 5 years.

Article 190-1: Circulation of deliberately false concoctions, slandering the Soviet State and social order, is punishable by depravation of freedom not exceeding one year, or by a fine not exceeding 100 Rubles.

> *(Article 70 is applied in cases where fundamental criticism has been made, such as the USSR's record on Human Rights.*
>
> *Article 190-1 is frequently applied to Christians who have written or spoken of the persecution of the church or have been involved in the circulation of documents detailing violations of religious freedom and other human rights.)*

D. **Other Articles Used** - covers offenses that are neither religious nor political, such as "parasitism" or "prohibited trading."

Article 162: Engaging in a prohibited trade.

2- If committed on a significant scale, is punishable by deprivation of freedom for a period not exceeding four years with or without confiscation of property.
(The unofficial printing of Christian literature is considered a "prohibited trade.")

Article 190-3: Organization of. or active participation in, group actions which disrupt public order, is punishable by deprivation of freedom for a period not exceeding three years, or by correctional tasks for a period not exceeding one year, or by a fine not exceeding 100 Rubles.

(This can be applied when Christians assemble in public for example, when locked out of a church or conducting an open air baptism.)

Article 209-1. Malicious evasion of fulfillment or decision concerning arrangement of work and discontinuance of parasitic existence, is punishable by a depravation of freedom for a period not exceeding five years or by correctional tasks for the same period.

(Some Christians cannot work because of discrimination, or they are supported by unregistered churches. Prosecution is possible under this article if work is not found within one month of an order issued to that effect.)

II. Forms of Punishment

1. **Correctional Tasks**
2. **Detention in a Labor Camp** - There are *(were)* four "regimes" (types) of labor camps.
   1- Ordinary,
   2- Intensified,
   3- Strict, and
   4- Special
   (Obviously, the stricter the camp, the more unpleasant the conditions. Many Christians upon the second offense were placed in Strict Regime Labor Camps.)

5. **Detention in Prison**
6. **Exile**
7. **Detention in a psychiatric hospital**

Appendix III
Recommended Reading List

Alone with God
by Richard Wurmbrand

Beyond The Wall
by Hank Paulson with Don Richardson

Escape from North Korea
by Paul Estabrooks (From Open Doors)

God's Smuggler
by Brother Andrew

Praying with the KGB
by Phillip Yancey

The Black Book of Communism, Crimes, Terror, Repression
by Courtois, Worth, Panne', Paczkowski Bartosek and Margolin
Harvard University Press

The Case for Christ
by Lee Strobel

The Night of A Million Miracles
by Paul Estabrooks (From Open Doors)

Tortured for Christ
by Richard Wurmbrand

Endnotes

1. Phillip Yancey, "Praying with the KGB, *A Startling Report From a Shattered Empire,*" (Portland, OR, Multnomah Press, 1992) 67

2. Ibid., p 23

3. Avraham Shirin, "The First Guidebook to the USSR - to Prisons and concentration camps of the Soviet Union," (Stephanus Edition Verlags AG, CH-Seewis/GR, Switzerland, 1980) *(translated from the Russian)* 103

4. Richard Wurmbrand, "Tortured for Christ" (Bartlesville, OK, The Voice of the Martyrs Inc, Living Sacrifice Book Company, 1967,1998) 34

5. ibid., p 34

6. Lt Gen. Mihai Ion Mihai Pacepa, "Red Horizons - The True Story of Nicolae & Elena Ceausescus' Crimes, Lifestyle and Corruption" (Washington D.C., Regnery Gateway, 1987) 280-281

7. Lee Strobel, "The Case for Christ - a Journalist's Personal Investigation of the Evidence for Jesus," (Grand Rapids, MI, Zondervan, 1998) 97

8. Ibid., p 24

9. Josh McDowell, "The New Evidence, That Demands A Verdict" (Nashville, TN, Dallas, TX, Thomas Nelson Pub. TX, 1999) 193

10.) Ibid., p 193

11.) Ibid., p 125

12.) Strobel, The Case for Christ - *a Journalist's Personal Investigation of the Evidence for Jesus,* p 82

13.) Ibid., p 83

14.) Ibid., p 85

15.) McDowell, *The New Evidence, That Demands A Verdict.* p 121

Bibliography

Andrew, Brother with John and Elizabeth Sherrill. *God's Smuggler.* New York, NY: SIGNET, Penquin Books USA Inc., 1967.

Boltman, Bud and Harold Pickett. *Revolution by Candlelight – The Real Story Behind the Changes in Eastern Europe.* Portland, OR: Multnomah Press, 1991.

Bornstein, Jerry. *The Wall Came Tumbling Down - The Berlin Wall and the Fall of Communism.* New York, NY: Arch Cape Press, 1990.

Courtois, Worth, Panne', Paczkowski, Bartosek and Margolin. *The Black Book of Communism.* Cambridge, MA: Harvard University Press, 1999.

Estabrooks, Paul. *The Night of a Million Miracles.* Santa Ana, CA: Open Doors International, 2008.

Foxe, John, Rewritten and Updated by Harold J.Chadwick. *The New, Foxe's Book of Martyrs.* Gainesville, FL: Bridge Logos Pub., 2001.

Knox, John, edited by Guthrie, C.J. *The History of the Reformation in Scotland.* Edinburgh, Scotland; Carlisle, PA: Banner of Truth Trust ed., 1898, 1982.

McDowell, Josh. *The New Evidence, That Demands a Verdict.* Nashville, TN, Dallas, TX, et.al: Thomas Nelson Pub., 1999.

Pacepa, Lt. Gen. Ion Mihai, *Red Horizons - The True Story of Nicolae & Elena Ceausescus' Crimes, Lifestyle and Corruption.* Washington D.C.: Regnery Gateway, 1987.

Shainberg, Maurice. *Breaking from the KGB.* New York, NY: Berkley Books, 1986.

Shitrin, Avraham. *The First Guidebook to the USSR - to Prisons and Concentration camps of the Soviet Union*, Stephanus Edition. Verlags AG, CH-Seewis/GR, Switzerland *(translated from the Russian)*, 1980.

Society for the Study of Religion Under Communism. *Soviet Christian Prisoner List*. Orange, CA: SSRC/Keston College, 1981 (Out of print).

Strobel, Lee. *The Case for Christ - a Journalist's Personal Investigation of the Evidence for Jesus*. Grand Rapids, MI: Zondervan, 1998.

Sweetman, John. *Ploesti: Oil Strike*. New York, NY: Ballentine Books Inc, 1974.

Wurmbrand, Richard. *Tortured for Christ*. Bartlesville, OK: The Voice of the Martyrs Inc, Living Sacrifice Book Company, 1967, 1998.

Yancey, Phillip. *Praying with the KGB, A Startling Report from a Shattered Empire*. Portland, OR: Multnomah Press, 1992.

Personal Journal, Notes and Recollections. 1980-1983.

The New American Standard Bible. The Lockman Foundation, 1960, 1962, 1963, 1968, 1971, 1973, 1975.

The New Open Bible, Study Edition, New King James Version. Nashville, TN: Thomas Nelson, 1982, 1983, 1985, 1990.

Wikipedia, accessed by Google, 2012.

"O God, You have taught me from my youth, and I still declare Your wondrous deeds. And even when I am old and gray, O God do not forsake me. Until I declare Your strength to this generation. Your power to all who are to come. For your righteousness, O God reaches to the heavens, You have done great things; O God who is like you?" (Psalms 71:17-19)

For:
My Mom and Dad
My Family
Bill, Nona & family
John, Mickey, Elijah & Talitha Lane
Mike Lee & family
Mike, Marilee, Jeff & Joe
Randy & family
Ray, Russ, Pam and family
Tim, Ron and families
Paul, Denise and family
Walt, Barb, Anna, Abby and Noah
Art, Pam and Family

"I beseech you therefore, brethren, by the mercies of God, that you present your bodies a living sacrifice, holy, acceptable to God, which is your reasonable service. And do not be conformed to this world but be transformed by the renewing of your mind. That you may prove what is that good and acceptable and perfect will of God." (The Apostle Paul, Romans 12:1-2)

Made in the USA
San Bernardino, CA
12 May 2018

Made in the USA
Middletown, DE
28 July 2024